PRAISE FOR

Death in the Air

"Kate Winkler Dawson's *Death in the Air: The True Story of a Serial Killer, The Great London Smog, and the Strangling of a City* is a stellar examination of a turbulent time in the city's history.... Dawson's background in documentaries and journalism makes this journey more than just a retelling of the facts. She tracked down people who lived it, and now readers will vividly experience that period as well."   — Associated Press

"Deeply researched and densely atmospheric."
                                        — *The New York Times Book Review*

"A gripping read that illuminates two dark crimes: the political scandal of London's Great Smog of 1952, which killed an estimated 12,000 people; and the frightening deeds of a human killer both demented and mundane."   — *The Dallas Morning News*

"For five days in December of that year, London was blanketed by a yellow toxic vapor that smothered its inhabitants. Journalist Kate Winkler Dawson has written an intriguing book about this silent disaster, which was borne out of a perfect storm of freak weather patterns and environmental ignorance.... The lessons for the present, Dawson suggests, are as clear as the air in front of our eyes."   — Maureen Corrigan, NPR's Fresh Air

"What's scarier: a murderous madman (now known to be John Reginald Christie) or an environmental disaster?"
                                        — *Los Angeles Times*

"*Death in the Air* is an enlightening look at two lesser-known but important events in British history, for both had far-reaching consequences." — *StarTribune* (Minneapolis)

"In her debut book *Death in the Air,* University of Texas journalism lecturer and Austin native Kate Winkler Dawson weaves together two terrifying events: the Great Smog that settled over London for five days in 1952 and the gruesome discovery that a serial killer, John Reginald Christie, had been living coincidentally in the city at the same time. Dawson spent two years researching the book, delving into everything from autopsy reports and trial transcripts to eyewitness accounts by people who survived the fog." — *Austin Monthly*

"Ms. Dawson, a journalist and documentary producer, is an assiduous researcher...her portraits of the ordinary people confronted by the depredations of the fog and Christie are moving. Ms. Dawson cogently argues that the Conservative government's response to the crisis was shameful: it did everything it could, seemingly, to cover up the extent of the catastrophe and avoid addressing the emergency." — *The Wall Street Journal*

"*Death in the Air* by Kate Winkler Dawson is a fascinating, beautifully researched, and compulsively readable book, which tells the entwined stories of the Great London Smog of 1952 and a serial killer, John Reginald Christie, who exploited the fog as a cloak for murder. This is a portrait of London at one of its darkest and most desperate times. Not since *The Devil in the White City* has a book told such a harrowing tale."
— Douglas Preston, #1 *New York Times* bestselling author of *The Monster of Florence* and *The Lost City of the Monkey God*

"How have we forgotten this incredible story? A deadly environmental disaster visited upon modern London, a serial killer stalking women at its zenith—this is a tale dying to be told. *Death in the Air* is a stunning debut by a writer you will be hearing about for years to come. It's just a great book."
— Bryan Burrough, *New York Times* bestselling author of *Public Enemies* and *Barbarians at the Gate*

"A killer fog. A killer loose amidst it. Dawson does what skilled storytellers do: drops you in a London peopled by finely etched characters and keeps you turning pages through the twist and turns of a harrowing case."
— Joe Drape, *New York Times* bestselling author of *American Pharoah* and *Our Boys*

"A London peasouper hangs over the city as a serial killer stalks its streets! This is a true tale of criminal violence against the backdrop of one of the worst environmental disasters of all time, one that led to the death of 12,000 people. It is a narrative that has relevance to the world's pollution problems of today and is also an engrossing read."
— Christine L. Corton, author of *London Fog: The Biography*

"I was seven, and living in London, when these two dreadful and murderous events uncoiled, and I—asthmatic as a result—remember them still. It seems to me that only an outsider, a non-Londoner, could possibly bring them so vividly, so excruciatingly, and so unflinchingly back to life. Kate Winkler Dawson has done the history of my city a great service, and she is to be commended for telling a terrible tale memorably and brilliantly."
— Simon Winchester, *New York Times* bestselling author of *The Professor and the Madman*

"Dawson deftly weaves the tales together in an engrossing narrative that reads like a thriller....readers will remain hooked on this compelling story and will eagerly await Dawson's next book."

— *Kirkus Reviews*

"A deranged maniac plays Fleet Street's reporters like a fiddle at the same time that an industrial-age climate disaster explodes into a full-blown humanitarian crisis. Richly detailed and shrewdly told, Kate Winkler Dawson's *Death in the Air* is as suspenseful as it is chillingly relevant."

— Robert Kolker, *New York Times* bestselling author of *Lost Girls*

"Just when you think true crime can't get more interesting, here comes Kate Dawson with her imaginatively conceived and meticulously researched tale about Reg Christie, the fastidious, soft-voiced London clerk who embarks on a vicious killing spree in 1952 just as a deadly fog descends on London. But *Death in the Air* is hardly another study of a depraved serial killer. It's also a riveting history of London in the years after World War II — a city beset by political cover-ups and misguided police investigations. Dawson's ability to weave together so many separate strands of one story is simply magnificent."

— Skip Hollandsworth, author of *The Midnight Assassin: The Hunt for America's First Serial Killer*

"Kate Winkler Dawson has a born storyteller's gift for building suspense and momentum and a keen eye for telling details, and her narrative poses a powerful moral question: who's the worse killer — a madman who strangles seven women and a baby, or government officials whose staggering indifference allows thousands to die in the Great London Smog of 1952? Dawson captures the whole sad mess in a heartbreaking, page-turning account that almost literally grips you by the throat as the government, the police, the press, and the medical profession all fail in their fundamental duty to preserve and protect the city's most vulnerable residents."

— Glenn Frankel, Pulitzer Prize–winning journalist and author of *High Noon* and *The Searchers*

"Dawson has reached deep into the past and pulled forth a spellbinding, darkly gothic tale of two serial killers—only one of which was human. *Death in the Air* surprised me, entranced me, and changed the way I see one of the most urgent issues facing the world today." — Alexandria Marzano-Lesnevich, author of *The Fact of a Body*

"This dark and disturbing tale of murder, deception, and killer smog in 1952 London serves as a vivid warning about what can happen when we destroy the environment, systems break down, and, well, a couped up, dormant serial killer feels the need to act out his twisted fantasies—again." — Dean King, bestselling author of *Skeletons on the Zahara* and *The Feud*

"What's great about *Death in the Air* is not just its stunning premise, but also its deep reach into the life of London in the mid-twentieth century. It's a wonderful read. Welcome to the metaphysics of fog." — S. C. Gwynne, *New York Times* bestselling author of *Empire of the Summer Moon* and *Rebel Yell*

"Evocative…vividly atmospheric….The narratives add up to a grim, Dickensian portrait of postwar London: broke, grimy, dejected, deranged around the edges, and gasping for breath." — *Publishers Weekly*

"Tendrils of sickening fog creep everywhere in this book, and terror lurks in the shadows. Dawson skillfully weaves these two events into a substantial narrative that will appeal to all types of readers."   — *Library Journal* (starred review)

"Journalist Dawson writes the parallel, shocking histories of the suffocating smog that menaced London, ultimately killing thousands, in December 1952, and a serial killer's salacious murders and trial the following year. Focusing on the powerful press's response to both killers and offering food for thought on what constitutes crime, responsibility, and progress, Dawson delves into heated parliamentary debates between Churchill's Conservative cabinet and Laborite agitators; first-person accounts from doctors, policemen, and other smog survivors; court records; and Christie's own, jaw-dropping account of his murders."
                    — *Booklist*

DEATH
IN THE
AIR

THE TRUE STORY OF A SERIAL KILLER, THE GREAT

LONDON SMOG, AND THE STRANGLING OF A CITY

KATE WINKLER DAWSON

hachette
BOOKS

NEW YORK   BOSTON

Hachette Books
Hachette Book Group
1290 Avenue of the Americas
New York, NY 10104
hachettebooks.com
twitter.com/hachettebooks

First trade paperback edition: October 2018

Hachette Books is a division of Hachette Book Group, Inc.
The Hachette Books name and logo are trademarks of Hachette Book Group, Inc.

The publisher is not responsible for websites (or their content) that are not owned by the publisher.

The Hachette Speakers Bureau provides a wide range of authors for speaking events. To find out more, go to www.hachettespeakersbureau.com or call (866) 376-6591.

Library of Congress Cataloging-in-Publication Data

Names: Dawson, Kate Winkler, author.
Title: Death in the air : the true story of a serial killer, the great London smog, and the strangling of a city / Kate Winkler Dawson.
Description: First edition. | New York, NY : Hachette Books, [2017] Includes bibliographical references and index.
Identifiers: LCCN 2017020079| ISBN 9780316506861 (hardcover) | ISBN 9781478923138 (audio download) | ISBN 9780316506854 (ebook)
Subjects: LCSH: Christie, Reginald. | Serial murderers--England--London--Case studies. | Smog--England--London--History--20th century. | London (England)--Social conditions--20th century. | London (England)--Environmental conditions--20th century.
Classification: LCC HV6248.E75 D39 2017 | DDC 364.152/32092--dc23
LC record available at https://lccn.loc.gov/2017020079

ISBNs: 978-0-316-50683-0 (trade paperback); 978-0-316-50685-4 (ebook)

LSC-C

Printed in the United States of America

To JWD—I'll always hold your hand
through the fog.

Contents

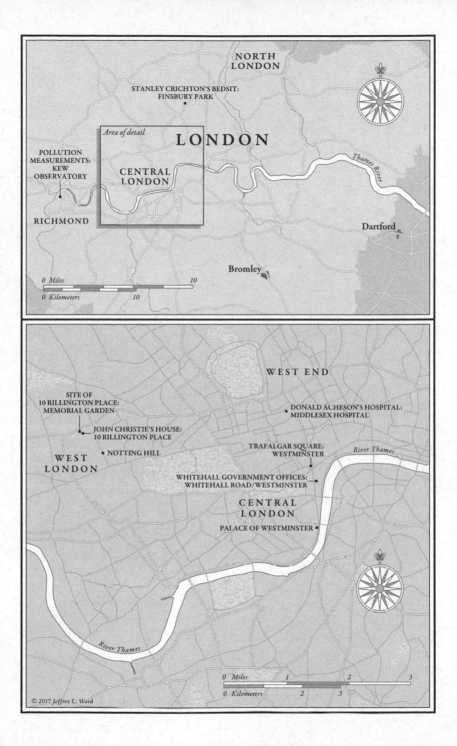

NORTH LONDON

STANLEY CRICHTON'S BEDSIT:
FINSBURY PARK

Area of detail

LONDON

POLLUTION
MEASUREMENTS:
KEW
OBSERVATORY

CENTRAL
LONDON

Thames River

RICHMOND

Dartford

Bromley

0 Miles 10
0 Kilometers 10

WEST END

SITE OF
10 RILLINGTON PLACE:
MEMORIAL GARDEN

DONALD ACHESON'S HOSPITAL:
MIDDLESEX HOSPITAL

JOHN CHRISTIE'S HOUSE:
10 RILLINGTON PLACE

TRAFALGAR SQUARE:
WESTMINSTER

River Thames

WEST
LONDON

NOTTING HILL

WHITEHALL GOVERNMENT OFFICES:
WHITEHALL ROAD/WESTMINSTER

CENTRAL
LONDON

PALACE OF WESTMINSTER

River Thames

0 Miles 1 2 3
0 Kilometers 2 3

© 2017 Jeffrey L. Ward

The Shiver

Fog everywhere. Fog up the river, where it flows among green aits and meadows; fog down the river, where it rolls defiled among the tiers of shipping and the waterside pollutions of a great (and dirty) city.
— *Charles Dickens,* Bleak House, *1853*

The teenager carefully avoided broken shards of glass, barely held together by cracked window frames, as the mist dampened her hair. She balanced on bricks and gently braced herself against the frame of the house. It was 1952 — London's winter wind, chilly and biting, prompted a shiver that began at her scalp and traveled to her toes. Thirteen-year-old Rosemary Sargent listened for the distant call of her younger brother as the mist thickened into a fog. She hopped across old pieces of wood full of rusty nails — materials that once held together a lovely house just a few homes down from her own. Now it was a bombsite, the perfect playground for mischievous kids hoping to avoid boredom. As she looked at the bricks, she could recall what her life had been like during World War II.

During the late summer of 1944, the Nazis had unloaded on Rosemary's working-class neighborhood in southeast

London—she had been just five. Her family had decided to stay, had *refused* to be driven out…and it was a miracle they survived. Years later, her parents still had their Morrison bomb shelter, a giant metal cage that sat in their parlor. Rosemary's mother had draped a cloth over it and called it a table.

The teenager's dream was to become a schoolteacher, a goal that had sprouted in her family's front garden during the summer the Luftwaffe sent a "doodlebug" right over her house. Rosemary recalled gripping a piece of chalk, dragging it down her new chalkboard, and then hearing a hum. It was the buzz that triggered such anxiety in Londoners. She could still remember how it looked, like a torpedo with wings. It was really a V-1 flying cruise missile, carrying a warhead that weighed close to two thousand pounds. She hadn't seen one in years, but she could imagine the thing quietly hovering over her house as she stood beneath its tail. She could recall her mother racing from the kitchen to the parlor door and shrieking: "Come in, come in, come in!"

The boys were making a ruckus nearby. As a light fog drifted in, Rosemary played hide-and-seek in the corpse of her neighbors' house.

⁓

The year 1952 suffered a somber beginning in Britain. King George VI had died on February 6 at the age of fifty-six, leaving a war-scarred country in mourning. Albert—that was his given name—had been crowned almost fifteen years earlier, at a time when the public had little faith in the monarchy, after suffering through a royal scandal that rocked the institution to its core. Albert's elder brother, Edward VIII, had ascended the throne first, in 1936, after their father died. Later that year, King Edward abdicated so he could marry an American divorcée, Wallis Simpson. Albert had reluctantly become king the following year.

But Albert had risen to the demands of what seemed at first to be an untenable position. When his nation needed a leader, King George VI had become a monarch the British could all stand behind. He had ushered the nation through World War II, through the bombings of London that had scarred the city's landscape as well as its psyche, and through the messy aftermath of war. When his people needed a voice, he spoke for them, despite a debilitating stammer. King George VI's funeral at Windsor Castle was impressive. The country was devastated by his death, but there was reason for optimism. His elder daughter, Elizabeth, ascended the throne as Queen Elizabeth II, ushering in a sense of excitement among the British. At just twenty-five, Elizabeth was the future of the monarchy, and the nation's hopes and dreams all seemed to be exemplified by the young, pretty queen, her dashing husband, and her adorable children. Britons looked forward to her lavish coronation, set for the following summer.

But in truth, seven years after the end of World War II, London was still in crisis. Nearly seventy thousand civilians across Britain had been killed during the war—forty thousand from air raids alone, and almost half of those had been in London. The British government still faced an enormous war debt. Rationing of sweets and sugar remained in full force. Smoking tobacco was chic, one small luxury amid the fiercely regulated reality of everyday life. And there was another war sapping the country's resources. More than twelve thousand British troops were fighting alongside American soldiers in Korea. In London, crime was becoming an epidemic in much of the city, as bombed-out buildings gave criminals safe havens. Police were increasingly outnumbered.

And yet there was one industry that was already booming to prewar numbers: coal. For years, coal had fueled the country's growth, and by 1952 there was at least one coal fireplace per home—meaning that in London, millions of domestic grates were stuffed into an area of just six hundred square miles (just under twice the size of New York City). The fuel was cheap, effective, and crucial—it was the only major source of domestic heating in the city at that time. But the smoke could be suffocating, and the sulphur dioxide released into the air was deadly. It triggered acid rain strong enough to bend iron, erode statues, poison land, and contaminate waterways—the pollution could destroy lungs and cause cancer. But still the coal burned. In 1952, almost forty coal-fired power stations kept London electrified and more than twenty thousand steam locomotives kept the city moving.

The politics of Big Coal were no less murky than the air it produced. Coal, it turned out, was one of the few thriving international industries remaining in postwar Britain—more than 250 million tons were mined domestically every year; it was a key export for the country at a time when national budgets were tight. More than seven hundred thousand workers were employed in British coal mines. Politicians weren't ignorant of the environmental concerns of burning huge quantities of coal every year, but their hands seemed tied.

The Conservative Party, also known as the Tories, was led by Prime Minister Winston Churchill, the country's ailing but still potent leader. The Conservatives knew that any attempt to constrain the coal industry could be devastating to a vulnerable British economy. Their main opposition, the Labour Party, was anxious to use the country's massive debt as a weapon in the upcoming election. So the government was keeping up a brisk pace in international coal sales, but it was selling its best domestic coal to other countries and reserving the cheaper coal for its own people. This cheaper coal, a brown dust with bits of coal, was a soft material, a poor replacement for the more expensive black coal still being rationed. It went by the nickname "nutty slack," and though it was far inferior to black coal, it was all that most Londoners could afford in those desperate postwar times.

It took enormous amounts of nutty slack to heat the average home—the cheaper brown coal was inefficient and much dirtier to burn, which created more smoke and more pollution. But most politicians in Parliament were certain that exporting black coal and selling the nutty slack domestically was a crucial cost-saving decision. Britain was desperate: smokeless fuel wasn't economically realistic, or widely available. In 1952, London entered winter with its largest stock of coal, of all grades, in any postwar year—nineteen and a half million tons.

As Londoners warmed themselves by their fires that December, they couldn't have possibly known there was a deadly killer gathering strength across London, around their homes—a lethal pollutant plotting to devastate an already crippled city.

❧

But in early December of 1952, as the London air thickened and smothered the city, another killer—devious, sick, and unrepentant—eyed his next victim. He was trapped with her in that horrid fog. When the smoke lifted, she would die, three more would soon follow. It was no trouble. He had killed before.

Most mornings, fairly early, he would sip tea in his tiny kitchen while his wife tidied up their sad, filthy flat in Notting Hill. It had been such a genteel district once, but certainly not by 1952. Gamblers and prostitutes filled its homes, joined by every shade of shifty character available. Most blocks were slums, with decent people drowning inside eroding row houses. The police force seemed hopelessly inert.

Six days a week, the awkward middle-aged man with the horn-rimmed glasses bade good-bye to his wife and tried to ignore the litany of loud curses and complaints from his upstairs neighbors. He despised them. He rode the Tube to his job as an invoice clerk at a large transport company. The work was mundane, he thought, but he was lucky to have such a stable position. He wasn't good at keeping jobs. He loathed his life, for so many reasons.

The man was quiet, meek—overlooked by most people who passed him in the neighborhood. He haunted the streets of Notting Hill like a spook, desperately searching for some time alone, away from his skittish, clingy wife. It was so suffocating, being trapped with her in that nasty flat. If he didn't find enough of those quiet moments...someone might die.

❧

This is the parallel story of two killers. As different as these murderers were, their similarities were striking. Both strangled their victims. Both eluded suspicion. And both nearly escaped justice. Each changed law in Britain and, in many ways, around the world. One was a toxin that ignored race, wealth, and age—a mass murderer that asphyxiated thousands of Londoners and sickened hundreds of thousands. The other was a psychopath, a serial killer, who terrorized one of the world's most important cities. There were miscarriages of justice with both. Yet only one of the two remains infamous—the other has been all but forgotten.

Telling the stories side by side, there's a sense of what life was like after World War II in the British capital—and what Londoners actually valued. The characters are a sampling of a society that influenced the world. And the braided narrative reveals something about the way in which humans experience fear: one man was more terrifying to Londoners than a deadly fog that strangled thousands—a naïveté that only benefited newspaper editors (promoting their salacious headlines) and the politicians who tried to cover up the choking smog that was largely of their own creation.

⸏

CHAPTER ONE

Pressure

A great chocolate-coloured pall lowered over
heaven...there would be a glow of rich, lurid
brown, like the light of some strange conflagration;
and here, for a moment, the fog would be quite
broken up, and a haggard shaft of daylight would
glance in between the swirling wreaths.
— *Robert Louis Stevenson*, The Strange Case of
Dr. Jekyll and Mr. Hyde, *1886*

It was like electricity, the power unleashed by the wind surging
across the waters of the Atlantic Ocean. The intense, warm rush
pushed, yanked the waves in a maelstrom and then whirled,
forcing them in the same direction. Combined with the spin of
the earth, they unified into a powerful weapon that could trigger
tropical storms, sink ships, and swallow up men. Thousands of
ancient vessels, many treasure-laden, littered the reefs along its
path—the victims of naïve captains, whose ill-fated crews were
sucked under by its waves. And it spawned some of history's
cruelest storms. The Gulf Stream was one of the most powerful
ocean currents in the world—the same remarkable "river in an
ocean" first recorded by Spanish explorer Juan Ponce de León in
1513 as his ships tried to navigate its waters between the Florida
coast and the Bahamas. The legend claimed he was on a quest
for the Fountain of Youth, a mythical water source purport-

edly capable of reversing the aging process and curing sickness. His only barrier was the Gulf Stream. Ponce de León's fleet was pushed backward by the strong, fast-moving current of warm seawater—his smallest ship was missing for two days.

The Gulf Stream has since shaped destinies. Explorers and merchants used the current to explore and colonize new lands, including Florida and the Dutch colonies of New York. But if captains ignored its power, they suffered. A change in wind direction or strength could have devastating consequences. Many navigators couldn't harness its power—they only hoped to survive it. The current started in the warm waters of the Gulf of Mexico, then moved northeast, branching off into three different currents that headed toward Africa, Europe, and Newfoundland. The northeast extension of the Gulf Stream, the North Atlantic Current, concentrated its force on the United Kingdom.

The British Isles jutted into the middle of the warming waters, right in the current's path. It made the winters warmer and the summers cooler than those of the central European countries, thanks to the heated water. Farmers in Devonshire, England, on the southwest coast, grew lemons in December for curd to pair with their famous clotted cream. Palm trees thrived in Cork, Ireland, in January. Without that current, the United Kingdom would feel as cold as Canada. The mild winter temperatures pleased most Britons—until it turned on them.

The first week of December 1952, the Gulf Stream was spewing warm, moist air toward London—misty stuff that hovered, lingered above the city, and waited, patiently, for its deadly companion.

London was a city in recovery, even seven years after the end of the war. There was more optimism, certainly—the Luftwaffe planes had retreated, and the air raid sirens fell silent; there was rebuilding and repair in the aftermath of bombs that had ravaged much of London. Despite the impact of war, a certain innocence still remained in the city, at least outwardly. Children strolled to school alone. Housewives left their doors unlocked. Kids shuffled cards and tossed dice on pavements without a parent nearby. Adults were addressed as "mister" and "missus." For teens, sex was forbidden and obedience was demanded, though those rules were often ignored, of course.

But it was difficult to overlook the shabbier side of the capital, even though most upper- and middle-class residents certainly tried. Across the city, crumbling tenements were packed with new immigrants from nations all over the world, many of whom found themselves living in destitution in a strange land. Many white Londoners were bitter, habitually underemployed, and constantly struggling in ghettos supported by slumlords. The impoverished districts in London were neglected by politicians and plagued by violence. Horrible crimes played out on the streets and inside private homes—like scenes from a Dickens novel. And soon, the crimes of one of British history's most heinous serial killers would be splashed across the front pages of newspapers around the world.

Still, for much of respectable London, British society promoted the wartime ethos of restraint and respectability—this was the time to conform and push forward. For children who matured in the midst of battle, however, it was hard to forget the carnage. They were surrounded by its relics, and often reveled in them. Most boys had wooden Tommy submachine guns or sometimes the real thing—a memento from the war with the firing pin removed. Woolworths sold replica fighter jets, tiny soldiers, and plastic submarines. Comic books were filled with stories about soldiers hunting German U-boats. War films lit up the cinema.

Soldiers and Londoners experienced reciprocal respect—an empathy created by a communal, terrifying experience. Any person older than thirty-five had already lived through two world wars. If they hadn't been in battle, they knew someone—a son, a brother, a sweetheart—who had been. War had touched every Brit in some direct way, but none as directly as Londoners, who had been subjected to the worst of the German bombing for years during World War II. Large swaths of the population were, quite literally, shell-shocked.

Perhaps as a direct result of all the chaos, by 1952 British society still insisted on deference toward the well-heeled superior. The King and Queen were revered for their decision to remain in London during the Blitz. The Conservative government—under celebrated Prime Minister Winston Churchill—had recently returned to power. The famously tough Churchill had led Britain through World War II, but his party had been ousted in 1945, near the end of the war. He had only recently been reelected in the 1951 election, which handed the Tories a slim majority in the House of Commons after six years of opposition rule. The heavyweights in the opposition Labour Party were aging and bickering. The party was showing cracks, but the Conservatives promised to keep some key Labour changes, like the National Health Service, implemented in 1948, and the nationalization of important industries like railways and coal mines.

Internationally, Britain was flexing its muscle, despite its beleaguered economy. The UK tested its first nuclear bomb off the northwest coast of Australia, making Britain an atomic power, just behind America and the Soviet Union.

When United States President Harry S. Truman warned Americans they were "moving through a perilous time" as long as Communists held power, Churchill gave him a standing ovation. The British Conservative government was preparing for the Cold War, but as 1952 progressed, there would be many more trials much closer to home.

The summer of 1952 heralded a string of disasters that tested the country's sense of calm. In August, the south of England was deluged by a severe tropical storm, which brought with it traumatizing scenes and great devastation. The low-pressure system dumped an unprecedented nine inches of rain within twenty-four hours on an area of moorlands. Ninety million tons of water roared through the nearby town of Lynmouth like an avalanche, hauling along boulders and crashing through homes. The flood dragged bodies out to sea, never to be recovered. Thirty-five people were killed and Lynmouth had to be completely rebuilt. The entire nation was stunned.

Within weeks came another national tragedy, this time at the prestigious Farnborough Air Show. Pilot John Derry was already a legend. Four years earlier, he had been the first British pilot to break the sound barrier, and he was going to do it again that September day. It started off just as planned; Derry and a flight test observer were in the cockpit of a Hawker Siddeley Sea Vixen, a two-seater fighter jet, as they broke the sound barrier at the air show. Their flight created a sonic boom that shook the eardrums of the people on the ground, who were staring upward in delight. The crowd erupted in applause, but the clapping stopped quickly. During a second pass at about five hundred miles an hour, the nose of the jet lifted and the plane suddenly disintegrated, sending heavy debris plummeting down toward more than one hundred thousand onlookers. Derry and the flight test observer died, but the real carnage was on the ground below; the accident killed thirty-one spectators, prompting tighter regulations to protect audiences at air shows. The entire nation mourned the deaths.

One month later, the country was again grieving—the Harrow and Wealdstone rail crash in London would lead the papers for days. The driver of an overnight express train from Scotland missed a warning signal and two danger signals in the dense fog as the locomotive barreled toward the city. Before he could apply the brake, it slammed into a delayed passenger train parked at the station, sending it hurtling across the tracks into another oncoming train. Passengers heard a great boom of clashing metal, bending and breaking. Those who could crawl from the cars stared at a mangled pile of train carriages. Witnesses said it was impossible to drag out some of the bodies. The crash killed more than one hundred passengers and injured 340 more. It was the most catastrophic railway accident in England—and fog was the suspected culprit.

That disgusting fog. It came most days in the winter, and as autumn approached and the days grew shorter in 1952, the whole country braced for the fog's return, London in particular.

The fog was omnipresent in the country's capital. Young Londoners lived in the stuff. They played hide-and-seek in a yellow haze—the fog made it easy to ambush a playmate desperately looking for a hiding spot. Kids, boys mostly, would swipe fruit from rickety wooden stands in the street market on Portobello Road. They used the smoky air as a valuable resource—stores were cloaked by fog so thick that the chemists and toffee makers could barely see their own boots when they locked up early. The children coughed into their mittens and carried on. It was obnoxious, the dirty air, but most Londoners accepted that it was their penalty for living in the world's most urbanized and industrialized city.

On Thursday, December 4, 1952, fog slowly appeared like a thin specter, circling Big Ben just before two thirty. The smoke smothered the sun early that morning. Any glimpses of light were chased away by the dusky apparition slithering around Parliament. That night, the politicians inside those beautiful buildings had no idea the fog would cause such outrage in the House of Commons—or how it would change the air they breathed. The minute hands on Big Ben ticked forward, and the quarter bells rang the Westminster Chimes, from Handel's bewitching oratorio *Messiah*.

⌘

Inside the Palace of Westminster's House of Commons, a veteran politician eyed Winston Churchill and his cabinet. Norman Dodds wasn't an especially patient man. That night, the forty-nine-year-old Member of Parliament (MP) shifted in his seat, a cramped two-foot area on the iconic green benches covered in Moroccan leather. A card with his name sat inside its slot, signaling that this was his seat for the day. He surveyed the room and glanced at his companions, the other MPs of the newly minority Labour Party. They were outnumbered by thirty-two votes, and the deficit alarmed Norman almost daily. The Conservative government was misleading voters on so many issues, he thought. He routinely accused the Tories of abandoning the commoner and obeying the wishes of big industries, to alleviate the country's enormous postwar national debt. Norman and his Labour Party had fewer members, but they were ready for a new fight—one he was happy to lead. He was feisty when he entered the Commons Chamber each day—his eyes gleamed as he listened.

"Lord, the God of righteousness and truth, grant to our Queen and her government, to Members of Parliament and all in positions of responsibility, the guidance of your Spirit," the Speaker's Chaplain read as he intoned the prayers that brought government into session. Norman and the MPs turned and faced the wall, a custom nearly four hundred years old. It was thought to have started because sixteenth-century politicians had problems kneeling for prayers due to the swords they wore.

But while the MPs still followed the trappings of history and tradition, the walls themselves were newly rebuilt. The Nazis had bombed the Houses of Parliament no fewer than fourteen different times during the Blitz. In May 1941, incendiary bombs had exploded above the Commons Chamber and set the roof of Westminster Hall on fire. The Chamber had been destroyed. A small bomb struck Parliament's clock tower and shattered the glass on its south face, but the bells continued to toll. By the following morning, there was little left of the great House of Commons. More than seven hundred years of history had been relegated to rubble.

The Chamber needed to be redesigned, but thanks to a tight postwar budget, the seat of British government now had a more practical aesthetic than before. Gone were the ornate stained glass windows; they were now replaced with plain glass. The walls were decorated with simple oak paneling. The Palace of Westminster was now warmed by a central heating system, doing away with almost all of the one thousand open fireplaces that had once burned; only six were left. The new House was only two years old, but it still felt cold to Norman. The high ceilings didn't help—they created an acoustical nightmare during raucous debates and lowered the temperature inside during winter months.

But if the weather outside that night was brisk, the political climate inside the Commons was biting. The Labour Party—Norman's party—had launched an attack on Prime Minister

Winston Churchill, one of its most vicious during this session. The politics were arcane, but the stakes, Norman felt, were high: His party had accused Churchill of waffling on appointing a Supreme Allied Commander in the Mediterranean, the senior military leader of more than twenty countries. A spirited debate had escalated to an all-out shouting match: MPs began bobbing up and down, attempting to get the Speaker's attention for a comment. This was the sort of brawl the reporters upstairs in the Press Gallery savored. More than two hundred journalists roamed Parliament when they expected MPs to make big decisions. Or cause controversy. It was heavy lifting for writers hoping for a scoop. Author Charles Dickens was a cynical teenaged reporter in both Houses in the early 1830s, when reporters were relegated to a cramped area, far from the debates.

"I have worn my knees by writing on them on the old back row of the old gallery of the House of Commons," complained Dickens.

The typewriters of House reporters clicked and dinged, churning out zippy pieces on everything from the death penalty to complaints about a new levy on long underwear. The correspondents shoved themselves inside the Commons' wooden telephone cubicles and phoned in stories to their editors for the morning edition paper.

As the prime minister exited the hall with the Government Chief Whip, a storm of noise surged from Norman Dodds and the Labourites. Churchill halted, swung around, scanned the room, and revealed a slight smirk. When the opposition unloaded a torrent of boos and hisses, Churchill's face fell and he stomped over to the dispatch box. He demanded to know if booing was an appropriate response for gentlemen lawmakers.

"What else can you say to a goose?" barked back Scottish

Labour Party MP William Ross. This sent off a fury of response from both sides. Churchill's voice lifted above the others.

"May I say, with great respect and with the indulgence of the Committee, that I do not in the least mind being called a goose? I have been called many worse things than that." Name-calling was fine, but the prime minister wouldn't tolerate booing.

The House of Commons, the Victorian building rich with history and conflict, was Norman Dodds' battleground. The cacophony of hoots came from his compatriots—those politicians who vowed to represent their constituencies with vigor, like soldiers protecting their platoons during a battle.

When Norman rose from his seat in the second row, other MPs either smiled or grimaced. People in the public gallery leaned forward, hoping to catch a glimpse. Norman's power in Parliament came from his speeches—he punched words constantly, sometimes indiscriminately, with spittle flying from his mouth. He wasn't a tall man or especially handsome. He was a bit portly, with thinning hair and a double chin. But his rhetoric, delivered in a working-class accent, was dramatic and convincing. His constituents believed him. Since his election in 1945, he had asked more than fifteen hundred oral questions and made even more queries on paper—an extraordinary amount for any politician. He was nicknamed "the cavalier of Question Time." Members of both sides of the aisle criticized him for playing to the press gallery for the past seven years.

"They expect me to deny it," said Norman, "but I don't. My only trouble is that I'm running short of ideas." In a matter of days, that would change.

Tonight, the dramatic moaning, amplified by a microphone connected to loudspeakers, bounced off the Chamber walls and settled inside Norman's ears. He looked across the aisle. Harold Macmillan wasn't there for tonight's debate, not unusual. The room was growing cooler. The fog was slinking along the outside of the windows, hanging above Norman.

⚬

It began simply enough. Meteorologists at the Kew Observatory watched the small ridge of high pressure as it crept, slowly, over the British Isles, first to Ireland and southern Scotland, over cities like Glasgow, then onward to northern England. As it traveled, that ridge of high pressure circulated wind—a lot of wind. It whirled in a clockwise motion around an eye filled with high atmospheric pressure. About a hundred years earlier, scientists named that type of storm an "anticyclone." The label may have sounded alarming to the layperson—cyclones were often associated with tornados, those destructive wind tunnels that tore across open plains, leveling homes and killing families. But an anticyclone, almost always, was fantastic news for Londoners.

When the high-pressure system drifted over the city, the days were sunny and the air was dry. The skies were clear because the air was sinking, so no rain or clouds could form. But those clear skies also sent temperatures plummeting at night. The air turned frigid. And there was the fog that would surely come from the moisture in the air; that was nothing new. But then a breeze would typically arrive, blowing the system away as discreetly as it appeared. An anticyclone would usually conjure up a perfect winter day for a Londoner.

But this year, something was different.

The high-pressure weather system was just a few hundred miles from the center of London by Thursday, the day the sun disappeared into haze and the grey wisps stalked Big Ben. British meteorologists tested the volume of smoke and sulphur dioxide in the atmosphere daily—it was normal. Scientists at the London Meteorological Office in Kingsway watched the system's progression, along with a low-pressure system following behind it in the North Atlantic. They thought, they *hoped*, that its smaller companion would push the anticyclone past London. There was no reason to think it wouldn't. They predicted the high pressure would simply blow away. It always had before. If it didn't, the city would be devoured by one hell of a peasouper—the nickname for thick, dark fog. If that anticyclone stayed for more than a day, forecasters predicted, there would be some minor issues with traffic, perhaps some additional patients complaining of respiratory problems. Londoners sighed, prepared for some minor inconveniences, and carried on, as they always did.

∽

The ground in December was hard, solid, and cold above her. When someone happened to shuffle across it, the thin top layer of soil crunched, shifted just slightly. She stayed still, though—no matter how many cracked flowerpots, broken bricks, or random bits of rubbish were dropped above her. A thin root from the yellow-flowering Philadelphus bush wrapped around one of her vertebra; it would be difficult to untangle. Ripped pieces of a penny newspaper dated July 19, 1943, were lodged between her bones. A knotted section of rope was nearby.

The air that Thursday night, December 4, grew sharper, darker, even somehow heavier, but it made no difference to her. The clouds masked her from suspicious neighbors, even though it wouldn't have been very difficult to find her, with a shovel. She was trapped, less than two feet under, so she stayed hushed. She languished under a layer of fog.

Ruth Fuerst was once striking, really, but not because of her beauty. She was slender, with olive skin and short, dark hair, along with deep brown eyes shaped like ovals, always revealing bits of sadness and pain. She was in fact rather plain-looking compared to the posh socialites that strolled along the High Street; Ruth was tall and, at around five foot nine inches, she matched the eye level of many men. That pleased her. She also had deformed legs from childhood, which made her all the more intriguing. Ruth guarded secrets, hidden by her mercurial tendencies. At only twenty-one, life had already abused her, so the manner of her death might have been expected—except he was just so dreadful to her. She was his first.

Ruth was Austrian, and in 1939, at the age of seventeen, she had been separated from her family when she became a refugee from Nazi persecution. The Third Reich labeled her a Mischling—someone who was half Aryan and half Jewish—and she fled Austria while she still could. The following year, when invasion loomed, she was sent briefly to an internment camp with other Germans and Austrians on the Isle of Man, an island in the Irish Sea between Britain and Ireland. After Ruth's release, she began a descent into various traumas: She had a baby out of wedlock with a Greek waiter, a little girl named Christina Sonya, who was immediately sent away for adoption. Ruth anguished over her parents, who she thought had been slaughtered by the Nazis in a concentration camp. They had actually immigrated safely to New York. She lived in poverty in London, much of the time.

Ruth's temperament was perplexing to anyone who spent time with her. She was bright, but also shy and frequently morose, bordering on depressed. One employer said she had a poor work ethic and was frequently absent, and then she resigned unexpectedly. But Ruth carried on. She worked at various hotels and restaurants, while studying nursing books in her off time. She could never seem to develop strong friendships—she liked privacy. But she appreciated male attention, frequently. "A girl who could be easily influenced by a stronger character," remarked one of her friends. She always seemed to need money— her earnings at a munitions factory weren't enough for rent.

The older man watched her while they stood at David Griffin's Refreshment Room, a snack bar in Ladbroke Grove. He bragged he was a special constable with the War Reserve Police—in fact, he had been awarded two commendations for distinguished service over the past four years. He was confident.

It was August of 1943—the month before, the Allies had bombed Hamburg and Benito Mussolini's fascist government had collapsed in Italy. Ruth and the special constable had both survived the Blitz in London, two years earlier. Ruth Fuerst smiled as he introduced himself as "John." He was perhaps in his forties and he seemed charming, if a bit strange—but not bad-looking, especially if she compared him to the goons who loitered in the neighborhood. They met several more times while he was on his beat, even at his house—they had sex. She knew he was married, but it didn't concern her. He stood close to her in his sharp blue uniform and official cap. Ruth admired the way he looked in it. She sensed the responsible war constable might be willing to help her, unlike the other men in her life. He liked to brag about his income.

"John, will you lend me ten shillings? I am short of my rent this week," Ruth asked. He agreed, but said she must visit him at his home in Notting Hill, close by. Ruth arrived promptly to the appropriate address: 10 Rillington Place. It was late August when she stood on the sidewalk of the shabby tenement apartments in the cul-de-sac. The building was butted against a brick wall, and smoke churned from the factory on the other side. They went inside his first-floor flat, stepped into the kitchen.

"My wife is visiting her brother up north," he told her. They sipped tea and chatted, and then he handed her the shillings. She said she wanted to be closer to him, a true relationship—not just casual sex. They could run away together. Ruth peeled off her leopard-skin coat and followed him to the bedroom.

"The poor girl did not dream she was walking into the room of her death," he would later say. They began to have sex. His fervor quickly changed—it was too intense, more than just passion this time. He reached over and grabbed a piece of rope. She felt it wrap around her neck. Her trachea crunched. The rope was squeezing the air out. Her eyes grew wider when he pulled the rope. He stared at her. Ruth fought, tried to overpower him. She thrashed, but he squeezed harder. Her stamina finally slipped away. One last gasp and he had killed her. He gazed down.

"There is a peace about death that soothes me," he later said. "A corpse has a beauty and a dignity which a living body could never hold."

But he was startled—there was a knock at the door. It was a boy, carrying a note that alarmed the man. His wife would soon arrive with her brother. He thought quickly, then pulled up the floorboards of his parlor at the front of the flat and placed her body there before replacing the boards. He moved hurriedly; he wouldn't have privacy for much longer. Later that evening, his wife and her brother appeared. His brother-in-law hoped to spend the night. *Yes,* was the reply, *in the front parlor is fine.* The brother lay down in the front room, just feet from Ruth's body.

"I became worried, wondering whether he would suspect anything," the man remembered. She stayed there until the next afternoon, until his wife and her brother left the flat for a bit.

He took up the floorboards and carried Ruth into his tenement garden's washhouse, a small building with a sink, mostly used for storage but rarely by the other tenants. Late that night, around ten o'clock, he told his wife he needed to use the lavatory, another small building in the garden, near the washhouse. He walked outside and quietly took a shovel.

"Neighbors watched me digging," he said. "They nodded 'cheerios' to me." When they left, he dragged Ruth from the washhouse and rolled her into the grave.

In 1952, nine years later, she was still there, secluded by the fog—just another object planted in the garden. His garden. She was lying beneath him, many days. The war constable with a large forehead, thinning hair, and startling voice frequently dragged a rake less than two feet above her. His steps disturbed the dirt. He shoved plants into the ground just inches from her face—he fancied himself a talented gardener.

One day, he was digging and misjudged where he had buried her, thrusting his shovel through her neck, cracking part of her vertebra, and breaking off her skull. He picked up her head and tossed it into an old dustbin for burning. He didn't have an innate process, the perfect way to murder someone. Not yet. In December 1952, the fog drifted above Ruth Fuerst, brushing over the dead leaves lying on the ground. It was a ghastly final resting place for a troubled young woman. Even more alarming—she wasn't alone.

CHAPTER TWO

Blackout

The yellow fog that rubs its back upon the window-panes,
The yellow smoke that rubs its muzzle on the
   window-panes,
Licked its tongue into the corners of the evening,
Lingered upon the pools that stand in drains,
Let fall upon its back the soot that falls from chimneys,
Slipped by the terrace, made a sudden leap...

   —T. S. Eliot, "The Love Song of J. Alfred Prufrock," 1915

Tendrils of smoke wafted up above his head, then coiled around it and expanded into a thin veil that enveloped him. Fat flakes of soot stuck to his jacket like paint. His sword tarnished. It was a despicable way to treat such a gallant figure.

Admiral Horatio Nelson was an eighteenth-century British war hero—a Royal Navy man who famously defeated the French emperor Napoleon Bonaparte's soldiers during the Battle of Trafalgar. In 1843, the British government erected a sandstone statue of Nelson in Trafalgar Square. Standing more than 150 feet tall and chiseled in Dartmoor granite, Nelson's Column was flanked by four bronze Barbary lions. They were his guardians as he gazed south toward the Palace of Westminster. Lord Nelson was a tick on a tourist's London itinerary—an essential visit. Children from all over the world flocked to the monument. They gazed up at him, and climbed atop his lions for a ride.

Nelson was more than a symbol of the British victory over the French and Spanish—he was yet another reminder of the fall of Nazi Germany. If Adolf Hitler had invaded Britain, he had infamously planned to move the beloved statue from Trafalgar Square to Berlin as a show of force. It would have been an unbearable humiliation for the fiercely proud Londoners, and through the dark years of the Blitz and the bloody end of World War II, Nelson's likeness had taken on near-totemic meaning. Today, seven years after the end of wartime aggression, Commander Nelson's statue was admired and positively revered by the city's populace. But that morning, December 5, the Admiral quietly, discreetly disappeared.

The dark, suffocating fog crept around him overnight and into the early hours of Friday. Temperatures dropped more than ten degrees from the previous day. At the same time, the barometric pressure suddenly rose to its highest level in more than a week. The night sky clouded and the thin fire in gas lamps flickered, highlighting the grey mist against the blackness. The pigeons fluttered around Nelson, kicking up small plumes of smoke. Chimneys, puffing out fumes mixed with soot, furiously working to keep away the creeping cold, dotted the buildings around him.

A Member of Parliament, hoping to start his day early, might peer upward as he entered the storied halls of British government, expecting to see Nelson welcome him as he did every morning. The MP might squint through his spectacles as fat flakes of soot stuck to the lenses. He would notice that the smoke forged a shroud around the column and climbed upward. As the haze thickened, the war hero faded, then finally vanished.

No matter, the MP might mutter as he trudged toward Parliament, *just another London particular.*

∽

On Friday, December 5, Londoners awoke to a blanket of grey fog covering the city. Along the River Thames, the smoke was not merely thick, but impenetrable. Just a few hours earlier, the government shut down all traffic on the river. Ships were ordered to stay docked. Commuters shivering on the platform of the Liverpool Street Central Line Underground Station could see less than fifty yards. But they still stepped onto their trains, ready for a full day of work. As the morning dragged on, instead of dissipating, the fog thickened. By early afternoon, the Underground trains were running on their normal schedule, but the public buses were beginning to experience delays. The city's coal-burning railway engines vomited smoke. Traffic in Central London slowed as drivers navigated through the fading daylight. Richmond Bridge was closed. In some parts of the city, all bus and trolleybus services were suspended indefinitely. At home and in offices, Londoners hoping to stave off the frigid temperatures sparked more than one million fireplaces, piled with that brown coal. The city's power plants churned out electricity, fueled by cheap, lower-grade coal. Smoke poured from their chimneys.

In the House of Commons, MPs debated the country's agriculture policy and then left a few hours early, to avoid being abandoned by commuter rails. Two trains were delayed as they carried animals from Scotland to compete in the Smithfield Fat Stock Show at Earl's Court. Criminals began using the fog to their advantage. A group of burglars bound and gagged a female cleaner before cracking open a safe in an office building in Little Britain, a small district in Central London.

And there was an especially foreboding bit of news from Parliament: Iain Macleod, the minister of health, sent a memo to all hospitals forbidding them from increasing their staff without prior approval. "It must be shown that the increase is justified by exceptional circumstances such as serious under-manning," wrote Macleod, "and that the need cannot be met by reorganization or in any other way that would avoid the employment of additional staff." He also demanded they cut non-medical and non-nursing staffs by 5 percent over the next year. The government was trying to control its bloated debts.

The fog was hardly mentioned in the city newspapers. They printed stories about compulsory crash helmets for motorcyclists and the introduction of a new stamp marking the reign of Queen Elizabeth II, but nothing about the smoke and fumes. The *Manchester Guardian* did proclaim: "the first real fog of the year has enveloped London today, an old-fashioned peasouper: thick, drab, yellow, disgusting." Yet the reporter described the conditions as rather pleasant for some drivers. "It was possible to drive through the West End at a speed which left a wide safety margin and yet reach one's destination more quickly than usual. There was plenty of parking space too."

As Friday morning carried into the afternoon, the soot worked in concert with the mist. The flakes were large enough to be expelled by a puff from a lamplighter's mouth. Eyes ached, reddened in the fog's miasma. Throats burned, as if specks of iron were caught in mid-swallow. Christmas lights on trees that decorated stores in the West End seemed to hang midair, but holiday shoppers pushed on. Scientists at twelve pollution-monitoring sites across Greater London recorded their daily readings. They found the new data troubling, particularly at a station on the Thames near Westminster Bridge. In less than twenty-four hours, the amounts of smoke and sulphur dioxide in the air had increased more than five times. More disturbing—the machines used by the Air Ministry to record air pollution tracked only sulphur dioxide and smoke. There were other deadly gases—carbon dioxide and carbon monoxide—belched out by exhaust from thousands of vehicles that were going unmeasured. And diesel oil engines from the city's eight thousand double-decker buses spewed out vanadium compounds that caused bronchial irritation. As the chemicals in the air increased, so did the number of deaths.

The fog drifted along the bottom of the Thames Valley, across the city, building its power. On Friday afternoon, it was mostly just an irritant—like those famous London fogs that had enchanted literature lovers for hundreds of years. But soon, a simple peasouper would throttle the city.

cofifco

Rosemary Sargent gazed through the window of the red double-decker bus as it snaked through London. Less than an hour earlier, her teacher, Ms. Atkinson, had peered outside and frowned as the dark clouds swirled. *Time to leave.* The thirteen-year-old had just finished up lunch at Catford Central, a secondary school for girls in Catford, Lewisham, in the southeast part of the city. Rosemary thought the early release was a tad premature—it didn't seem like one of those fogs that would turn from inconvenient to alarming. But Rosemary was accustomed to the curt interruption of her secretarial studies. She was learning shorthand and typing—skills she could eventually use to secure a good office job. She was such a smart girl—if she made good grades, in a few years she would take the General Education "O" Level and Secretarial exams in individual subjects. Passing the "O" was considered a huge achievement, and earned students (and their parents) bragging rights. But today, the exam was the last thing on her mind.

Rosemary and the other girls, bundled by their mothers in warm sweaters, long woolen socks, and leather shoes, were told to clear out. Teachers ordered them to board diesel buses, recently rolled out by the government. There was no panic, just acceptance. She shivered. It just seemed so much colder than the day before. The fog was a nuisance to girls Rosemary's age. They often wore white petticoats under their cotton dresses and the smoke tinted their hems black—it took hours for their mothers to clean them. Rosemary's hair was grimy, coated with soot. The stuff seeped into her skin, like a thin layer of lotion that refused to be scrubbed away with soap flakes. It was god-awful, that fog. But she lived with it, as she would a lifelong flatmate.

The sun hung in dust. Rosemary glowered. She could see the small particles floating, even without a real breeze. The bus windows were screwed tight, but that smell haunted her— acrid, filthy, and burning, like taking a whiff from the inside of a chimney's brick throat. The heavier the cloak of fog, the more it burned. It scorched her eyes and her nose, and then squeezed her throat. On the street, trendy debutantes wrapped their chiffon scarves across their mouths, their pearls dangling just below, in a futile effort to stop the rancid air from choking them. But even their upscale woolen coats wouldn't cut the chill on this day. Londoners scurried along Bromley Road, gripped their shopping bags, their umbrellas, and their children. Rosemary's daily trip home to Bromley felt longer than its usual twenty minutes, but she couldn't imagine the diesel buses would be running much longer. The police might soon be forced to use torches, a practice adopted to guide vehicles through the fog. Their black overcoats, tall woolen hats, and white, double-strapped fog masks were a common sight in the winter. The pollution tarnished their polished silver buttons. Dapper young men sporting Teddy Boy suits slipped downstairs to the Underground, but the subway service might be suspended soon, too.

Rosemary stepped off the bus that afternoon just as the fog descended; she was already struggling to catch her breath. The air was dark yellow, not quite brown or black, but somehow thick. She turned her head quickly left and right. Aggravated, she squinted. She couldn't see her house—she couldn't even see her front gate, let alone her family's modest garden packed full of potatoes just under the surface. The smell had worsened to a dirty, sooty stench. It addled Rosemary's brain. She shuffled down the garden path, trying to orient herself. As she got closer, she scanned the front of her split-level terrace home—a small building on a block of mirror-image redbrick houses with shared sidewalls, London's answer to its dense population.

Rosemary stepped inside the front parlor to find her three siblings. The coal fireplace in that room was cold and dormant, as always. Her family couldn't afford to light coal in two hearths, so they spent much of their time near the fire in the family room. The Sargents, a clan of six, weren't well-off but they weren't hard up, either. They were upper working-class—Rosemary's father, Albert, was a skilled cabinetmaker who earned a good living. Rosemary didn't have a "best pair" of shoes or a "school pair," just that one pair—those black brogue-style shoes that seemed to last a lifetime. But her father could afford to have her feet measured, so she wasn't wearing hand-me-downs that pinched her toes or left gaps at her ankles, the bane of so many children her age.

The fog was swirling at the window—an unwanted visitor lurking outside. Her mother, Edna, didn't switch on the radio for a news update. *Why?* A peasouper was commonplace, almost customary—an entrée to Christmas. Her only question: *How late will Albert be tonight?* Rosemary strolled into the family's small gallery kitchen as her mother was preparing supper.

Edna Sargent was a bona fide British matriarch: a spitfire with a temper—a wordsmith during rows with her husband. She and Albert had the occasional flare-ups during fifteen years of marriage—quarrels largely ignored by the children, but always peaceful at the end. There was a mutual respect between them, and Edna was always pleased to see him step across the threshold into their parlor, usually around half past six. That Friday night, Rosemary looked through the room's glass pane. When the foggy air permeated a clear December night, Albert was frequently several hours late. Occasionally he was able to slip away from work to use a public telephone box, that red booth with a rotary phone inside, outfitted with coin slots. But most of the time Albert didn't bother; he just began walking home. Edna wondered if his supper would need to be warmed later.

Rosemary and her siblings proceeded with their afternoon, looking forward to spending the weekend making holiday paper chains for the parlor fireplace's hearth with their father. A tree would soon arrive, with colorful lights and cheap tinsel. Rosemary suspected her parents had already finished their holiday shopping—she dreamed of new winter gloves lined with real rabbit fur. The fog couldn't stop the holiday preparations across the city. Fathers haggled over petite spruces in Covent Garden Market. Selfridges' "Father Christmas in Toy Town" window displays thrilled young children. Little girls begged their mothers for Mickey Mouse dolls. Boys gawked at Lionel trains in Hamley's Toy Store. London was dressed in swaths of red and green—it was a glorious time of year, especially in the midst of a painfully slow recovery from the war.

In the Sargent household, Rosemary was the eldest child and, at thirteen, the most defiant. She had a sharp wit complete with snide retorts that bordered on insubordination, at least according to her mother. They had an uneasy kinship that was generally subdued, thanks to mediation from her father. After greeting her mother, Rosemary checked on the youngest Sargent, five-year-old Sue, then chatted with eight-year-old Malcolm and eleven-year-old David.

The last glimmer of sun faded behind the gusts of grey clouds. The fog trickled through the cracks of the wooden frames, dragging along that stench, soon to be absorbed by the cotton curtains. Still, the family carried on with the evening, waiting for Albert. Six days a week, Rosemary's father toiled inside a London bus garage in Camberwell Green, about a twenty-minute bus ride from their home. Inside the redbrick warehouse, Albert Sargent mended the wood frames and upholstery on the city's diesel buses. He was a carpenter by trade, but after World War II employment was scarce, so he had joined up with a transport company. It was a good job—his wife didn't have to work and he could support his four children.

Tall, slender, and agile, the forty-two-year-old had been born four years before World War I. After his mother died, his father had raised him for a bit in the East End of London—a neighborhood synonymous with poverty, overcrowding, disease, and crime. The legend of Jack the Ripper, the notorious serial killer of the 1880s who was never caught and brought to justice, still haunted that area's crumbling buildings. Albert's father was a publican; he managed alehouses in the neighborhood and sampled his wares a bit too often, at least for a single parent. Rosemary's grandfather then moved Albert and his siblings to Dulwich Village in inner London, an area that would be devastated by German V-1 flying bombs and V-2 rockets decades later. Albert became a streetwise kid who grew into a conscientious man.

When Albert was a boy, his father would scrape together enough money to take the family to visit an aunt and uncle on the island of Mersea in Essex on the Suffolk border. Rosemary's mother, Edna, lived there, and less than two years after meeting over coffee, she and Albert married. The year Rosemary was born, 1939, twenty-nine-year-old Albert tried to join the army, along with more than one million other Britons at the outbreak of the World War II. He failed the physical miserably.

He had a nagging cough, a hack that could turn into a bark near a fire, especially a fire fueled by that cheap coal dust peddled by the government. He blamed it on his younger days, cycling through the streets of Dulwich in the foggy, urban air when he was a teenager—his lungs had never been very healthy. When the British Army discovered he was plagued with respiratory issues they rejected him—too much of a risk. Instead, in 1939 he was assigned to an aircraft factory at Langley Airfield in Slough, a town about twenty miles west of Central London.

Albert worked in the upholstery unit inside massive aircraft hangars, plying his trade on the famous Supermarine Spitfires, the single-engine fighter planes manned by the Royal Air Force. There was irony in that assignment: He worked with hot glue most days, and the poisonous gases in the factory made him wheeze as much as any chlorine gas unleashed by the Germans during World War I. That was his job for much of the war, and though the hot glue was toxic, he felt proud knowing he had contributed to the war effort in some important way. The factory was too far to allow him to live at home in Bromley with his family, so he rarely returned to the city. Then the bombings began—Rosemary and her family were told to leave London.

During the worst of the Blitz, government tried to empty the densely packed cities of mothers and children through a mass evacuation. About eight hundred thousand young people were forced from their homes and moved to the countryside, where there were fewer targets for German bombers and much less devastation. Many were gone for up to six years, for the remainder of the war. Rosemary's mother packed up the family's few belongings and moved with the children to rural West Murphy in Essex where her parents lived. The children were without a patriarch, in a strange town without friends. Rosemary's grandparents were devout Methodists—they attended church three times a day, most days. Rosemary and her brother came along. The humble local school was bursting with evacuees; there was little learning, but quite a lot of chaos. Rosemary thought of her father often while she was with her grandparents.

She knew he was serving as an air raid warden in London, one of the men who proved themselves indispensable and heroic during the Blitz. Whenever the sirens blared in London, wardens like Albert helped people into the nearest shelter—then, despite the bombs, shrapnel, and masonry falling from the skies all around, they toured their sector to be sure all civilians had cleared out. When explosions leveled buildings, Albert pulled people out of rubble. *A hero*, Rosemary thought.

She was back in a London grade school when he finally arrived home six years later in 1945—she had grown in inches and pounds. She was now the spitting image of him: blonde, attractive, and slender, with deep-set eyes and soft features. It was a different life for them, now that he was back. Her mother explained that many children lost fathers to the war—they were very lucky. Rosemary knew it; she was so grateful to be with him, to get to know him again.

By the time the fog slowly invaded their home that Friday night in December 1952, Albert Sargent had been back with them for seven years. The teenager looked out the window for her father, a futile exercise considering the muddiness of the air.

It was seven o'clock ticking toward eight—her mother quickly prepared dinner. She didn't seem worried. By nighttime the fog was so thick that even a policeman's flashlight was nearly invisible. Rosemary knew it would take Albert hours to walk in that fog from his bus garage in Camberwell Green, about five miles away. Her mother wasn't concerned about the distance. It was that nagging cough of his—that hacking, forced choking sound that was guttural. It was a clear sign of a bronchial infection. He just couldn't shake it in the winter—most Londoners couldn't.

It must have taken Albert at least two hours to walk those five miles home through the putrid air. And it was bleak, just below freezing outside. Rosemary knew his route through the hamlets, filled with families warming themselves by fires. Well after eight o'clock, Albert plowed through the door, wheezing and desperately searching for breath. He dragged inside with him the moldy air, and the family quickly bundled him in and shut the door. The fog lingered in the air after the door had been closed, and tendrils of it crept under the window frames, which were closed tight against the chill outside. Rosemary grimaced as her father choked and wheezed, tears flowing down his cheeks. He was her hero, though they were still learning about each other. She saw an extraordinarily good man who was suffering. Her mother tried to calm him, asked him if he wanted supper.

"I don't want anything to eat, I'm going to bed," he replied.

Her mother rolled her eyes—his plate was already on the table—but she didn't protest aloud. Albert climbed the steps to the small master bedroom. The rest of the family soon retired for the night to the chilly upstairs rooms. When Rosemary peered in to check on him, she saw her father stretched out, still fully clothed, on her parents' bed. He was completely exhausted from the walk.

Rosemary listened to each labored breath as she lay in a twin bed in her small room—she was the eldest and rightly entitled to privacy. She could hear her brothers and sister next door in their bedroom—the boys climbed into their double bed while Sue curled up on her small bed. They were all cold. It was like an icebox upstairs, almost year round. There was no heating, no fireplace—only a few woolen blankets that offered little comfort. The windows' cheap frames ushered the warm air out and invited harsh wind inside. Her father's cough echoed through the house.

∾

It was a similar scene in houses, flats, and rooms all across London, including Maura and Stanley Crichton's small bedsit in North London.

Maura Crichton was quite a willful woman—a cantankerous spirit simmering under the auburn locks of an Irish beauty. When something angered her, her husband naturally stepped backward, just a foot or so. She relished their debates—the affectionate bickering. And he loved her. Her temperament was why Stanley had married the twenty-two-year-old earlier that year—that and her gorgeous singing voice. Maura's sweet Irish lilt illuminated whichever song she selected, whether she was singing in their tiny place in Finsbury Park or performing on stage in her native Waterford. And when she was well, her voice was as pure as the crystal that made her hometown famous. Not this night, though. Her voice, which had once produced beautiful melodies, had turned gruff and hoarse—and then she had no voice at all. That fog ruined it all, really.

This wasn't a new problem for Maura, the coughing. Just a whiff of smoke at their favorite pub forced her to gasp and choke.

A thick peasouper might send her to the hospital, if she didn't stay inside. Maura's asthma was misery for a young singer and frightening for her husband—a police officer, fresh from the academy. Twenty-year-old Stanley glanced out their window toward Finsbury Park. There it was, just as the forecasters on the radio had warned. The next few days were certain to be miserable for both of them—but for very different reasons. The Victorian gas lamps, peppered across more than one hundred acres of the park, should have stood tall and flickered, illuminating a young couple out for a stroll. Now, the flames quivered like tiny fireflies from a children's book. The outlines of the light posts softened. The flames just lingered, engulfed by the smoke.

The dark clouds drifted—approached Stanley's windowpane, demanding to be allowed inside. Without invitation, the smoke slipped under the wooden frame and into the room—it dragged with it that bitter smell. Stanley turned and watched Maura throw on her winter coat. She tried to swallow a wet cough. He sighed and braced himself. "You can't go out right now, that's mad," Stanley said.

"But *you're* going on shift, so can I," Maura snapped back.

"Yes, but I'm not coughing up that yellow mess."

They were both scheduled to work that Friday—Stanley was assigned to patrol Holloway, a seedy district nearby. Maura was an auxiliary nurse at the Great Ormond Street Hospital Children's Charity, where she tended to young patients. They both worked the night shift. Maura wheezed, then glared at her husband. "I'm going."

Stanley raised his voice. "By the time you get to the end of the road, I will have lost you!"

Maura repeated, "But you're going to go!"

"Yes, but I know my way better than you, now come on," he insisted.

Maura coughed, clutched her coat, flung open their front door, and disappeared. Stanley raced to the stoop—his eyes searched for her. She was stumbling on the street just a few feet away, clutching her throat. She suddenly dropped. The smoke slowly nudged past Stanley in his doorway. He jumped into the haze, lifted his wife, and carried her like a helpless child back inside. He laid her on their small bed and ordered that she control her breathing. She was quite beautiful to him, even in this state—and he was truly worried. But he had to go. He had joined the Metropolitan Police just a few months earlier and he was still on probation. He had to leave right now or risk losing this job they needed so desperately. She wheezed.

"Just stay there," he said. "I'll come round in a few hours."

Maura nodded.

Stanley strapped on his white cotton face mask, opened the front door, and buttoned his black Yorkshire coat. He could feel the wooden baton inside his wool trousers, his only weapon. He readied himself for the mile-long walk to Hornsey Police Station, on the other side of the park. He looked up at the window that guarded Maura from that noxious smoke—he couldn't see the light inside. The grey mist had smothered it.

✑

As night settled in, the people began showing up in emergency rooms all across London. Doctors saw a substantial increase in respiratory and cardiac diseases from the day before. Ambulance calls had increased by a third. As the temperatures plummeted, Londoners were forced to burn more and more of the cheap, dangerous, sooty brown powder—almost 40 percent of Britain's coal supply was nutty slack. But Londoners, like their ancestors, were accustomed to coal-smudged skies and thick smog.

Until the thirteenth century, wood was the main fuel source in London. But as the city expanded, the outlying trees were cut down for new homes, and wood soon vanished. Londoners then collected the so-called "sea coal" that washed ashore off the northeast coast of England, near Newcastle. It was soft, bituminous coal that could heat their homes and fuel their factories. It was used to churn out a variety of products needed by the English, everything from beer to soap. Lime kilns blasted poisons into the air. But the cheap coal wasted most of its energy making smoke instead of providing heat.

Sea coal contained high levels of sulphur, so when it was burned it released large amounts of sulphur dioxide, carbon dioxide, nitric oxide, and soot into the air. If the weather conditions were right, smoke from London's thousands of chimneys and factories combined with the fog to create a deadly concoction that could last for days. And kill for months.

None of this was a surprise to Londoners; they had been coping with the ill effects of burning this cheap coal for centuries. In 1257, the British royals were warming their drafty castle in Nottingham with coal fireplaces when huge clouds of smoke disseminated throughout the building. The fumes forced Queen Eleanor from the castle. In 1272, King Edward I forbade the use of sea coal by threatening to torture or execute anyone caught with it. The royal edict didn't stop Londoners, even when the first offender was executed—most couldn't afford the expensive wood. It was simply a matter of economics. Anthracite coal— the black stuff—was of higher quality, but too costly. The royals offered commoners no real solution, only intimidation.

King Richard III and Henry V both had attempted to ban sea coal, but failed.

As London expanded over the centuries, so did its dependence on coal. It became the dominant source of heat, and by the fifteenth century Londoners were constantly overcome with smoke. Seventeenth-century astrologer John Gadbury kept a daily weather diary and labeled particularly smoggy days "great stinking fogs." Three hundred years later, Australian scientist and historian Peter Brimblecombe compared those dates in November 1679 with death records for London during the same time period. The highest death rates coincided with weeks following those "great stinking fogs." It was evident that smog was a killer.

It also attacked young Londoners—even through the 1950s. The fogs blighted out the sun, the best source of vitamin D for growing kids. Without vitamin D, the body can't absorb calcium and young bones don't develop correctly. Children were afflicted with bowed legs and deformed pelvises, ribs, and limbs. The fogs created an epidemic of rickets in poor kids, who had diets without calcium-rich foods. During the 1600s, more than half of the city's children had rickets.

In 1661, influential writer John Evelyn distributed a treatise, one of the earliest works on air pollution, entitled *FUMIFUGIUM: or the Inconvenience of the Aer and Smoak of London Dissipated*. In the pamphlet, Evelyn begged King Charles II and Parliament to do something about the burning of coal in London. "And what is all this, but that Hellish and dismall Cloud of SEACOAL," he wrote, "so universally mixed with the otherwise wholesome and excellent Aer, that her Inhabitants breathe nothing but an impure and thick Mist accompanied with a fuliginous and filthy vapour." Despite Evelyn's pleas, the government did nothing.

Religious leaders were even executed over those fogs. In the 1600s, the Church of England's Archbishop of Canterbury, William Laud, fined several coal-burning brewers so he could repair smoke damage to Saint Paul's Cathedral. He was beheaded in

1645. When the Industrial Revolution reached Britain in the late 1700s, coal was king and the environment was irrevocably damaged. By the nineteenth century, more than a million Londoners were shoveling soft coal onto their grates. Winter fogs were persistent and so was the smoke. In 1873, smog smothered the city for days—almost three hundred people died from bronchitis—sending the mortality rate soaring 40 percent beyond normal. Another fog six years later blocked the light from the city for four months. Londoners in the East End were usually the most affected because of the dense population, cheaply made buildings, and the plethora of factories. It was also low-lying, so the fog took longer to burn off. By the turn of the twentieth century, smoky fog was endemic. In 1905, Dr. Henry Antoine Des Voeux coined the word "smog."

During both world wars, smoke became a defense strategy. In some areas of England, pollution was produced with the intention of masking the city from enemy bombers, like the smoke screens that armed forces used to hide the location of military units during combat. As German planes circled British cities, local factories churned out smoke, creating a dense layer of protection—a blackout of pollution.

There were critics, like influential members of the National Smoke Abatement Society (NSAS)—a lobby group that had existed, in various forms, since the 1880s. The NSAS admitted that smoke screening could be an effective strategy, but argued that the smoke was as much of a nuisance to British forces defending cities from the air and on the ground. And the pressure on industry to accelerate productivity during the war caused even more smoke. Factory owners began to force their steam boilers to exceed their design capacity—smoke restrictions were generally ignored. Pollution dirtied the air, not just in Britain but also around the world. And as industry ramped up and factories got bigger in scale, they used more coal and spewed out more carcinogens. The smog got more deadly. But as disgusting as it was, black smoke was also appreciated by some, like novelists.

Deadly fog was the muse for famed Victorian authors. They harnessed it as a literary device, symbolizing confusion and claustrophobia coupled with oppression and the blurring of roles in society. Charles Dickens weaved fog into his plots, molding it as a living character. When Robert Louis Stevenson penned *Dr. Jekyll and Mr. Hyde,* he used the fog itself to show the mutation of identity—the nightmarish landscape protected the murderous Mr. Hyde as he committed his crimes. When the fog drifted away, the civilized Dr. Jekyll reappeared. And the mention of Jack the Ripper evoked images of Victorian Whitechapel, smothered under an ominous cloak of fog—never mind that each of the murders happened on perfectly clear nights.

Swirls of fog were romantic and beguiling to Londoners, whose affinity for an open fire was virtually a requirement for being British. A coal fire in the hearth was an old companion who called on them every winter. Fog could be a nuisance, yes, but it also became the city's trademark. For centuries, few in England had paid much attention to those who cautioned about the dangers of bad air. The National Smoke Abatement Society had harassed the government for years about air pollution, but in the past, Parliament had only responded with ineffective committees and rules, which promoted the status quo. Sooty buildings, greasy hair, and dirty shirts were understood to be the price of progress. Smoke particles had floated through London's air since medieval times—and Britons didn't expect that to change.

But even the most stalwart gas lamplighters, those men who

illuminated London streets on a gloomy night with a torch on a pole, would likely admit the fog on this day was certainly more than just a bad peasouper.

✆

It was dark, dismal now, on this cold night in early December. It seemed similar to those blackouts the British government imposed during the Blitz, when all lights had been extinguished—homes, factories, streetlamps, even the Palace of Westminster, where the order originated. The blackouts had acted as a sort of camouflage from German bombers searching for targets in the darkness. Those nights had been frightening for Londoners. Cars traveling without headlights careened into pedestrians. Residents tumbled down stairs. Criminals took advantage of a vulnerable city. It was prudent to stay inside behind locked doors.

But there wasn't a government-ordered blackout this Friday night, the first night of the fog. There were no signs posted signifying when the lights could be turned back on. Tonight, the London air was black—thick, like ink, and there was no way to gauge when the fog would end. Meteorologists predicted it would blow away by the next day. It wouldn't.

Acrid smoke churned from the chimney of the dreary apartment at 10 Rillington Place. The plumes pushed down, tumbled over John Reginald Christie's private garden. If "Reg" were to glance down from his kitchen window that night, as he often did, his small plot would be almost indistinguishable, smothered by the fog. The swirls born from the coal were bewitching. And the fog was once his accomplice, such a reliable conspirator. He drew inspiration from its noxious fumes—it had helped him murder her, the second woman, after all. The back garden's broken pots, dead plants, and general rubbish usually visible out his back window vanished in the fog—the fence, which could barely stand on its own, faded like a lost memory.

If Reg screwed up his eyes, adjusted his spectacles, and made careful calculations, he might visualize something odd about that fence, a strange stick that helped brace it. It was a bone— a thighbone, actually. It didn't belong to the first girl, the flirty one who had been infatuated with his uniform. It came from the other one, the woman who had arrived at his home the following year—and never left. It was her thighbone bracing a section of Reg's fence—so many people had strolled past it over the years, including Scotland Yard investigators. If they had just looked down at her bone, haphazardly lodged into the dirt, perhaps he would have been stopped. If only they had noticed.

Muriel Amelia Eady had been so different from his first: short, plump, and quite average-looking. She had short, wavy brown hair and a squished face—and, at age thirty-one, she was older than Ruth Fuerst. Muriel didn't want his money; she had a good job—actually, that's where they met. And she didn't need his company—she had plenty of male companions. This affair, as Reg would call it, would require some effort and planning. And patience. He plotted. Muriel was quiet and restrained as she worked on the assembly line at Ultra Electric Ltd, a factory in northwest London tasked with building radios before the war began. She helped construct military equipment, including parts for the combat planes used to attack the Nazis.

It had been 1944 when Reg met her. That summer in Normandy, the Allies launched the largest seaborne invasion in history, known as D-Day, beginning the liberation of parts of Nazi-occupied Europe. There was hope in London—prayers that this war would soon be over. In a factory spanning more than 150,000 square feet, packed with more than a thousand workers, Reg had noticed her right away. He gazed at Muriel as she stood in the canteen; he asked her to join him for a cup of tea. She invited a male friend over—Reg smiled. He invited them both to tea at his home with his wife, Ethel. Muriel and her friend visited 10 Rillington Place several times, happily chatting about life in London. The four of them even went to the movies. He could be charming, when he needed to be. Slowly, Muriel grew to trust Reg. She believed that he was honorable—he was a former War Reserve policeman, he mentioned.

That "quiet, peaceful thrill" he experienced from his time with Ruth—that's what Reg yearned for again. But this time would be very different—he would stay in control. He was willing to wait, to plan appropriately. As October 1944 began, the weather turned foggy and smoky as it often did that time of year. Rain soaked the streets, dripped down the gas lamps. Muriel coughed quite often. Reg noticed and smiled, feigning concern. He was working it all out now.

"A really clever murder," he would later murmur. "Much cleverer than the first."

At home, away from his wife's inquisitive glances, Reg prepared for Muriel. He found a mask and then a square glass jar, punched two holes in the tin lid, and attached two rubber tubes. One led to steaming water in the jar, which was infused with Friar's Balsam, a compound that smelled like alcohol; it was used to treat breathing issues like bronchitis. It might smell familiar to her, perhaps soothing.

But there was more to his invention. He attached the other rubber tube to the mask; that hose was longer, and its source wasn't immediately evident to someone sitting at his kitchen table. In fact, that second tube stretched behind his stove to the gas pipe projecting out of the wall—inside it was coal gas. When the metal seam cap was unscrewed, it churned out lethal carbon monoxide, the same stuff that puffed out of his chimney on a cold night. It was a brilliant plan, really. Reg stashed his equipment and waited.

Muriel complained about her cough again one morning. Reg smiled and explained he had a medical background—he had earned a First Aid Certificate and kept a book handy from St John Ambulance for reference. *I have something that can cure that cough*, he promised. She was grateful and agreed to meet him, without her male friend, at his home over the weekend. He arranged to take sick leave from the factory—nine days beginning on Monday, October 2. Before he left, he told Muriel to come to his home that Saturday for a treatment, when he knew his wife would be working—she worked at Osram's light bulb factory as a typist during the war.

Just a few weeks earlier, Londoners had turned back their clocks for daylight saving time—the evenings were longer, the light faded earlier. Muriel lunched with her aunt on Saturday, October 7. Around four, she slipped on a jacket and quickly left the house, calling out, "I shan't be late." It was a week before her thirty-second birthday—her aunt would clearly remember that detail.

Reg opened the door. Muriel had dressed nicely for him—a black dress with a pink collar and a camel-colored coat. He welcomed her, invited her to sit in the kitchen. *Ethel's gone to visit family*, he said. Reg proudly showed her the jar with the tube and explained that her cough would be cured in no time. He handed her the tube and put a scarf over her head. He suggested she breathe deeply. *The Friar's Balsam will help*, he assured her. She didn't seem to notice that other tube, the one that stretched to his coal-gas pipe. Reg reached over and released the bull clip he had left clamped on the tube. It might seem strange that a woman with any common sense could have trusted him. It was simply a testament to the confidence he was able to muster when properly motivated. The coal-gas pipe pumped out carbon monoxide as she inhaled the Friar's Balsam.

"She had no suspicions at all she was about to die," he later said.

Soon, she went limp. She wasn't dead—that wouldn't have suited Reg—but she was helpless.

"This was the moment I was waiting for," he remembered.

He lifted her carefully. He laid her on the bed and did what he had done with Ruth—except this time he reached for a pair of stockings. It was part of the excitement. He knew its potential, what it would feel like to squeeze her throat until she was gone. It took relatively little energy to kill her, which surprised him. His body wasn't healthy—he had loads of aches all over and he was recovering from bronchitis. He hoped to kill her with the least amount of effort. She never opened her eyes; there was no fight. "She made no objections at all."

It was the most exhilarating feeling—"No regrets," he said. "I dismissed it from my mind."

His inner hubris was peculiar, particularly for a cowardly man.

"For the second time in my life, I looked down at the still, lifeless form of an attractive woman who had died at my hands," he said.

Muriel spent several hours inside his washhouse in the garden—but he didn't want to keep her there long. That wouldn't be smart. Later that evening, with Ethel still out, Reg quickly disposed of her in a familiar manner, plopping her into a shallow grave near the back of the yard. They were so close to each other, Muriel and Ruth, crammed together in that tiny garden, along with an array of animal bones from pets long gone.

But tonight, more than eight years later, in December of 1952, the first night of that god-awful fog, Reg's trophies evaporated in the smoke, created by the coal fires inside 10 Rillington Place. For now, the women were only recollections to him—beautiful memories. And yet quite soon, they would resurface.

CHAPTER THREE

Restrained

We saw the greasy, heavy brown swirl still drifting
past us and condensing in oily drops upon the
window-panes…"look out this window, Watson.
See how the figures loom up, are dimly seen, and
then blend once more into the cloud-bank. The
thief or the murderer could roam London on such
a day as the tiger does the jungle, unseen until he
pounces, and then evident only to his victim."
—*Sir Arthur Conan Doyle,* The Adventure of the
Bruce-Partington Plans, *1908*

"**S**hit!" screamed the man at the other end of the radio. The
dispatcher punched buttons, tried to muster up a calm response.
The receivers were blaring, perhaps a bit too loudly considering
the profanity erupting from the speakers. The crackly reception
punched through the brick walls and echoed around the halls of
the famous Victorian building, sitting on the bank of the River
Thames. It was officially called "New Scotland Yard," but Londoners settled on simply "Scotland Yard" or "The Yard." It was
the headquarters of the distinguished Metropolitan Police Service,
the department for those officers who served Greater London.

The fog on Saturday, December 6, was maddening for members of Britain's police force. Those officers, who pledged to
protect one of the world's most important cities, were essentially
crippled by smoke and soot. For much of the morning, colorful

expletives flooded the "Information Room," the nerve center for emergency calls in the United Kingdom.

Met investigators boasted of their acumen in tracking down criminal masterminds, all while battling fog and rain. Yard detectives starred in Alfred Hitchcock's suspense films. They solved murder mysteries in Agatha Christie plays. They were charming, erudite inspectors in Dickens stories. They were mildly belittled in Sir Arthur Conan Doyle's famous Sherlock Holmes novels — after all, no one could be as brilliant as Holmes. But even Doyle assigned them some redeeming characteristics.

The Met was the world's first modern police force, founded in 1749 as the Bow Street Runners. Before the Runners, private citizens had been in charge of punishing criminals — the streets were chaotic and vigilante justice prevailed. Two hundred years later, London was a safer city, thanks to the Metropolitan Police.

In 1888, Chief Inspector Frederick Abberline and his detectives worked tirelessly to unmask Jack the Ripper — and failed. Met police juggled countless cases of murder, prostitution, and robberies in Victorian London. Even Scotland Yard's own building was wrapped in mystery. During its construction in the late 1800s, while the Ripper was lurking in Whitechapel alleyways, workers found the torso of a woman in the Yard's cellar. The murder was dubbed "The Whitehall Mystery" — the victim was never identified and detectives couldn't find the killer. If Met police weren't able solve the crime, it was unlikely anyone could.

In 1952, Scotland Yard enjoyed a reputation around the world as a symbol of efficient policing. And its leaders demanded civility from its officers. Unfortunately, there was little of it to be found inside the Yard during the second day of the fog.

After an extremely cold and windless night, Londoners awoke to find themselves engulfed by a dense, dark yellow vapor that extended at least twenty miles in every direction from the city center. The belt of high pressure stretched from Spain, across England and Wales to Germany. Rural areas saw glimpses of sun, but London was still drowning in smoke and fumes.

It was thicker than the day before—at Kingsway Observatory in Westminster in Central London, visibility was less than thirty yards. At Kew Observatory in Richmond, near the Thames, it was nil. Scientists recorded their daily pollution measurements— the amount of smoke and sulphur dioxide in the air near the Palace of Westminster had increased by more than 20 percent over the past twenty-four hours. The level of poison was now seven times higher than it had been forty-eight hours earlier, an astounding increase in such a short period of time. And it was colder, too. The temperature at Kensington Palace didn't warm past thirty-two degrees Fahrenheit, almost twenty degrees below average. But there was no wind—a blessing because of the temperature, but the lack of circulation compounded the toxicity of the air. To battle the chill, Londoners layered their clothes, closed their doors, and piled more coal nuggets onto their fires.

But despite the deepening crisis, British newspapers were still covering the situation in a cursory way. The *Manchester Guardian* buried the smoke on page ten, with a three-hundred-word piece entitled "Traffic Delayed by Fog." The *Observer*'s only headline about the fog on Saturday was "Fog and Ice: Cars Left by Roadside." The *Times* featured a similar story, with concerns about delayed traffic. Londoners coughed, wheezed, and did their best to get on with their day—until they truly began to suffer, by the thousands.

Forecasters projected Sunday's weather: "the fog may persist near large towns for much of the day, but most places will have sunny periods after mid-morning. It will continue cold or rather cold." It was a naïve prediction. Every form of transportation was impaired. Overnight, planes at London's three main airports were grounded. Transport workers halted double-deckers in mid-route and escorted them back to their garages using flares. Officials with the Automobile Association said it was the worst fog they had ever known—they demanded that drivers stay home. The Underground was deluged with passengers, but trains sat on the tracks; the weather delayed service by hours. Police officers lit torches along the city's main thoroughfares. Thousands of street gas lamps were sparked and it was still almost impossible to navigate empty roads. Drivers abandoned their cars on the streets, like frightened teenagers hiding from a ghoul in an American horror film.

But if the papers were still largely overlooking the disaster, those working on the front lines were acutely aware of the crisis. As it became darker, the black mist adhered to the windows of Scotland Yard. Detectives sparked cigarettes as they walked out of the redbrick building; they cupped their hands—and inhaled their own smoke. Inside the Yard, grey streaks of fog clung to the ceiling. It was a huge building, more than four stories tall, and most rooms had a fireplace, resplendent with glowing coals. As the spate of swear words continued over the radios, Met police dispatchers barked directions—*Go this way or that* and *Get a move on!*

"No, we're lost! We're lost!" was the most common response from the beat cops. In less than a day, the "London particular"— the fog that Scotland Yard had hoped would blow away quickly—had spiraled into a disaster. Officers were leaving behind their patrol cars; the smut stuck to their windshields like paint. They rode bicycles to respond to emergency calls, or just began walking. They donned white jackets so they could be seen more easily.

Met police had spent the last two days working constantly.

There were no cots or warm showers—none expected to spend the night in the Yard, but most did. The Metropolitan Police had a force of about sixteen thousand working the streets of London in 1952—about 15 percent fewer than prewar levels, despite a much heavier workload. In 1938, the police cleared about 50 percent of the nearly 290,000 indictable offenses. By 1951, the crime rate had almost doubled, and the city had far fewer officers available.

"Scotland Yard Information Room," answered a calm voice through the phone receiver. The officer jotted down some details on a form stuck to a clipboard. Police cadets, teenagers mostly, hovered over four large wooden tables, representing the four quarters of the city. Each table was covered with a map of that quarter of Greater London, marked up with every street, even the tiny alleyways. The boys stared at small plastic disks strewn across the drawings. Each numbered disk represented a Metropolitan Police car, responding to calls reported through the emergency line 999. The cadets' main responsibility that day was to slide those disks around the maps as radio operators deployed those officers to the scenes. Phone operators would take a call: *Car 5P heads to Commercial and Fournier Streets.* The disk would be shifted to the new spot and the dispatcher would relay the details to the patrol car. *Robbery in progress: 84 Commercial Street in Spitalfields.* The whole process took about two minutes. The patrol car would soon arrive at the emergency—in theory. Not this day.

The hoodlums and the police shared the same frustration—neither could see a thing in that wretched fog. But that certainly didn't stop criminals from preying on Londoners. The radio dispatcher took detailed notes. An officer reported that a man sneaked out from under a railway bridge in an outer suburb and stabbed a fifteen-year-old female shop assistant in the back with a stiletto heel, leaving her in serious condition. Rescuers arrived after hearing the girl's screams. The ambulance was forced to travel at a walking pace through the fog; it took two hours to drive four miles. By then, the girl's attacker had vanished into the smoke. Police were patrolling the length of the Thames, searching for bodies of people who had drowned in the cold water because they slipped off the bank. A young police cadet inside the Information Room stared out through a window. The river was right there, just below them—but it merged with the black air, rendering it invisible. There was little those officers on the bank could do—it was impossible to fish out a corpse they could scarcely find in the fog.

A train ran over a gang of railway workmen near Norwood Junction, just south of London. It killed at least two of them and trapped others beneath the engine and coaches. It took almost an hour for the ambulances, guided by attendants with torches, to arrive. The ambulance service had 334 emergency calls on Saturday night—about one hundred more than usual. Supervisors appealed to off-duty drivers to relieve the emergency crews that had been operating an additional twenty-two ambulances.

Meanwhile, the calls continued to pile up at the Yard. Thugs attacked people on the streets, smashed shop windows, snatched purses, and burgled homes. Someone robbed a post office in the West End. A judge slipped off the platform at Liverpool station—he was treated for shock. Deadly car crashes frightened drivers. Cops were furious. They struggled to respond quickly to the radio calls and to the flashing police call boxes on the streets. They wanted to grab the phones inside, respond to the demands from their sergeants that they help Londoners. Many didn't—they couldn't take control and fulfill their oath to protect innocent people. They could hardly stumble back to their patrol cars. They groused, loudly. It was exhausting and bewildering. The police faced an adversary that was defending criminals. The fog was everywhere now.

⁓

Saturdays were usually filled with joy in the Sargent household, the bustling headquarters of adventure for the four kids and their father. They played loads of board games, painted pictures, pulled weeds in the front garden, and chased around chickens in the backyard. Rosemary went on grand expeditions with her brothers, Malcolm and David, exploring a bombsite up the road from their house. They pretended they were on a safari in a foreign land. Four houses on her block had been attacked during the Blitz, and a blast had shattered the windows of her own home.

Like most British families, the Sargents couldn't afford a television, so they often gathered around the radio to listen to a BBC program. And Rosemary's father was an enthusiastic reader—she loved flopping down on the couch next to him, snuggling up and losing herself in the book as he read. After a long day of playing, Albert would bathe the younger children, and then he would patiently lather and wash Rosemary's long blonde hair. Her beautiful locks stretched down to her waist—they were exhausting to detangle. But night after night, her father plopped down in front of her and gently, slowly combed out the knots. Rosemary wouldn't allow Edna near her hair—her mother was heavy-handed, yanking clumps out in frustration. Her father had taken over those grooming duties when he returned from the war and Rosemary adored him for it.

That was one of Albert's critical roles in the family—he

played arbitrator in the delicate relationship between a teenage girl and her mother. He was quite strict, but Edna Sargent was downright draconian. When Rosemary snapped at her one day, she took away the girl's school bus fare and lunch money for a full month. When Albert found out, he berated his wife and handed his daughter a shilling. Rosemary knew to ask her father first for permission—he was always more likely to donate additional funds for the cinema or an extra sixpence for a treat. But he was also apt to give her a hiding if she was caught doing something silly, like playing hide-and-seek in a dangerous bombsite.

Albert resisted alcohol. He was married to a Methodist teetotaler, and Edna forbade drinking in her house. Besides, his father, the pub manager, had been a violent drunk, and Albert wasn't interested in being that type of man. But he was a smoker, despite those winter bouts with bronchitis. Rosemary happily purchased a pack of Player's Weights at the store up the road each weekend. Despite the occasional feuds, they were a happy family. But none of their normal traditions, their routines, happened this Saturday. Her father didn't swiftly hop down the stairs for breakfast, ready for a half day at work. He was still in bed by mid-morning, coughing in a way that rattled her mother's nerves, those already frayed from raising four children. *Take him something to eat.*

Rosemary was tasked with hiking up and down the stairs most of the day, supplying her father with drinks and meals. She felt optimistic in the morning about his condition but, as he continued to struggle, she worried. *He's not getting better.* He was barking, laboring for breath.

"Are you all right?" Rosemary whispered.

"Yes, I'm all right, don't worry," was the reply, accompanied with a weak smile.

She knew he wasn't. She ran downstairs and cornered her mother. "I don't think Dad's very well."

"Oh, he'll be all right," she replied and handed Rosemary a glass bottle. "Take this up to him."

Rosemary gripped the diabolical brown mixture that most British mothers kept in a medicine cabinet, called Liqufruta. Chemists sold the stuff as a cough expectorant—it contained loads of garlic, so the taste was horrible. It was easy to figure out which child had a sore throat at school because he reeked of it. Her father managed to swallow a spoonful in between coughs, but it didn't help. As nightfall approached, her mother finally ventured upstairs and wandered through the black mist in the hallway to check on Albert herself.

The teenager listened and worried. For as long as Rosemary could remember, her mother had nagged her father nearly around the clock. Not tonight. Edna stayed silent—Albert's coughs resonated in the hallway. Edna carefully climbed down the stairs, refocused, and began her work in the kitchen. She was a brilliant cook, particularly with beef roasts and York-shire puddings. But a savory pie was her specialty—one she had perfected during the war. It was stuffed with inexpensive sausage meat and could easily be sliced into six pieces, perfect for her family. Rosemary's favorite treat was suet roly-poly, a Victorian dessert made of a steamed roll of suet dough filled with jam. Her mother made it for her, but only rarely—rationing made it difficult to get butter or sugar easily.

Rosemary spent most weekends picking vegetables from their front garden for weekly dinners: carrots, cabbage, cauliflower, and parsnips. She fed her father's chickens for him; she and her brothers would lovingly name each bird, then Albert would promptly decapitate them right before the holidays. Rosemary could hear their soft clucking in the backyard—she knew their time was coming. The kitchen filled with wonderful smells as the teenager glanced at the fireplace near the kitchen. The clumps of coal smoldered; their smoke floated up and was joined in the chimney by obstinate fumes from the outside, determined to push through the fireplace and into the house. It didn't matter whether she read a book in her parlor or kicked a ball across her garden, Rosemary couldn't escape the poison.

She wasn't sure when she had last seen the coal man, the worker with the filthy leather bag strapped to his back. He hauled around the brown, crumbly stuff like Saint Nicholas might carry new toys in his sack. She knew his lorry had rolled up recently, because his wares were shoved inside their coal shed at the bottom of the garden. Her mother constantly moaned about the sad nuggets and their high price, but each week she collected the requisite number of pennies and, as the coal man lumbered down the alleyway, she met him to make the exchange. Once the coal was dumped inside the fireplace, her father would supplement it with old newspapers and small bits of wood he collected from the yard. One strike of a match and the coal would soon gleam.

By early Saturday night, the house grew colder—there was a silence only broken by her father's violent coughing and her mother's futile attempts to comfort him. The fog pushed through the upstairs windowsills into her parents' room.

⟋⟍

In the West End, on the corner of Mortimer and Cleveland streets, sat Middlesex Hospital, London's premier teaching facility. It was established in the 1700s by one of the world's most famous surgeons, Charles Bell. Four giant oil paintings welcomed visitors to the reception area, a collection entitled the

Acts of Mercy. One of them depicted orphans being cared for by nurses. Another showed injured World War I soldiers waiting to be treated—this was a safe haven where patients begged to be cured. Soon, it would be a final resting place for fog victims.

The six-story redbrick hospital was chronically drafty. The cold winter winds didn't just lightly blow through the windows—they burst through the doors, towing along streams of smoke. The fog was dragging filthy scum through the clean hallways and into sanitized rooms, places meant to be safe for delicate patients. Nurses in short-sleeved blue dresses and starched aprons scurried through the wards. They pulled on white masks that blackened almost immediately in the smoke. The doctors issued a public appeal: *If you have respiratory problems, leave the city.* But most Londoners couldn't even stumble their way to a local train. Summoned by the hospital, extra nurses hurried over from their living quarters on Foley Street, which were connected to the hospital by underground tunnels to allow safe access for the women at night. The fog hadn't yet seeped underground, so most didn't realize there was a problem until they emerged from the exit and into the smoke-filled hospital.

Twenty-six-year-old Donald Acheson jogged from room to room; he was one of the city's nearly two thousand general practitioners—most were on duty that weekend. The slight, dark-haired resident medical officer simply couldn't stand still. He traversed the maze of hallways, quickly assessing the conditions of patients and directing them to appropriate wards. Every available bed was taken. Some patients, waiting on doctors, prayed in the hospital's huge chapel. But soon even the sanctuary was requisitioned. The air was filthy—Donald yelled orders to the junior doctors around him. The smoke-filled wards through which he moved were a far cry from his privileged upbringing in Scotland. He had been born in Belfast, but he had attended Edinburgh's finest prep schools before becoming a star student at Oxford University.

Donald would soon join the Royal Air Force Medical Branch, the doctors who helped during search-and-rescue missions and on emergency relief flights. He would leave next year, but today Donald was already in a battle. The Ambulance Service was a mess. During the night, it had issued a radio appeal for all off-duty drivers to return to their stations. Twenty additional ambulances were sent out, only to quickly return without patients. The vehicles simply could not navigate through the turbid air. Drivers and attendants were approaching physical exhaustion. Patients staggered through the hospital doors, bringing in a torrent of smoke. Just a decade ago, they would have been lucky to receive hospital treatment.

The creation of the free National Health Service in 1948 had improved the quality of medical care in Britain, especially for the elderly, women, and the poor. Suddenly, virtually all health services were free. Doctors were better educated. Sanitation, water, and food safety regulation reduced the number of communicable diseases. The pharmaceutical industry developed new drugs for mental illness, and the introduction of antibiotics gradually eradicated many epidemics, like tuberculosis and cholera, which were major killers. Death tolls shrank, particularly for infants. But there were no vaccines that could protect Londoners from air pollution. Donald stared at the smoke.

"The fog itself swirled into the wards, and seemed to consist principally of smuts, so that the wash basins and baths turned darker and darker grey," he remembered. The film was so thick that Donald took his finger and wrote his name on one of the tubs, like a child marking his property in wet cement. The smell was there—sulphur dioxide, a pungent, irritating odor. It reeked, like getting a whiff of a lit match.

And it was no wonder the scent was so strong. The amount of sulphur dioxide in the air had more than quadrupled since Thursday, from one hundred parts per million to five hundred and fifty. And the amount of smoke had increased from four hundred micrograms per cubic meter to sixteen hundred. Donald's ward in Middlesex Hospital was less than five miles from the Battersea Power Station, the third-largest energy plant in the UK. This was the third day that Battersea spilled, along with the city's other pollutants, more than one thousand tons of smoke particles and two thousand tons of carbon dioxide into the air.

The Borough of Westminster, where Middlesex Hospital sat, suffered from the most pollution. The level of sulphur dioxide in the air was the highest in London—so high that, the day before, pollution-measuring devices were useless in some areas. Donald watched a wave of patients walk through the doors— "middle-aged and elderly people, principally men, gasping for breath," he later recalled. Many had ventured out in the smog to find resources for their families; others had been forced to walk long distances when public transportation shut down. Donald noted the illnesses: pneumonia, bronchitis, tuberculosis, and heart failure. Many patients arrived with preexisting conditions, including asthma. Some died of respiratory distress. Asphyxiation and cardiac distress killed others. Junior doctors were responsible for filling out death certificates; most labeled the cause of death as "acute respiratory failure" or "coronary heart disease." No mention of fog. The victims who didn't die struggled with chest pains, lung inflammation, and diminished breathing ability. Donald guessed they would likely suffer permanent lung damage; perhaps he would see them later, in the throes of asthma attacks.

A patient near him was frantically trying to breathe. He put his stethoscope against the man's chest—startled, he listened again. He expected to hear rales and ronchi, the rattles and wheezes characteristic of chronic respiratory illnesses.

"Usually when one listens with a stethoscope to the chest of people with asthma or other respiratory illnesses, one can hear these noises in the chest…there were none," he recalled.

Why? If it wasn't a respiratory illness, what was it? It was clear to Donald that the larger bronchi in the man's chest weren't affected. Something else was causing the coughing. He saw patients with the same complaints—they were all hacking. Their throats burned, their chests ached, their flesh felt scorched. The sight of the smoke terrorized them, like children spotting a rabid animal at the window. And there were so many more out there—dying. The fog was murdering Londoners.

∾

It was a small lie, really…just a harmless bit of dishonesty from a middle-aged man who worked diligently to appear truthful—particularly when he was being deceitful. But compared to his other fibs, this was a minor one. No one would question it. John Reginald Christie typed the one-paragraph note carefully, in his usual exacting manner, being mindful of smudges. Its recipient's name and title were printed in the upper right corner—every word was spelled correctly. Now it had to be delivered. The fifty-three-year-old buttoned his jacket, adjusted his brown trilby hat, closed the door behind him, and gingerly stepped onto the sidewalk in front of 10 Rillington Place. The fog besieged him, and then swallowed him up.

This was the heaviest peasouper Reg had seen since he moved to West London's Notting Hill almost twenty years earlier. He slowly shuffled toward the Ladbroke Grove Underground station—this fog seemed more deceptive than those in the past. *When would it end?* It made him uneasy. The air was a sickly shade of dark yellow, thick and sour, like the fumes from rotting eggs decaying inside a wooden pail. Reg waited for the train— at least he would find some tranquility away from his home, if only for a few hours. He loathed that building and every person inside—it was an appalling place to live. And in one week, for one tenant, it would become a terrifying place to die.

Rillington Place was a small street that dead-ended in a cul-de-sac—ten dismal houses lined each side of the road. They were all virtually identical: large Victorians with peeling paint and cracked façades of crumbling brick and sandstone. Every building contained small, cramped flats—each as depressing as the one below. Rillington Place homes were the epitome of squalor in London's tenement housing plan. Reg's home was the last at the end of the cul-de-sac; it sat flush against a factory wall. On the other side, coal smoke poured out of an iron foundry's chimney and into his house. During summer days, the pollution created mounds of grit on his windowsill. To the north of the street was the Metropolitan Railway Line; the trains rumbled through Notting Hill, shaking the flimsy homes, jostling the residents.

Reg and Ethel had moved to Rillington Place fifteen years earlier, renting the ground-floor flat. There was a large Victorian bay window facing the street, poised at the front of their living area. The Christies' tiny bedroom was behind it, overlooking the back garden, and then a small kitchen was at the rear of the house. Ten Rillington Place had three levels: the Christies rented the flat on the ground floor, and seven other residents lived on the two floors above, along with their frequent visitors. At the back of the building, near the Christies' flat, was the entrance to the small garden. Laundry could be done in the washhouse, which was a small building just inside the garden. The Christies had the only key, although "key" was a loose term. It was really just a piece of metal they used to flip open the lock, a lock that rarely worked anymore. Behind the washhouse was a small building with a toilet and sink, a lavatory that was shared by all nine residents.

Reg had almost no privacy. The building was tiny and over-crowded, so it seemed impossible to have a conversation above a whisper without other tenants overhearing. As an attorney once quipped, "there is not enough room to swing a dead cat in the kitchen." The street was no more peaceful. Many Saturdays, it was swarming with a menagerie of characters; they were fre-quently loud and, much of the time, doing illegal things. Notting Hill was later reinvented as a tony district for the well-heeled, but in 1952 it was a crime-ridden skid row. There were homeless people yelling at one another, prostitutes lingering in doorways, and burglaries in the middle of the day. Police hurried to domes-tic violence calls, sometimes involving former servicemen who had smuggled their service weapons home after the war. And the number of young working-class criminals in prison had in-creased dramatically after World War II, up 250 percent.

But on that cold December day, despite the vibration of trains and the screeching of degenerates, the streets of Notting Hill were almost deserted, thanks to that fog. Dim gas lamps il-luminated specters on the sidewalk doing God knows what. "Leave your homes only if necessary," warned Scotland Yard. The fog was protecting criminals as they broke into homes. Police in Notting Hill staggered through the fog around Lad-broke Grove, Pottery Lane, and Portobello Road.

He shouldn't have been out that day—it wasn't safe—but he was determined to deliver that letter. Reg stepped onto the train and the doors closed. His life was already intolerable, but this fog was so upsetting. It seeped into the Underground, shrouded him wherever he went. It spawned a layer of grime that coated virtually all the surfaces of Reg's home, like they were smeared with tallow and then dusted with black flecks. He couldn't escape the smoke—it was smothering him. And he knew that it would trap him in his horrible little flat with his bothersome wife. The fog was odious—rancid air blowing around a decaying flat inside a condemnable Victorian townhome, nestled in a slum.

Notting Hill had once been a nice district filled with large middle-class homes in the Victorian years. Eventually the economy changed, the houses lost their value, and they were divided into numerous dwellings. Luftwaffe bombs had badly damaged much of the area during the Blitz, and Notting Hill had never fully recovered. Now, the district was synonymous with shabby, overcrowded housing coupled with lawless renters and squatters. Atop those worries, there was racial tension and hostility after an influx of immigrants had begun arriving from the Caribbean four years earlier.

In 1948, the SS *Empire Windrush* carried almost five hundred African-Caribbean passengers from Jamaica to London's Tilbury docks. After World War II, Britain encouraged immigration from Commonwealth countries to help rebuild. There was a shortage of cheap labor, and many of the immigrants were ex-servicemen who had served in the Royal Air Force during the war. The image of West Indians marching down the gangplank was published on the front page of British newspapers. "Welcome Home," declared a headline in the *London Evening Standard*. "Five Hundred Pairs of Willing Hands," announced another paper. But hospitality quickly turned to hostility.

Within four years, the number of Caribbean immigrants had exploded from a few hundred to several thousand. Their presence exacerbated the severe housing shortage already plaguing the city in the aftermath of World War II. Many resentful white Londoners viewed the immigrants as haughty, lazy, and indecent—they blamed the West Indians for turning respectable areas into ghettos. Landlords hung signs declaring "no coloureds" and "no West Indians." "Keep Britain White" posters and graffiti became commonplace. Reg and Ethel prayed they would all pack up and leave—live anywhere but in Notting Hill, on their block. Instead, West Indians moved into their little building. And they would create such a problem for the Christies.

Despite the blanket of fog and the aggravating train delays, Reg dutifully reported to his job in the accounts department at the British Roads Services in its Hampstead Depot, about five miles from Rillington Place. It was his third month at this station working as an invoice clerk for Britain's largest road transport company; he earned a good salary of eight pounds a week. It was a tedious appointment, yet one that suited a fussy man like Reg. He was fastidious and intelligent—very intelligent—but also odd.

Reg walked into the office of George Burrow, his superior. Burrow was satisfied with Reg's performance at work, but tired of his hissy fits and complaints; he was far from an easy employee. He had gone home with a cold on his first day of work, complaining there was no heater. He was socially awkward and prone to loud outbursts; he was overzealous when he refereed company football games, irritating coworkers with haughty, aggressive calls on the pitch. Yet around women, Reg was tongue-tied. He once joined his colleagues at a social function and was encouraged to ask a girl to dance. Instead, he wilted and slunk to a corner. He was constantly emasculated. He might have seemed a bit smarmy to most women, and perhaps weak, but not threatening, particularly compared to the rough characters in Notting Hill. Little did they know.

When Reg glanced in the mirror, he saw a decent-looking man: lean-jawed, tall and lanky with a balding head—but he was so insecure. Exposure to mustard gas during World War I had left him blind for five months, he claimed, and with a voice that was weak, whiny, and effeminate. He had a girlish bounce to his step. His smile read like a forced grimace—he had a sallow complexion, a long nose, and ill-fitting false teeth. He was never considered handsome and he frequently felt dejected. When he did manage to attract a woman's attention, it was only because he could offer her something, like money—they were usually desperate. It was such an unsatisfying life.

Reg handed Mr. Burrow the short, typed letter.

"Sir, I wish to give my notice to terminate my engagement, this notice to expire on December 6th 1952. J. R. Christie, Invoice Section. Group Office."

Burrow read the note and looked up. Reg explained that he and Ethel were moving to Sheffield, where her family lived. Ethel's brother, Henry, had secured a better job for Reg there with an engineering firm—he would start in three months and receive National Assistance unemployment benefits in the meantime. *Ethel doesn't feel safe in our neighborhood anymore*, he explained. Ethel Christie, his plump wife of thirty-two years, was a smidge older than he. Her round, pudgy face and squinty eyes were framed by old-fashioned, mousy hair. She had been quite fetching in her youth, but she hadn't aged well. Despite all that, Reg said he truly loved her, though her rows with the other tenants caused him such stress.

In 1950, the owner of 10 Rillington Place had sold the building to Charles Brown, an immigrant from Jamaica. As Brown accepted renters from the West Indies, the demographic of the house's residents changed. The Christies were incensed, unnerved by their new neighbors. It was quite agitating for a couple that already suffered from near-hysteria over simple disagreements. Their doctors labeled them "nervous-types." Reg fretted that Rillington Place, once a home for three proper families, was now a flophouse for countless prostitutes and paupers, he claimed. Ethel and he were the only decent folks, Reg often thought.

"When Mr. Brown took over the house he put some odd bits of furniture which he brought into each room, the four upper rooms, and then let them to coloured people with white girls," said Reg. "It was very unpleasant because one or two were prostitutes."

Reg complained to the city, furious that the West Indian tenants used the communal toilet in the outdoor lavatory, six to nine men at a time, and then refused to flush. He lamented that dogs would run loose, allowed to defecate where they pleased. He accused some of the female residents of spitting in the hallways. He and Ethel began putting disinfectant down on the linoleum. Reg fumed as the tenants filed in and out of the building at all hours—he claimed they laughed loudly, fought viciously, and cooked food that smelled disgusting. He complained they were stealing his milk bottles and newspapers. His landlord, Charles Brown, seemed apathetic and, much to Reg's outrage, even accused *him* of causing the conflicts. Brown called the police when the Christies would refuse to pay rent.

"Our lives here have been and still are made intolerable by the persecution of Brown and the coloured people who are certainly doing all possible to make it impossible for us," complained Reg. "We were persistently persecuted by the niggers."

And then, suddenly, there was good reason for Reg's chronic hysteria. Brown demanded use of half the back garden to store building supplies—Reg's special garden. Even more concerning, Brown also planned to excavate the sad little patch of land to make it level. Reg panicked—Ruth and Muriel were still buried there, just inches under the dirt. He hired an attorney, who scared Brown into dropping the issue.

By 1952, two years' worth of endless bellowing and distressing arguments with the landlord and his tenants had frayed Ethel's nerves and tripped off immense anxiety. Not only could she not sleep because of the "raucous behavior" of her neighbors, she accused several tenants of physically assaulting her. The Christies' physician, Dr. Matthew Odess, prescribed her two sedatives, potassium bromide and phenobarbital, to help her rest. She had taken drugs for the past three years, but they didn't seem to help what became a catalogue of maladies. Her hands were arthritic and prone to cramping. She complained of varicose veins, rashes, and migraines. She was agitated over the neighborhood and distressed about the building. On October 10, she wrote her brother that the landlord wouldn't repair cracks in the ceiling, but bragged that Reg did it himself.

"If we could only get somewhere else to live it would be better for us," she wrote.

Because of her fragile health, Ethel stopped visiting her sister Lily's home in Sheffield, about 160 miles away. She no longer worked at Osram's light bulb factory. Aside from one neighbor living next door, Ethel had few friends. Reg and his wife were together in that flat frequently—which infuriated him. He tried to bring girls around for trysts (he was always able to offer them something they needed). But Ethel wouldn't leave. She was so scared of the neighbors that she seldom ventured outside. He was rarely alone.

Near the end of 1952, Ethel spiraled into a depression that suffocated her husband. The stress was almost too much for the Christies to endure—they were both in such bad health. He popped folic acid tablets several times a day at work. "These keep me going," Reg told his boss.

That Saturday, December 6, 1952, the second day of the fog, as he and Mr. Burrow stood inside the British Road Services, they bade each other good-bye. Reg strolled out the door and disappeared into the mist. His body frequently ached. Most days his stomach burned from enteritis. Pain plagued his lower back. He couldn't sleep, and he had problems with his memory. In the twenty years Reg had been visiting Dr. Odess' office, none of the remedies he had prescribed had really helped. He was prone to fits of crying, sobbing, giddiness, amnesia, and flatulence—sometimes all at once. His head pounded incessantly. He hadn't been able to work for eight months at his previous job, thanks to fibrositis and enteritis. The symptoms were worsening. Reg hadn't touched his wife in more than two years, since she had reached menopause. He was perpetually insecure with women who weren't paid to be with him. He traced it back to his teenage years.

"I was never what is described as a 'sexy type,'" Reg once said. "I often had my leg pulled by other boys because I did not go out with girls. Some of my friends made suggestions which I resented."

When he was a young man, his friends had encouraged him to walk with them through Savile Park, along a sort of lovers' lane nicknamed the "monkey run," in his hometown of Halifax. They all hoped to pick up girls there. Reg, seventeen at the time, found one and invited her to walk alone with him.

"I remember that we kissed and cuddled, but I heard later she told my friends I was 'slow,'" said Reg.

The following week, the girl was intimate with one of Reg's close friends. She compared the two boys, very publicly. Reg quickly earned the nicknames "Reggie-no-dick" and "Can't-do-it-Christie."

"I wondered at the time whether my lovemaking would appear ridiculous to a girl," he remembered. "And all my life since I have had this fear of appearing ridiculous as a lover."

He learned early on that he desperately needed complete control during sex, or the taunts were unbearable. Women could be so loathsome, he thought, unless he was paying them—or they were dying. As December 1952 dawned, he felt the walls closing in on him from every side—but he could glance at his garden. Muriel and Ruth had been together for eight years now, all alone. He had certainly paid for women—which was ironic, because he complained about the women who stayed with his neighbors. Just days ago, he had taken lurid, obscene pictures with two prostitutes he met outside a pub. He rented a small photography studio. He needed that release so much—as if he had been holding his breath for weeks, only to finally exhale. But it wasn't enough. The thrilling memories of those dead girls in the garden were the only lovely things in his life now. But those recollections were fading. He desperately needed a new adventure. Resigning his job was the first step. He was ready to take the next one, very soon.

On this Saturday afternoon in early December of 1952, Reg was home again in Notting Hill, having officially resigned. There was nowhere to go now—that hateful fog paralyzed the entire city. So many troubles consumed him—his own ailments, his sickness from the fog, Ethel's neurosis, and the neighbors' contempt. They preyed on his sanity—muddled and manipulated his mind. The fog circled the outside of the house slowly, like a pacing predator. As the night settled in, it continued to spill into his flat at 10 Rillington Place. The factory next door erupted with smoke. The street's chimneys discharged fumes. He was trapped, maybe for days. That thought might have driven him mad, disabled his common sense. Floating around the flat, amid the sooty flakes, was that little fib, the lie that seemed so innocent, but would change so much. There was no promising job with an engineering firm in Sheffield. In fact, he had no intention of moving his wife anywhere.

CHAPTER FOUR

Trapped

The yellow fog came creeping down
The bridges, till the houses' walls
Seemed changed to shadows, and St Paul's
Loomed like a bubble o'er the town.

— *Oscar Wilde, "Impression du Matin," 1881*

By one o'clock on Sunday morning, the fog had oozed through the windowsills upstairs and into thirteen-year-old Rosemary Sargent's bedroom in southeast London. Tucked beneath wool blankets, bracing against the chill, Rosemary slipped into sleep. She knew there would be no church services for them today.

It was a break from the Sargents' normal routine. Every Sunday, twice a day, the family boarded a bus to their local Methodist church for a weekly dose of sermons and Bible study. Her mother would sit quietly in the pews, holy book in hand, gazing ahead as the choir sang. Rosemary and David would quietly play the "church and steeple" game with their fingers, hiding giggles. There were no play dates or birthday parties on Sundays, but quite a lot of worship.

While fashion styles and social mores had evolved over the past decade, Sundays in London were still staunchly Victorian—

a day for family meals, self-reflection, and prayer. Religious adherence had dropped since before the war, but there was still a sense that churches represented faith, community, and respectability. On Sunday, December 7, however, most churches, chapels, and cathedrals were vacant. A veil enshrouded the statue of Queen Victoria standing outside St Paul's Cathedral. The spire atop St Martin-in-the-Fields, almost two hundred feet tall, could be seen only briefly, as the clouds of smoke traveled. Many Londoners prayed at home.

Another custom in the Sargent household would also be delayed. Sunday mornings, Albert would take Rosemary and David to see his father in a hospital in Dulwich, an area of south London about five miles away. Rosemary's grandfather was dying of cancer, drifting in and out of consciousness; he wanted to see his eldest grandchildren—in fact, the trio had made the trip just the week before. This was a special journey for her father; it seemed good for his soul. Albert tried to visit his father often, despite their strained history over the elder Sargent's excessive drinking. Albert's mother had proudly raised him in the Church of England, but once she died, his visits to religious services fell off. As an adult, church wasn't a priority for Albert, but he was devoted in other ways. He worshiped his family, and their house was his sanctuary. He tolerated the strict Methodist church, for Edna's sake, but preferred to stay home with the younger children and allow his wife to attend services. Every so often, he would wrangle Sue and Malcolm on a Sunday, plant them on a bus seat next to him, and join the rest of the family in a pew, but only if there wasn't a good football game on the neighbor's television. But this Sunday there would be no church, no football game.

"He's turning blue!" Edna cried.

Just before dawn, Rosemary sat up in bed when a series of bangs jarred her from sleep. It was her mother, Edna, shouting and pounding on the wall they shared with their neighbors, the Taylors.

"Get help!" she screamed.

The children stayed silent, secluded under their covers. Rosemary didn't venture outside to question the frantic orders. The siblings were restrained, hesitant during any disagreements—kids raised by rigid parents who abided by the belief that children should be seen and not heard. Their neighbors rang the family doctor from a nearby telephone box.

"I'm making my rounds on foot," Dr. Walker reported. "I'll come when I can."

Albert coughed, cried, and whooped through the early morning. Rosemary was right—no church. Instead, she prayed alone in her bedroom.

~ ~ ~

Sunday was cold and wet, even for Londoners accustomed to the damp weather. Stepping outside was like being tossed into an ice bath, then yanked out and left to dry without a warm towel. It was the third day the city had endured the suffocating, dreadful fog—the third day of anguish and death. The bitter air, slightly below freezing, added more agony to the whole mess. The weather not only forced Londoners to inhale smoke, but each breath was so biting that it made them gasp, and then gag. The sun had vanished entirely. The city's transportation system was now crippled. The London Underground's tracks were still busy, with cars smashed full of travelers trying to avoid the smoky streets, but only essential personnel were needed. The vermin that lived among the rails had a reprieve from the ferrets released by city workers to drive the rats into nets. The "fluffers," women who prowled the Tube tracks in their overalls and hair bandanas to rid the rails of debris, were told to put down their wire brushes and stay home; the nightly cleaning of the tunnels would need to wait. It was a startling contrast from Friday, when police fought to untangle traffic in Piccadilly Circus and Trafalgar Square. Today, merchants and shoppers left streets deserted. Most sporting events in the city were canceled—no rugby, racing, or football. The Automobile Association's rescue vans found it almost impossible to locate the thousands of members who telephoned for help. Londoners were finally starting to realize that this fog was no ordinary pea-souper.

The fog swelled as Sunday dragged on, becoming increasingly foul and lethal. Visibility of more than a yard was rare. At a time when record quantities of imports and exports passed through the city's docks, the Thames had been almost desolate for more than forty-eight hours, save for a collision between a ferry and another boat. All area airports were closed. The pollution levels were staggering. The amount of smoke and sulphur dioxide in the air had increased by almost ten times within seventy-two hours. And the poisons were still trapped in the city.

"The most recent case of such a long period of fog in the London area was in 1948, when it lasted four and a half days," reported the *Times*, "but temperatures were not then so low." Warmer temperatures meant less coal was needed—less pollution in the air. And yet even now, on the hills of London, still within the city, there was beautiful sunshine. At Wimbledon Common, less than two hundred feet above sea level, the sky was blue. But if a hiker stood at the top of one of those hills and peered downward—he would see a floor of dark clouds sitting below.

This was the same quality of fog, with the same tainted smell, that had bewitched artist Claude Monet fifty years earlier. At the turn of the century, the French impressionist had carried his canvases and paints to London. He visited in the winter, when the city was clouded with fog and steeped in the smoke from coal fires. Monet dipped his brush into browns, greys, and blacks and painted the Houses of Parliament as silhouettes cloaked in the misty sky. Blue swipes peeking through a sea of orange and yellow represented Charing Cross Bridge.

"Without the fog," Monet declared, "London would not be a beautiful city. It is the fog that gives it its magnificent breadth. Those massive, regular blocks become grandiose within that mysterious cloak."

Monet might have been less entranced with this particular fog. His canvas, set up near the window of his room in the West End's trendy Savoy Hotel, would have quickly blackened with smut. That Sunday, the *New York Times* published a flattering book review of *Winter in London*, author Ivor Brown's description of four months in the dreary capital. The article's headline was "A Dingy, Haunting Beauty." Those adjectives defined the landscape of the city—the fog could be both enchanting and degrading.

The smoke muffled London and left it hushed and eerie. A curious visitor, at first hesitant, might screw up enough courage to venture out that Sunday morning into the fog for an early tea and scone. He might reminisce about a scene unfurled by Charles Dickens or T. S. Eliot, as he inched along unfamiliar buildings, lingering in the shadow of a gas lamp—the only light he could find on his trip. He could hear clock chimes through parlor windows and unfamiliar footsteps several yards back. The fog might feel romantic to a couple, clutching each other in the mist, like a scene from *Casablanca*. But for someone alone— it was could be terrifying.

❦

That Sunday, December 8, was John Reginald Christie's first full day of unemployment—he should have felt liberated. He was free from that job, the one that had thrust him into a group of judgmental coworkers. He had had few friends there. But today he was cornered by that nasty fog, like the other tenants of 10 Rillington Place in Notting Hill.

The smoke and fumes choked them all for a third day—the newspapers couldn't, or wouldn't, predict when it might end. "The fog is as thick as any Northerner, but not as acrid," stated one story. "The prospects for tomorrow are appalling." Reg and the rest of the city would have to wait and wonder when the predictability of their lives might return. The fog sickened him. He was morose, which was alarming because, to many people, he wasn't particularly pleasant under most circumstances. This time of year, with its biting winds and dreary fog, afflicted Reg—it forced him to recall some very unpleasant memories.

Three years earlier, in 1949, Reg had been a ledger clerk with the Post Office Savings Bank at Kew, before he had worked for the transport company from which he'd just resigned. Back then, before Mr. Brown and his West Indian tenants, there were only three families living in 10 Rillington Place—an older man on the floor above theirs, and a young couple with a baby on the top floor. It was relatively peaceful for the Christies.

The weather that November 8, 1949, was cold, as Novembers in London tended to be—rainy and, yes, foggy. They combined to make the night blurred, muddled. A criminal could make quite a lot of devilry in that kind of weather. Reg couldn't seem to sort out what had happened that night, after he lay down and closed his eyes. All day he had been distressed. The physical maladies that had plagued him for much of his adult life were particularly acute that winter. It was his second week on the sick list at work—he was in tremendous pain. Reg began to visit his primary physician, Dr. Matthew Odess, every Tuesday. The doctor was constantly giving him notes to extend his sick leave or handing him a prescription for relief; he even recommended that Reg register as disabled.

"He was an unfit person," recalled Dr. Odess. "He could hardly get off the chair sometimes; I had to help him up."

That Tuesday back in 1949, Reg had been in bed, in his pajamas, with a fire in the room from dawn until dusk. He listened for any movement outside the flat—the only people he saw were his wife and some workmen making repairs to the building (those laborers would become important later on). Earlier that afternoon, he had shuffled to the parlor and briefly saw his neighbors, Beryl Evans and little Geraldine, through the front bay window. He would normally manage a smile when he saw them—greet them the way any Londoner might on a cold winter day. They weren't significant to Reg—not just yet. Soon, their lives would become tangled, and for such awful reasons. With the exception of the jarring noises caused by the building repairs, 10 Rillington Place was relatively tranquil that afternoon. About half past five o'clock in the evening, Reg had gathered himself, put on some proper clothes, and taken a train to see Dr. Odess at his office in Colville Square. He had returned home less than two hours later, along with Ethel, whom he had collected at the public library on Ladbroke Grove. It had been such a fitful day—he was in a tremendous amount of pain.

"I was unable to lie down for any length of time, and I had to keep getting up," he remembered. "And I used to sit in front of the fire and try to get it to my back to get some relief, and then I would go back and lie down again in bed."

Doctor Odess was also concerned about his painful enteritis, an inflammation of the small intestine. Reg could hardly bend at the waist.

"I had to crawl out of bed, and if I wanted to pick up anything off the floor I had to get on my hands and knees to do it," said Reg.

It was a pathetic existence, so the physician suggested a starvation diet consisting only of milk, toast, and barley water for more than a week. After Reg was settled, Ethel had prepared a drink for him; she carried the glass slowly to their bed, then promptly slipped, flopped onto the floor, and spilled it everywhere. Not only was Reg in agony, he was now wet and hungry. It was a dreadful, depressing night. By ten o'clock, Ethel and Reg were finally asleep, lying next to each other as the rain dripped down their window.

Suddenly, around midnight, they both heard a thud—like someone dropping a sack above them. Reg would have sprung up if he could have, but given his discomfort all he could manage was a slow pivot on his knees. Moving aside the curtains, he peered out the window behind the headboard, the glass pane overlooking his garden, with those two secrets buried beneath it. With Ethel squatting beside him, they both pressed their faces to the windowpane and tried to tilt their gaze up to the next floor above them. It was useless—there was really no telling what had happened. It seemed so strange, though, because the flat above them was empty. Mr. Kitchener, their longtime neighbor, had been its sole tenant, but he had been hospitalized for several weeks with cataract problems. There were only two families in the building on that quiet November night in 1949—the Christies on the ground floor and the Evanses, along with their daughter, in the flat at the top of two narrow staircases. The Christies weren't particularly close with the family, but they were fond of the little girl, Geraldine. Ethel occasionally watched over her when her mother needed help.

Twenty-five-year-old Timothy Evans and his wife, Beryl, had been married less than a year when they moved to 10 Rillington Place twelve months before, in 1948. Despite being newlyweds, they were having a rough go of it. Violent rows punctuated their short marriage, thanks to the Welshman's quick temper, his fondness for drink, and his feisty wife.

Tim had been born in Merthyr Tydfil, a working-class borough in South Wales, to a single mother, who raised him with his two half-siblings. Young Timothy was troubled: an accident in his youth triggered an infection in his right foot; the painful treatments resulted in repeated absences from school, where he already struggled with slow speech. Even as an adult, Tim said he couldn't read or write anything other than his name. To compensate, he embellished stories about his life. He was ready to brawl with anyone who snickered when he puffed out his chest. Beryl was just eighteen when they married, and a year later Geraldine was born. The pretty, petite brunette proved to be a dismal housekeeper: their flat was littered with garbage, old clothing, baby diapers, and spoiled food. Tim frequently accused her of mismanaging their finances, though he drank away some of his wages as a van driver for a food products company. Their fights echoed through 10 Rillington Place, permeating the walls of Reg's flat. Beryl declared to Ethel Christie, more than once, that she was leaving Tim for good—and taking Geraldine with her.

"All the time the Evanses have lived at our address there have been frequent quarrels," Ethel would say later. "After some of these quarrels Mrs. Evans would tell me that she had rowed with her husband over his lying to her, his associating with other women, and financial matters."

The landlord had taken out a summons against them for failure to pay rent—they were heavily in debt and discussed leaving 10 Rillington Place for good. One night, the Christies heard what sounded like a violent argument upstairs, but they couldn't pick up what it was about. Beryl later told Ethel that it had been over a woman.

"Mrs. Evans has told my wife and I on more than one occasion that he has assaulted her and grabbed hold of her throat," said Reg. "She said he had a violent temper and one time would do her in."

Ethel worried about the young family—she made it her duty to leave the hallway light on for them before she retired for the night, so they wouldn't stumble with the little girl as they climbed the staircase after visiting Tim's mother. And now Beryl was pregnant again. It was a mess: infidelity, alcohol, and money worries could act as a catalyst to violence. Yet, Tim was a doting father to Geraldine, according to his family. Reg listened to the couple's arguments.

"We think he is a bit mental," Reg admitted.

So that night in November 1949, the loud noise that came from above them was startling, but hardly unprecedented. Ethel and Reg turned to each other and tacitly agreed to lie back down and ignore whatever was happening above them. There was silence for a few moments, and then they both heard more movement upstairs.

"I thought that it sounded a bit like heavy furniture, something of that sort, that had been moved," he recalled.

Reg was groggy now—Dr. Odess had prescribed him some tablets for his back earlier in the afternoon, and they made him sleepy. He closed his eyes and forgot the whole incident.

At least, that's what he would later tell the police.

∽

More than three years later, and across town, the 1952 fog continued to torment Londoners. And in the Sargent household, the situation was particularly grave. Twelve hours—Edna Sargent had begged their neighbors to call a doctor *twelve hours* earlier. The family had suffered through twelve hours of coughing, crying, and tension. The children didn't leave the house; they stayed put, shielded from the smoke, at least the thickest of it. They watched the door, waited for the doctor's knock.

By late afternoon Dr. Walker, footsore and exhausted, finally arrived at the Sargents' home. The fog was now so thick that he could barely navigate between houses. Once inside, he gripped the handrail and climbed the stairs to greet Albert, still in bed. Dr. Walker was a comforting sight to the family. He had treated the Sargents for years, delivering three of the four children and traveling to their home to look in on them during illnesses. Like most doctors in London, he made house calls—seven shillings and sixpence a visit and worth every coin, as far as Edna was concerned. Over the years, he had treated them for measles, chicken pox, and mumps, all the childhood diseases that terrified parents.

Four years earlier, Dr. Walker had referred the family to a hospital specializing in kidney disease when five-year-old Malcolm contracted nephritis, an acute inflammation of the kidneys, which in 1948 was deadly for most children. Little Malcolm had spent almost five months away in treatment centers; Albert and Edna visited him every week, always praying he would recover—and he finally did.

Now, however, Dr. Walker looked grim. He unpacked a stethoscope and gently placed it against Albert's chest. The patient was struggling for shallow breaths, and the doctor was concerned. Heart failure was common for people with chronic bronchitis. He had already seen numerous dead patients, their bedsheets now funeral shrouds.

"He needs to be in hospital," Dr. Walker told Rosemary and her mother, "but they're all full up."

The ambulances were immobile, so transport wasn't available. And it would be a futile trip, anyway. Even if they could manage to carry him to Lewisham Hospital—an hour's walk down a long road on a clear day—there were no oxygen tanks left to help him breathe. Rosemary listened as Dr. Walker advised her to keep Albert in bed. He scribbled a prescription for a nitro-glycerin pill; it would dissolve under his tongue and help ease the strain on his heart. Rosemary was relieved to learn it would work quickly. Albert would likely feel better within five minutes. The doctor instructed Edna to pick it up from his office, about a thirty-minute walk from their house. She turned to Rosemary.

"Come with me."

⌒♋⌒

In North London, Police Constable Stanley Crichton watched the fog swirl around the halls of the Hornsey Police Station; it was the worst-smelling stuff he had known.

"This is horrid," he said, grimacing at his senior officer.

"We've seen this all before. Go on, get out of here," was the reply.

Stanley wasn't looking forward to this particular shift on Sunday evening. He knew what was happening out there, with that fog. The officers all overheard the calls coming in. One burglar had ransacked three different homes within hours in southwest London. He had quickly scaled the drainpipe of each one and forced open their windows, snatching thousands of pounds worth of clothing and jewelry. Another gang of thieves had sneaked into a posh hotel, swiping mink furs and money. Still another had climbed through the balcony of a colonel's home around six o'clock, beneath the fog's mask, and stolen all of the family's jewelry. Stanley was leery—he was worried about himself and his wife; she was still home alone with that cruel asthma.

He was on his own, with no partner and no weapon except for the heavy wooden truncheon he kept inside a long pocket in his wool trousers. He was trained in unarmed combat, but he was a slight man and, at five foot nine, he barely met the Met's height minimum. The department required all male recruits to be in good health, under thirty-five years old, and at least five foot eight inches, to ensure that they could handle the job's physical demands. It was a popular career choice, especially since the department had increased the pay of all officers the year before. If he couldn't do the job, there would be someone to replace him.

Stanley's territory was three miles long, in a rough inner-city district in North London called Upper Holloway in Islington, full of lower-income housing, cheap shops, and hooligans. He tried to be vigilant, but he knew his job was dangerous, especially in this dismal weather. Stanley was headed toward Seven Sisters Road, a busy shopping area on a typical Sunday. Now it was barren. Shopkeepers locked up their stores and hoped for the best. Butchers, in their straw hats and striped aprons, cleaned off their chopping blocks, iced their mutton, and padlocked the doors. The rag-and-bone men who collected unwanted refuse for resale to merchants hung up their sacks and kept their horses and carts off the streets. Milk and coal deliverymen didn't venture out.

Stanley walked deliberately, thinking through every step. He couldn't make out his feet; it was like shuffling through a cloud. He listened for people in front and behind. Stanley stopped, leaned up against a wall on Tottenham Lane, and thought about his route around Finsbury Park. He was counting the turns he needed to take when he saw a faint light a few feet ahead of him. There was the familiar grunt of a large diesel engine. He could smell the exhaust of a city bus. As the light approached, Stanley could see the silhouette of a fellow police officer in a long coat, swinging a hurricane lamp, guiding the bus. It was empty—the passengers had left long ago. Stanley greeted the cop and the driver, then walked alongside them for several miles. *What a miserable night, isn't it?*

He waved to the officer and continued along Seven Sisters Road, tapping on brick buildings, peering through the fog on the lookout for numbers. The row houses were identical, which made his job as frustrating as it was grim. He was responding to calls from doctors all over North London as they discovered the bodies of people dead in their flats. Stanley found an address and stepped inside. An elderly man was sitting upright in his living room chair, his eyes wide and blank. A doctor greeted Stanley as the victim's family huddled in a corner. The physician looked exhausted from making his rounds on foot.

"Oh, yes, they died peacefully in their sleep," the families would say. Physicians knew that the victims were not asleep but unconscious right before they died. Their bodies might have appeared to be calm, but their organs were failing, desperate for clean air. Stanley took down a report for the city's records. That was his main job in these cases, filling out paperwork and filing reports. Stanley nodded to the doctor and walked out. He visited home after home and examined the bodies. Many were in beds, tucked in beneath their sheets, eyes open. A few more were sitting upright in chairs, like the man earlier.

Stanley had already seen too much death before he became a police officer. He spent two years in the Royal Air Force, based at Netheravon in South West England, five years after the end of the war. He trained military police dogs, German shepherds, as part of his national service. When he was eighteen he had passed all of the exams to be an airman, those brave fliers who had manned piston fighters and strategic dive bombers for the RAF during World War II, but his mother was scared he would have an accident and refused to give her consent. She may have saved his life. One of Stanley's duties on the base was to help re-cover pilots who crashed their planes during training exercises, mostly during takeoff. They would burst into flames in nearby fields. Air crews would rush to the wreckage to retrieve the bod-ies. The eighteen-year-old corporal would grab hold of a corpse and pry it out of the cockpit. Once it gave way, he would drag it to a tarp and carry it back to the base.

It was a horrible job for a teenager who was barely a man, but death was inevitable in the RAF. Stanley knew he would cope with tragedies as a police officer, as well. Murders, assaults, and suicides were routine calls to the station. Still, there was something deeply unnatural about seeing people dead in their own beds. There were no bullet holes, no stab wounds, no faces bloodied from a fight. They had struggled to control their breaths, to suppress their coughs—but they were too weak. Their bodies finally failed them. It was heartbreaking.

Stanley offered condolences to the families. Some were angry, ready to blame anyone. Some were weeping, reciting scripture through their tears; others were stoic. At each home, Stanley filled out a report and left. There was nothing else to do. The coroners' offices were stuffed. There were no final resting places for these victims, at least not right away. Their families kept them at home, closed the door and prayed.

Stanley slowly made his way home toward Maura, moving as quickly as he dared. He worried about her asthma, her hacking and coughing. He had left her lying on the bed, begged her to stay inside. She could easily be one of the numerous victims he'd seen that day—dead in their marriage bed, alone. When he finally reached their bedsit, he found her exactly where he had left her eight hours before. Maura was still bedridden, still coughing, and still irritated at him for keeping her indoors. Stanley smiled at his wife, prepared her a basin full of hot water and menthol vapor. He gently covered her head with a towel and encouraged her to breathe in the steam and cough out the gunk.

"Breathe this in for a while," he told her.

His Irish bride may have been irked by his prudence, but after a night of counting the dead, he knew he was right.

⁂

On Sunday evenings, the noise was booming and rhythmic—even hypnotic. Millions of newspapers, filled with information for Monday morning readers, whipped through the hot metal rollers and plunked themselves onto moving belts. A monitor, dressed in a dark blue jumpsuit, sat to the right, quickly eying the copies as they zoomed across the platform and up a vertical conveyer. The printing press hummed with constant reverberations. The sounds were grating, like the hollow smack of a wooden paddle, two or three times per second. The rollers themselves produced a steady, unnerving drone in the background. There were thousands of parts, all moving seemingly in different directions for different purposes. The sounds ricocheted off the walls of the building, assaulted the ears of workers for hours, every night, year round—fog be damned.

Most of the city may have lain suspended in smoke, but Fleet Street in Central London was still a hive of activity Sunday night. The neighborhood was the storied home of Britain's national newspaper industry—the country's nerve center for journalism. London hosted seven daily papers, eight Sunday papers, and three evening papers, all desperately competing for the wallets of millions of readers. Customers could purchase a copy of the morning paper at midnight at one of hundreds of newsstands strewn across the city. The print media in postwar London was big business, a lucrative investment for publishers hawking the most dramatic headlines.

Just two days earlier, the Number Nine red double-decker bus serving Charing Cross, Piccadilly, and Kensington crept along Fleet Street, rolling through the smoky haze. Today, service was suspended. Editors sporting bow ties, gripping a cigarette in one hand and a broadsheet in the other, barked orders to cub reporters. The young journalists, mostly men, rushed galley proofs to their newspaper offices, tucked away on the side streets of Fleet. Veteran reporters dialed Scotland Yard's press bureau for last-minute updates on the latest murder or robbery. The press officer would release infrequent bulletins about different crime incidents—not nearly enough information for news-hungry reporters. There was a delicate relationship between Met press officers and journalists—neither trusted the other.

Reporters began to specialize, and most papers assigned at least one writer to cover the police; his job was to cultivate sources within Scotland Yard to secure exclusive interviews to fantastic crime stories. Once the editor signed off on the galleys, the final version was hurried back to the printing press for publication. It tended to be a whirlwind process, one that was exhilarating for a novice reporter.

Pubs and eateries welcomed weary journalists working late hours. The cramped Old Bell Tavern, known to the media simply as "The Bell," backed up to St Bride's Churchyard, once the official sanctuary for journalists hoping to squeeze in a prayer between interviews. The church had nearly been destroyed during the war. El Vino featured a steak and kidney pie that was a favorite among reporters, perched on stools at the smoke-filled bar. Only men could order there. Women were relegated to sit in the leather armchairs in the back. Both sexes gossiped about scandalous politicians, high-profile criminals, and unscrupulous journalists. Many papers had their preferred pubs, where reporters could buy a cheap snack of sausage, bacon, and fried egg late in the night. The Kardomah Café, near Chancery Lane, served soft herring roe on toast at lunchtime. Printers favored Ye Olde Cheshire Cheese.

As the nearby presses thumped and hammered away, the pubs erupted in chatter as hacks drank pints of beer or whiskeys straight—then drank some more. The papers were quickly bundled and loaded onto steam trains, fueled by coal, for distribution across the country. That's how news was made in London. But on Sunday night, most newspapers missed Britain's most important story. There were no pieces about overcrowded morgues and overtaxed doctors—no headlines that screamed about an overwhelmed police force.

The *Manchester Guardian* featured a front-page story on the fog, but the headline "Third Day of a London Particular" was anticlimactic, considering how many people were dying. "Transport Dislocated by Three Days of Fog," declared the *Times*. And that story was printed on page eight. The *New York Times* covered the smog more thoroughly than most British newspapers, but even though the reporter mentioned the uptick in robberies and the lack of milk supply to poorer areas, there was still nothing about deaths. The press didn't ask if people were dying. And British lawmakers, most safely tucked away in homes outside of London, may not have realized that the fog was strangling their city. The media had not yet learned the government's horrible secret: this was a catastrophe, worse than the cholera epidemic of 1866, when thousands had died. There was no reason for Londoners to panic, according to the press.

"The business of the city cannot cease just because of a fog," wrote the *Manchester Guardian.* The newspapers were wrong.

⤳

The teenager steadied herself—slipped on her coat and hat and swung open the parlor door. Rosemary and her mother stepped outside in the front garden, gripping each other with each step. They were alone now—just the two of them, making the most important journey of their lives. Rosemary's father needed that pill—now. His life depended on it. The sky was black. The air was stale. They found their path, ventured into a maze that seemed like another world—staggering, stumbling, and moving at a shuffle. With hands interlocked, they walked forward several feet, turned right, and touched the garden hedge. The grass had disappeared. Rosemary's eyes darted up and down—they burned. She couldn't see the garden where she and her siblings had played games for most of their lives. She couldn't see the pavement on the other side; she couldn't spot the curb. Her feet disappeared.

Before they had left, Rosemary's brothers, Malcolm and David, were sent next door to the Taylors, while little Sue was escorted down the street to the Hathams' house, where her best friend lived. They weren't told a thing—nothing about the vital trip their mother and sister were about to take. More neighbors watched over Albert in his bedroom. He was still gasping. Rosemary could tell that her mother was nearly panicked. She was scared of being disoriented in her own neighborhood, fearful of who might be out there in the fog. But Edna was most afraid of staying home and doing nothing—just sitting there, listening to her husband die. She gripped onto her daughter. Rosemary needed that pill—it would save her father.

But this fog was so disorienting, transforming their familiar neighborhood into a spooky, menacing landscape where a bogeyman might have lurked nearby—watching them. British parents often told bedtime stories of Bloody Bones to frighten their misbehaving kids. "Here comes the bogeyman dressed in black, carrying children with his sack on his back." The fog could have been hiding a monster. The teenager said little to her mother as they felt their way along the street toward the doctor's office, now just a few blocks away. It should have only taken thirty minutes—but they stumbled for an hour.

"We've gone the wrong way," Rosemary cried.

"No, we haven't! No, we haven't!" her mother yelled back.

Rosemary could sense her mother growing confused. The smoke burned their eyes and the acrid stench assaulted their noses. It was so hard to concentrate. They finally arrived at the doctor's office and retrieved the tablet. They made their way back home in silence—another hour dragged by. Rosemary finally calmed down.

They had been gone for two hours now, as they felt their way through their front garden, walking along the same path Rosemary's father traveled to and from work every day. Around six-thirty every night, she would hear his special knock on the front door, set to the tune of "Shave and a Haircut, Two Bits."

It was a knock cherished by his eldest child—the daughter who had waited six long years for his return from the war, looking forward to the day they might sit at their small table over a meal of beef and potatoes, the day she would once again have a father. As Rosemary and her mother climbed their front steps, there was silence inside—no sounds of hacking or struggling for breath. Into the parlor's doorway stepped a solemn pair of neighbors, the couple watching over Rosemary's father.

"He's died," they whispered. "It just happened."

Her mother let out a yelp, a sound like nothing Rosemary had heard before. Edna dashed upstairs to the room where her husband lay. She began to scream. Rosemary stayed downstairs in shock, listening to her mother's piercing wails. The teenager was confused. *They didn't act quickly enough. They should have walked faster. They waited too long to summon a doctor.* This small tablet should have cured her father. Now he was dead—lying upstairs, cold and stiff.

Her mother's shrieks rang in Rosemary's ears, cutting through the muffling fog that was now billowing into the parlor through the open door. Weeping, Edna emerged from the bedroom and ran down the stairs. The girl begged her mother to calm herself. Suddenly, Rosemary was furious—filled with rage that she embraced. She flattened her hand and swung at her mother's face, a quick slap providing a respite from the horrid screeching. Her neighbors stood in silence as Edna rushed to another room, sobbing. Rosemary took a breath and stared ahead.

She couldn't cry. She wouldn't talk. She focused, but refused to go upstairs—to see him like that. Rosemary collected herself and stepped through the parlor doorway, into the London fog.

CHAPTER FIVE

Bodies in the Mist

So heavy was the gloom, that gas was lighted in all the shop-windows; and the little charcoal-furnaces of the women and boys, roasting chestnuts, threw a ruddy, misty glow around them. And yet I liked it. This fog seems an atmosphere proper to huge, grimy London…
— *Nathaniel Hawthorne*, Notes of Travel, *1857*

T he stunning brunette with the full red lips grabbed her neck. She hacked, struggled while her guests stared. The room spun— she swooned near her French paramour. It was an odd episode, especially because it unfolded during a lavish affair at her salon; she was celebrating her recovery from a bout of tuberculosis. Her concerned suitor led her to a chair. She insisted that guests continue with the festivities, she would be fine. Then she began to sing, in Italian—her beautiful soprano voice strained, but strong. She turned, tried to engage the hundreds of people there to listen to her. She squinted, but their faces blurred, even those just a few feet away. A blanket of smoke engulfed them as fog poured through the doors.

On the stage of the iconic Sadler's Wells Theatre in Islington, North London, singer Marjorie Shires was radiant as Violetta, the lead character in one of the world's most famous operas, *La*

Traviata. That Monday, December 8, the actress indeed gave an authentic performance during the first aria, when her character clutched her throat in agony during a Parisian party. But there was little need to act. The beautiful society women, peering through brass opera glasses, hovered above her in their private boxes; now they were shadows, thanks to the stage lights and the heavy smoke. Only faded figures sat in the crowded orchestra, just below her. At the end of the first act, the music abruptly stopped. The conductor insisted they couldn't continue. His eyes burned—he could only make out the first row of musicians. It was impossible to direct them; the percussion and wind instruments struggled to compete with an ensemble of patrons, coughing just behind them.

As the gigantic red curtains closed, Marjorie hurried across the stage and begged the theater's manager to stop the performance; she feared the smoke would cause permanent damage to her lungs—and her most challenging songs were still to come. Laryngitis was certain. After just one act, *La Traviata* was abandoned. Well-heeled guests streamed out of the theater, grumbling about the fog and demanding the return of their money.

Sadler's Wells wasn't the only theater handicapped by the smoke—most cinemas turned off their projectors early when the screens became obscured. It was another dismal day to venture out. Monday would be the final day of full potency for the anticyclone. A mass of low-pressure air over Scotland stalked it, insisting that it move away from the city. The Air Ministry's forecast was optimistic: There would be improvement in the afternoon and perhaps a bit of rain. Not just yet. The fog wasn't quite finished with London—many more would die before it was compelled to leave. It thrived on being underestimated.

The Air Ministry's encouraging prediction convinced London Transport to allow many of its buses back on the road. After three days of being trapped, most business owners were anxious to see their workers return that morning. And drivers seemed to navigate the roads easily during the morning rush. The mist melted away and revealed a glimmering copper-colored sun; it teased Londoners that it would stay for a longer visit this time. Cars ventured out, crawled along the streets around Hyde Park and Piccadilly Circus. Then suddenly the smoke pounced, gobbling up the sunlight. Cars were once again abandoned— their owners surrendered. The fog was so fickle. There were clear skies in some places throughout the city, and impenetrable smoke in others. There was no logic.

The Ambulance Service struggled—officials put out another call for volunteers, begging them to work. "London at a Standstill," declared the *Daily Express* newspaper, "30-Mile Fog Belt Again Tonight." It detailed troubles with the roads and the struggle of police trying to direct traffic. No stories about the unusual number of deaths. "Chaos Again in Fog" was the *Times* headline. Editors dedicated an entire page to fog coverage, ranging from the spike in petty crime to the cancellation of sporting events. The *Manchester Guardian* had a similar story: "Third Day of a London Particular." But again, there was no mention of casualties.

Journalists may have called around to hospitals, inquiring about a spike in deaths, but their findings never appeared in a major paper. Yes, there were problems on the road and crime was a concern, but London editors overlooked their real lead story. The fog had killed thousands by now, and tens of thousands were seriously ill. Journalists now seemed to understand the inconvenience of the fog, but not its gravity. This was the worst health crisis to attack London in nearly one hundred years.

Despite the brief reprieve, the fog forced London to shut

down once again. It was still impossible for ships to navigate the River Thames. The overcrowded Underground trains were delayed and backed up from over the weekend. Local and long-distance trains were either postponed by hours or canceled. Transportation was becoming a crisis. The *Times* reported that at the Central Line station in Stratford, three thousand people were in line for tickets during afternoon rush hour. Extra constables were ordered to control the passengers. And the winter's first power cuts began that morning. For several months, in the darkest days each year, the government begged residents to use electricity only when necessary. But now the unusually cold weather forced the British Electricity Authority to shut down the power briefly in some places in southern England.

Big Ben's bells chimed two thirty—time for Parliament to begin its session. Norman Dodds and the other MPs traveled through the fog to the Palace of Westminster—even smoke couldn't suffocate the braying that would most certainly come from the Commons. Harold Macmillan, Norman's nemesis in Parliament, lamented traveling to London from his family's grand mansion, Birch Grove, in affluent East Sussex. He was hoping to go hunting.

"Another lovely day in the country," wrote Macmillan in his diary on December 8, "with impenetrable fog in London."

In the House of Commons, Norman argued with future prime minister Anthony Eden over fishing rights in Iceland and harassed the minister of food about the lack of milk supplies. They were relatively banal topics—no mention of fog. Norman was the MP who prided himself on fiercely protecting the needs of his constituency—and even he didn't recognize its severity. The Parliament session on the last full day of the fog was fairly humdrum, except for a curious question from another Labourite, a former coal miner who represented Durham, in North East England.

MP James Murray asked Geoffrey Lloyd, the minister of fuel and power, about nutty slack, those cheap, small nuts of brown coal mixed with dust; it was of even lower quality than the larger brown clumps that the government had rationed since the war ended. Britons complained to the National Coal Board—they needed more coal during the winter, but the government was planning to continue rations until 1958. So, ten days before the start of the fog, the British government had begun an intensive advertisement campaign to market nutty slack to domestic consumers, ration-free.

"Order as much as you like," read an announcement posted by the National Coal Board in the *Times*. "But don't wait until your ordinary coal allowance is finished before you buy Nutty Slack. Order your Nutty Slack this week in time for Christmas."

But the dust didn't burn well—it created more smoke and less heat. A housewife hoping to warm her home for the night would burn more nutty slack than the ordinary, rationed brown coal. In Parliament, MP Murray wanted to know if the minister of fuel and power thought nutty slack burned well on its own or if it needed to be mixed with higher-quality coal. *Of course*, he replied.

"Nutty slack is the cheapest solid fuel freely available," the minister of fuel and power reminded Parliament.

He assured Londoners that it would keep their families warm this winter. It was an unrestricted, inexpensive fuel. More than one million tons were available—consumers could buy as much as they wished for 30 percent less than the cost of rationed coal. But it was a horrible choice: Londoners could either wait for their higher-quality coal rations to arrive or buy that wretched nutty slack. Both of the fuels were dirty, both were deadly, and both were burning during those five cold days in December.

The silhouette of the Palace of Westminster looked seductive in that fog—when the sun peeked through, the smoke looped around Parliament's gothic peaks. Its beautiful decoration, cut into the stone, had been destroyed by years of acid-laden smoke. In less than two weeks, the ministers inside would be aghast by the aftermath of the smog; but that Monday they didn't seem concerned with the thick mist that draped them as they left for the evening. This was life in London. After a day of sun and fog, the *Manchester Guardian* noted that the banality of normal life seemed to have returned.

"Housewives were cleaning a layer of greasy grime that coated every surface in the house," the reporter noted. "Fair-haired young women made mousey by the fog were making appointments with hairdressers. Everybody had a fog story to tell, just as everybody used to have a bomb story."

Nowhere was printed the real truth, the evidence hidden within hospitals and inside homes. Thousands of Londoners were suffering and dying. The center of the anticyclone began to move east, but not quickly enough. As night fell, the fog gathered more, reducing visibility to a yard or less in most parts of London. By midnight, the city was enveloped again. The blanket spread across the outer ring of the city, about fifteen to twenty miles from Central London, then it vanished. All of the fog's spite was focused on London.

By the end of Monday, the death rate in Greater London finally reached its peak. Nine hundred people had perished over the past twenty-four hours alone. Almost three thousand had died since Friday morning. And the suffering wasn't over.

This was the fourth day of Police Constable Stanley Crichton's long five-day shift in North London. Over the weekend, he had entered dozens of homes, wealthy and impoverished, jotting down details of the dead people he found inside: name, age, and the cause of death—that part seemed obvious. When he returned home each night, he held his breath, hoping his wife, Maura, wouldn't be one of those poor victims—another name on his long list of dead. She wasn't. She was alive, but certainly not healthy. She still suffered from hacking fits, and her asthma seemed resigned to stay.

Monday evening, PC Crichton stumbled to his beat on Upper Holloway Road, which ended at Highgate, a suburb of North London. On a day that should have been busy with shoppers, the street was vacant, abandoned by shopkeepers and patrons. Stanley dodged in and out of freak thick patches of smoke so distinct that their edges morphed the clouds into moving walls. The sound of police whistles cut through the fog. He was disoriented, but he managed to spot an old police callbox about three hundred yards from a tailor's shop.

"I decided the best thing I could do was stand in the doorway in that area," he said. "If I needed help, I could go to the police box."

He stood there for hours, listening and watching, though it was futile. An old bobby trick was learning to sleep while standing—but Stanley wasn't safe enough to take a nap. Sound was muffled and visibility nil. When he stretched out his arm, his hand disappeared. He thought about Maura, alone in their home, with that yellow stuff seeping through the windows. He hoped his stubborn bride would stay safely inside. Then Stanley was jolted from a daydream. The abrupt crash of glass made him stumble backward and slam into the store's door. He leaned against it, shocked.

BODIES IN THE MIST • 101

BODIES IN THE MIST • 101

"I knew it was very, very close so I walked out of the doorway, still holding onto the sides of the windows," he said. "I found out that it was the window where I was standing beside."

He reached through the shards and began frantically tapping the bottom of the display, searching for a body. There was the only explanation: Some poor soul, bewildered by the fog, must have fallen into the glass. Stanley moved his hand through the display, left to right. He did it again, just to make sure. There was nothing there—quite literally, nothing. *Where were the reams of cloth in the display?* He knew they had lain there when he arrived, large sections of fabric the tailor hoped would lure customers inside. Now they were gone. Stanley glanced toward that police callbox. He needed help—now. He was frazzled, and then panicked. There was another crash, just a few feet to his left. Stanley whipped around.

"I heard another window go, and it was the shop next door," he recalled. "I couldn't see the people, I couldn't see anybody."

And Stanley didn't even hear the footsteps, right beside him. He was just inches from a criminal he couldn't see, much less arrest. The thief might have been armed—he was probably dangerous. At the least, he was brazen. And now he was gone. It was one of many smash-and-grab raids that happened that night, across the city. Stanley rushed to the callbox and picked up the phone.

"The windows have been broken through!" he yelled. There was a pause.

"Well, there's nothing we can do about it," was the calm reply on the other end. "We'll mark it down that you've made a report and we'll take it from there."

That was it. The burglar faded into the fog. Stanley inhaled the smoke, coughed into his black glove. He was alone again, struggling in that foul smoke. Stanley had been charged with keeping the people and businesses on this street safe. And he was failing, thanks to that fog.

❦

The wooden stairs just above Reg's kitchen creaked as the neighbors walked up and down. It felt like there were no walls, no seclusion. Ten Rillington Place was a strange little building. Because the single-family home had been renovated to house several families, whenever a tenant stepped through the main entrance, he had to pass the door of the Christies' bedroom and parlor—the hall of the Christies' flat was also the hallway of the entire house. Tenants ascending the darkened staircase did so directly over Reg's kitchen.

The noise, that incessant creaking and moaning of old wood, was enough to drive a balanced man to fits—let alone one inclined to agitation, like Reg. And it was still so cold outside, so suffocating with that fog. It seemed to never end—the smoke had eclipsed the beautiful sun for four days. He was still trapped inside with Ethel, still sick from the smoke. And his urges weren't waning— that photo shoot with the two prostitutes, days before, had been so tantalizing. But the rest of Reg's life was bleak, really, even after resigning from his job. And today was another anniversary of sorts, one Reg didn't cherish—not at all.

Three years ago to the day, on December 8, 1949, he had been seated at his kitchen table, facing a sergeant with the Metropolitan police. Rain showers had peppered a thin layer of snow on the ground, yet it was hot in his tiny kitchen, thanks to a fireplace stuffed with coal. Reg's hands ached from arthritis. Ethel sat near him—she listened as he described, yet again, the night a thud had awoken them.

Reg spoke slowly as Detective Sergeant John Corfield jotted

down every word; this was his third interview with investigators in a week. On November 30, 1949, metal had banged against metal, then scraping that made a dreadful sound—Reg had opened the front door. *What's happening?* Three police officers groaned, struggling to pry up the heavy drain cover underneath his front bay window.

"Have you seen Beryl Evans and her child?" asked DS Corfield.

"Not since earlier today," Reg replied.

"Where might they be?" asked the detective.

Reg knew the family spent quite a bit of time at Tim Evans' family home nearby. Every Wednesday, Beryl and Tim dropped Geraldine off with his mother, so the young couple could go to the cinema—they were likely there.

"Number eleven St Mark's Road," replied Reg, as he watched the men wrestle with the drain lid.

What were they looking for? What the detectives found, tucked away at 10 Rillington Place, would rattle Reg's life—and haunt him until he died.

∽

On November 30, 1949, Timothy Evans and his wife and daughter weren't at his family's home down the road. He was instead locked in a jail in South Wales more than 150 miles away, facing the most terrible of charges: murder. Earlier that day, the twenty-five-year-old had walked into the enquiry office at the central police station in Merthyr Tydfil, his hometown.

"Can I help you?" asked Detective Constable Gwynfryn Howell Evans.

"I want to give myself up. I have disposed of my wife," declared Tim. "I put her down the drain."

DC Evans stared at the handsome stranger with dark brown eyes.

"You realize what you are saying?" he cautioned. "Just think before you say any more."

"Yes, I know what I am saying. I can't sleep, and want to get it off my chest," insisted Tim.

DC Evans surveyed the young man. He wasn't tall, quite short actually, but intense.

"I will tell you all about it and you can write it down," Tim replied. "I am not very well educated and cannot read or write."

DC Evans and Detective Sergeant Glyndwr Gough sat down with Tim and asked him to repeat the details. Tim launched into a long story, one that took almost two hours to relate, to the annoyance of the Welsh investigators. Still, they wrote it down, word for word.

It had started, Tim said, the month before, in October. Beryl had told him that she was three months pregnant—she was upset.

"If you are having a baby, well, you've had one, another one won't make a difference," he told her. Beryl disagreed and vowed to abort it.

His wife bought a syringe, he said, and began injecting herself vaginally with a strange mixture. No success. "I'm glad it won't work," he told her. But she started taking tablets—he didn't know what they were—and he noticed that she began looking ill.

"She told me that if she couldn't get rid of the baby she'd kill herself and our baby Geraldine," said Tim. "You're being silly," he told her.

Beryl, frustrated that nothing seemed to work, insisted she would seek out someone who could help. Tim dismissed her rants, and left for his job as a driver for Lancaster Food Prod-

ucts. Now his story became peculiar—he described a very detailed memory of his chat with a man at a diner between Ipswich
and Colchester, while he was making deliveries, claiming the
stranger gave him pills for an abortion. Later that night, Tim
told Beryl about the stranger from the diner and the mysterious
tablets. She found them as she searched his overcoat pocket for
a cigarette—and kept them.

The next night, Tim returned from work to a darkened flat.
He put a penny in the coin meter to turn on the gas, then lit the
lamp on the mantel. He noticed Geraldine worming around in
her crib, and Beryl was lying on the bed. When he spoke to her,
she stayed quiet—she didn't move.

"I went over and shook her, then I could see she wasn't
breathing," he explained. "Then I went and made some food for
my baby."

The detectives looked at Tim, and then continued to take
notes as he slowly, calmly, described the rest of the evening. He
was certain that Beryl was dead.

"I fed my baby and I sat up all night. Between about one and
two in the morning I got my wife downstairs through the front
door," he said. "I opened the drain outside my front door that is
No. 10 Rillington Place, and pushed her body headfirst into the
drain."

He walked back upstairs, past the Christies' bedroom, sat
down beside the fire, and smoked a cigarette. Over the next few
days he "got my baby looked after," gave up his job, and arranged
to sell the furniture in his flat. Tim told his mother that Beryl and
Geraldine had gone for a holiday in Brighton, and after retrieving
money for his belongings, he took the train to Wales.

Detectives Evans and Gough peered at Tim as he signed the
confession. He seemed so detached, like he was describing a
trip to the corner store. There were so many problems with

his tale—to start with, it took entirely too long for him to explain everything. He struggled with details, as if he were making them up as he was going along. But perhaps he was trying to explain what had happened, carefully including all of the specifics. *Doubtful*, thought the police.

"A terrible liar," they said. They accused him of "telling a cock-and-bull story." Beryl Evans was dead, Tim claimed, but he hadn't mentioned his daughter. And the gift of abortion pills from a stranger seemed unbelievable. Now, DC Evans was not just worried about Beryl's location, he was gravely concerned about little Geraldine's safety. *Where is she?* he demanded to know. Tim was evasive. He claimed she was with friends in London or maybe Newport. When further pressed, he finally said that she wasn't with his friends, that he had actually handed over the child to his neighbor—John Reginald Christie. DC Evans jotted down the name, then immediately phoned Scotland Yard. Within thirty minutes, a Met police officer had typed out a telegram with information for local cops.

"He handed his 14 month old child to a man named Reginald Christie at the same address who stated he could have the child taken care of," read the note.

About half a dozen officers raced over to 10 Rillington Place, with all eyes on that drain cover, expecting to find a woman's body. They tried to lift it. It wouldn't move. They struggled, cursed, and pounded on the lid. Impossible. But they had to keep trying—there could be a woman down there, maybe with her daughter. The Met officers telephoned the Welsh police. *We can't do it.* Three strong men, making quite a racket, couldn't seem to remove that cover. DC Evans, in Wales, ordered them to keep at it. John Reginald Christie came outside to investigate the noise. He said he hadn't seen the Evans family lately. Police believed him.

With the help of tire irons, the drain was finally removed. A detective lowered a torch into the hole and peered down. It smelled disgusting—wet and rotten. He looked at the bottom. Nothing. The London police phoned DC Evans with the news—Beryl and Geraldine Evans were still missing. Now the detective was irritated with Tim.

"The drain which you say you put your wife's body down has been examined, and there is nothing there," said the detective.

"Well, I put it there," Tim insisted.

"I don't think you are physically capable of taking the lid off the manhole. It is as much as three men can do," said DC Evans.

Tim paused, looked at the detective and abruptly changed tack.

"No, I said that to protect a man named Christie," he said. "It's not true about the man in the café either. I'll tell you the truth now."

After listening to a stream of lies, DC Evans was grateful for the prospect of "the truth," but he would need to settle into his chair. Tim's second statement took even longer than the first to dictate—the pair sat across from each other for almost three hours. Listening to Tim was vexing. He spoke slowly, deliberately—"much surer of the facts," the detective thought.

"The only part that is not true in the statement I made to you this afternoon is the part about meeting the man in the café and about disposing of my wife's body," began Tim. "All the rest is true."

DC Evans doubted that.

Tim said that about a week before Beryl died, Reg had invited him into his sitting room, and had begun chatting with Tim about the pills Beryl was taking—she apparently had found those on her own, and had confided in Reg.

"I know what she's taking them for, she's trying to get rid of the baby," Reg was said to have told Tim. "If you or your wife had come to me in the first place, I could have done it for you without any risk."

But Tim said he was confused by his neighbor's offer. "I didn't think you knew anything about medical stuff." Reg assured him he had had training before the war—he had assisted other young women with unwanted pregnancies. Tim said Reg assured him that he would help, but warned that with "the stuff he used," one out of ten women would die. *No, thank you,* Tim told Reg. But the older man apparently convinced Beryl. Tim and his wife argued—he told her that an abortion was too dangerous.

"She turned round and told me to mind my own business and that she intended to get rid of it and that she trusted Mr. Christie," Tim said.

Tim didn't want to start a loud row, he claimed—they bickered too much already. And he had doubted she would follow through. Tim had spent much of that day at work, making deliveries. Ten hours later, he said, he dragged himself through the front door of 10 Rillington Place. The foyer was dark—the house was quiet. Tim said that Reg had been there waiting for him at the bottom of the narrow staircase, holding a light. His angular, pale face was macabre in darkness, like a ghoul on a visit from hell.

"Go on upstairs and I'll follow behind," Reg had whispered.

They climbed the two flights and walked into the Evanses' flat. It was dim with the curtain drawn, just some sparse shadows. Tim had sparked the gaslight in the bedroom. There was Beryl, lying on her side atop their bed, with a blanket wrapped around her.

"It's bad news. It didn't work," said Reg. "The baby's in the cot."

Tim said he had pulled back the eiderdown cover and stared down at Beryl.

"I could see that she was dead and that she had been bleeding from the mouth and nose and that she had been bleeding from the bottom part," Tim recalled.

He looked over at the cot, where his daughter lay. She was alive—and wiggling. He wrapped Geraldine in a blanket as Reg lit some coal in the kitchen's fireplace. The dust began to smolder.

"I'll speak to you after you feed the baby," Reg had reassured him.

Tim calmly boiled an egg and brewed some tea for his daughter, then asked Reg what had happened. Her stomach had septic poisoning, Reg explained—she had been dead for several hours. Reg had waited for him to return home, so they could discuss what to do with her body.

"He told me to stop in the kitchen and he closed the door and went out," Tim said. Reg had returned fifteen minutes later and explained that he'd carried Beryl downstairs to Mr. Kitchener's empty flat on the floor right below his, just for a moment while he gathered his strength.

"I'll dispose of it down one of the drains," Reg had promised. " 'You'd better get to bed and leave the rest to me. Get up and go to work in the morning as usual,' and that he'd see about getting someone to look after my baby."

DC Evans was confused again. *Three strong officers couldn't easily open that drain—how could a middle-aged man pry it up without help? And why would he help Tim, anyway?*

Both men, Tim explained, had been concerned about involving the police in Beryl's accidental death. Reg had previous convictions, though more than fifteen years old, for stealing. He also had spent time in prison for a violent assault involving an ex-girlfriend. Tim, too, had been a petty criminal, dabbling in fencing stolen items. And so, according to Tim's statement, began a series of events that were meant to cover up Beryl's death.

Tim wanted to give Geraldine to his mother, but Reg argued that it would cause suspicion. According to Tim, Reg knew a young couple in East Acton who would happily care for her. Reg ordered Tim to pack up some baby clothes and leave Geraldine with him the next day. He ordered him to resign from work, sell his furniture, and leave London. Tim had gratefully agreed—he told his mother that Beryl and Geraldine were on holiday. Within three days, he was boarding an overnight train leaving Paddington Station for Cardiff, South Wales.

So in less than six hours, Tim's story had greatly evolved. He'd dismissed the tale that Beryl accidentally overdosed on strange abortion pills in favor of this new account: that Reg, who was an occasional abortionist, had accidentally killed Beryl during a procedure, and then dropped her body in a street drain. And in the first scenario, Reg had volunteered to care for his daughter. Now, according to Tim, Reg's *friends* were actually caring for Geraldine. Tim was now the victim—Reg was the criminal.

DC Evans stared across the table. He may have been dumbfounded by the two conflicting stories, but he was absolutely clear on one thing: Timothy Evans was a chronic liar. He phoned the Met police in London—*come and take him, please.* While they waited for Scotland Yard detectives to arrive, DC Evans investigated Tim's time in Wales.

The detective interviewed the Lynches, Tim's aunt and uncle in Merthyr Tydfil, with whom he was staying. Part of Tim's story was truthful; he did arrive in Wales within a few days of Beryl and Geraldine's disappearances. His aunt had not seen him for at least three years, his uncle for nine years. Tim had told them that his employer's van had broken down in Cardiff and needed repairs—he would need to stay a while. When his aunt asked about Beryl and Geraldine, Tim told her they were in Brighton until after Christmas.

DC Evans learned that Tim had been having a fine time in Wales—he had visited pubs, performed in singsongs, and reminisced with family. And something strange—the detective also discovered that Tim had pawned a woman's wedding ring. Shortly after arriving in Wales, Tim had suddenly returned to London. He told his aunt and uncle that he had seen Beryl at their flat at 10 Rillington Place, but she had simply turned away and walked out, leaving Geraldine behind in the cot; he claimed he had paid a couple to look after the little girl, then visited his mother.

Tim is a liar, his aunt and uncle agreed. They wrote Tim's mother, repeating his story. His mother replied—and she was enraged.

"I don't intend to keep him anymore," she wrote. "His name stinks up here. Everywhere I go, people [are] asking for him for money he owes them. I am ashamed to say he is my son."

She denied seeing her son—and there had been no word from Beryl in weeks. The day his aunt and uncle received his mother's venomous letter, Tim walked into the Merthyr Tydfil police station and confessed to dropping his wife's body down a drain. And now here they were—on confession number two.

DC Evans was incensed, overwhelmed at the number of lies. He confronted Tim about his mother's claims.

"When did you last see your wife's body?" asked DC Evans.

"Just before Christie took it to Kitchener's flat," was his reply.

The detective fired off his most direct accusation. "Did you help Christie to carry it down?"

Tim looked at DC Evans. "Well, what happened was..."

Now, there emerged even more missing details. Tim claimed he'd heard Reg "puffing and blowing and went out and saw Beryl's body on the stairs." He had said to Reg, "What's up?" Reg had ordered him to pick up Beryl's legs, and together they had carried her body into the kitchen.

"That's the truth, and that's the last time I saw her body," Tim contended.

DC Evans stared back at him and declared: "I do not think you are saying the truth." Tim paused — he was resolute.

"I may have made a few mistakes but as far as Christie is concerned, I have said the truth."

Later that day, Scotland Yard investigators retrieved Tim and dragged him back to London for more questioning. Flanked by police as he stepped off the train at Paddington Station, Tim looked up and flinched. He was startled by press photographers, snapping his picture. Someone had tipped them off about his arrival. Tim was quickly escorted to Notting Hill Police Station. Now Detective Inspector James Neil Black, a twenty-two-year veteran of the Met, took over the interrogation. He was one of the investigators who had lowered a flashlight down the drain, searching for Beryl Evans' body late that night. When she wasn't there, DI Black had walked through that nasty garden at the back of the building, searching for signs of recently disturbed earth. It was dark and there was so much rubbish — *there was nothing there.* His eyes, probing the small back lot for signs of digging, never spotted the most disturbing sign of foul play: that thighbone holding up the garden fence. Of course, it didn't belong to Beryl or Geraldine but to one of those other doomed women buried in the garden. If only the detective had noticed it, the discovery could have saved lives in the years that followed.

DI Black ordered officers to search the washhouse, the one used primarily by the Christies — the one where both Ruth

Fuerst and Muriel Eady had been placed until Reg buried them. It was one of several blunders made by police: Black's officers failed to look inside the washhouse that night, blaming a series of miscommunications. If they had bothered to follow orders, they would have found two neatly wrapped packages waiting for them, now cold and stiff. Those packages would have to stay hidden a while longer.

That night, police questioned Ethel Christie in the couple's kitchen from about one until five in the morning, while Reg was whisked away to the Notting Hill station. Ethel recalled Tim's unstable marriage, and how Beryl had threatened to leave him just days before she went missing. The young mother had also told Mrs. Christie about her attempts to abort the baby. When Tim had arrived home from work on the night he said his wife had died, Ethel had heard him come inside. She had asked about Beryl—he'd told her that she and Geraldine were visiting family in Bristol. Ethel didn't believe him—and she didn't trust him. Now, as she spoke to investigators, she was outraged by Tim's accusation that her husband performed abortions.

"I have seen nothing to suggest that Mrs. Evans had had a miscarriage at our address, and I cannot think why Evans should suggest that she had and that my husband knew all about it," said Ethel. Referring to Tim, she said darkly: "I do know that he was always telling lies."

Officers showed Ethel some clothes—she picked them up. Yes, Ethel confirmed, they belonged to Beryl and Geraldine. During his own police interview, Reg explained that, after Beryl disappeared, Tim had bemoaned her absence, complaining she had left him. But the Christies weren't surprised, Reg explained. They knew Tim had been carrying on with a pretty sixteen-year-old blonde—even the neighbors down the street had heard the violent fight between Beryl and his young girlfriend, Lucy Endecott. It had made Tim furious—and violent.

"I'm going off the track," Tim had told neighbor Charles Vincent. "If I ever get hold of Lucy, I'll smash her up or run her down with my lorry."

Vincent also had witnessed rows between Tim and his wife.

"On several occasions I have heard him say to Beryl, 'I'll do you in.' But Beryl said he hadn't got the guts to do it," recalled Vincent. He told police that she had once had to use a bread knife to defend herself against her husband.

The Welshman was an embarrassment, according to Reg—a sloppy drinker with a dangerous temper. And, like Ethel, Reg claimed to be baffled by Tim's allegations.

"At no time have I assisted or attempted to abort Mrs. Evans or any other woman," Reg told investigators. "I cannot understand why Evans should make any accusation against me as I have really been very good to him in lots of ways."

Police searched Tim's flat and seized a briefcase that had been stolen from a nearby house—he said he was holding it for friends. Investigators also searched the Christies' flat, looking for evidence that Reg was an abortionist—among the clutter they found an old, decaying syringe that Ethel claimed as her own, along with Reg's St John's Ambulance First Aid book. The parlor's floorboards had recently been replaced, but there was nothing hidden underneath. It all seemed perfectly normal, at least for a vile tenement flat in Notting Hill.

The Christies were very helpful—and Reg was warned that he might be asked to testify. He would prove to be a model witness: a former War Reserve policeman with a steady job and a devoted wife. Sure, the prosecutor knew about Reg's past, those convictions for theft and assault. He would emphasize that those things had happened years earlier—and that since then, Reg had stayed out of trouble.

On December 1, 1949—just over three years before the choking fog of 1952—the Notting Hill police investigators closed the back gate and concluded their search of 10 Rillington Place. They had never scraped the surface of the small garden, the section in the back that fascinated John Reginald Christie the most. And they had never noticed that thighbone that was fastened to the fence.

CHAPTER SIX

Postmortem

Stand at the window here. Was ever such a dreary,
dismal, unprofitable world? See how the yellow
fog swirls down the street and drifts across the
dun-coloured houses.
—*Sir Arthur Conan Doyle,*
The Sign of Four, *1890*

Their breaths quickened, they wheezed and staggered. Their
attendants rushed over, jumped on their beds, and wrapped their
faces in whisky-drenched grain sacks with holes for the eyes. It
was a bizarre effort borne of desperation—and it didn't seem to
work.

Soon, the fits stopped and they collapsed, tongues hanging
to the side. News of these deaths appeared in papers all over
the world. Finally, the weather was triggering some alarm—over
cattle. "Fog fever," as it was dubbed in the media, had poisoned
prize-winning cows in London. On the first day of the fog, Friday, breeders trucked in hundreds of their valuable bovines on
trains to the Smithfield Livestock Show in Earl's Court, near
the city's center. Their owners brushed them meticulously, and
had fattened them for months for this world-renowned show.
The cows were young and in prime condition. Now eleven were

dead. The fog had suffocated three of them. Eight more showed signs of respiratory distress, and they were slaughtered at their owners' request. About 160 cattle were having problems breathing. Veterinarians ran from stall to stall. "More Deaths at the Cattle Show," reported the *Times*.

Nowhere was printed the larger truth, the evidence hidden within hospitals and inside homes. Thousands of people were suffering and dying.

❧

Most Londoners were asleep now—it was early Tuesday morning, December 9, 1952. Hours earlier, they had shut their doors, latched the locks, banked up fires with coal dust, and wrapped themselves with blankets. More than eight million people, crammed into London, hoped to stay warm through the night. In the previous one hundred hours, the fog had killed almost three thousand people—their friends and families watched them struggle, deteriorate, and then finally die. And so many of them died alone. Thousands more were doomed, still dying—it would take weeks, even months for them to succumb. But for now, in the dark hours of Tuesday morning, London's godsend finally arrived—a faint wind.

The breeze pushed the mass of cold, polluted air toward the south. The clouds picked up speed. The grit swirled and wafted upward. That little low-pressure system, the one that had spent days nudging the anticyclone from behind, had finally prevailed. By dawn, the soot-laden fog and smoke that had blacked out London for five days began silently rolling away. The temperature warmed above freezing, five degrees higher than the day before; the barometric pressure dropped slightly. The warm air, once trapped at the bottom of the Thames River Valley, slowly began to rise. Discreetly, without a fuss, the lid covering London was unsealed. The curtain that had isolated millions of Britons from the rest of the country, closed airports, blockaded the River Thames, and created hundreds of accidents was gone. By the time the morning rush hour approached, most of the city was clear of fog. The Thames immediately hosted a fleet of commercial ships, all headed by anxious captains, ready to raise their anchors and push off.

The world's most populated city was animated again. Bus drivers began their regular routes. The Underground operated without delays. City workers stored the torches meant to light the roadways for wayward drivers. Owners reclaimed their abandoned cars. The railways and airports ran on schedule. There seemed to be little concern on Tuesday, no wailing in the streets or protests in front of Parliament. But inside homes and hospitals, thousands of Londoners grieved for the dead. And their misery was just beginning, because soon they would find out why their loved ones died—who and what were responsible.

On Tuesday, Parliament convened promptly at two thirty to discuss boilerplate issues ranging from British troops in Korea to an increase in pension benefits for dependents of deceased police officers. MPs debated for more than ten hours, covering forty different issues, but none of them concerned the murders caused by a dirty fuel—a fuel the government itself had promoted as safe and cheap.

But coal did make a brief appearance in the House of Commons that day, during a lively debate. Edwin Leather, a Conservative from North Somerset, implored the ministers to make chest X-rays compulsory for a quarter of a million men working in hundreds of mining villages in South Wales and South West England. He argued that these miners breathed in excessive amounts of coal dust in the pits, which infected their lungs.

They suffered from coal worker's pneumoconiosis, also known as black lung disease, because the charcoal dust turned the organs dark before killing its victims. Leather begged the MPs for help, saying it would only cost the National Coal Board a quarter of a million pounds a year to order mandatory X-rays.

"Innocent men in the mines are today sowing the seeds of their own ruin in the later years of their lives," argued Leather. "Innocent men are every day causing irreparable damage to their lungs, which will make the later years of their lives a misery. Science has the power to stop it."

The long response from the government was detailed, but discouraging.

"We do not know fully what the cause of the disease is," replied William Joynson-Hicks, the parliamentary secretary to the Ministry of Fuel and Power. "Until one can tell the cause, one cannot be certain how to prevent the disease, let alone how to cure it."

Leather was furious. This was the third year he had approached Parliament on behalf of the miners, only to be rebuffed by the Ministry of Fuel and Power. The government insisted on more research before it would commit money to a prevention plan, even though the repercussions from mining were clear—men were dying from coal dust, even before it arrived in London to be sold. Coal was killing people from the moment it was extracted by miners deep below the ground in the Gloucestershire coal fields, to the instant a match was sparked by a housewife in Westminster. The fog simply escalated coal's daily assault on London.

The newspapers covered the smoke's retreat; readers could sense the relief of an entire country, but they did not yet realize they had been trapped for days by a phantom killer. On Tuesday, some statistics began to surface. The Automobile Association reported that it had responded to nearly five hundred calls from stranded or crashed motorists over the weekend. The ambulance service answered more than six hundred emergency calls within two days. The National Smoke Abatement Society claimed that the worst fog in living memory was costing the capital two million pounds every twenty-four hours. The antipollution advocates pointed to the losses suffered by airlines for grounded planes; the reduced patronage of cinemas, hotels, and restaurants; and the thousands of people who weren't able to report to work. For now, the casualties from the fog were measured in money and aggravation—not lives. For a final day, the newspapers highlighted crime, disruption, and freak accidents. "Hit By Duck" read one pithy headline; a mallard, blinded by the smoke, had crashed into a pedestrian, injuring them both. The victim was kind enough to take the crippled bird to the Royal Society for the Prevention of Cruelty to Animals for evaluation. Another story detailed how the Westham dog track was closed because the dogs were actually able to catch the mechanical hare. The man controlling the animal couldn't see the lanes in the smoke. There was one frightening headline, printed not in a London newspaper but in an Australian broadsheet, *The Canberra Times*. "Fears of Loss of Life in London Fog," it read. But the concern wasn't for the thousands of respiratory and cardiac victims.

"We fear when the fog clears we shall find bodies floating in the water," said a Port of London official. Met officers lifted eight people from the Thames using crooked wooden staffs as aids.

The amount of smoke was slowly decreasing across much of the city, but sulphur dioxide had hit its peak the day before and CO_2 levels in the air were still incredibly dangerous. Londoners were ill. Insurance claims for new sickness during the fog were almost 40 percent higher than average from the year before; the next week, agencies would complain that claims more than tripled. From the start of the fog through the following Friday—seven days—more than four thousand people died, two and a half times more deaths than normal for that week in previous years. The Great Smog of 1952 was officially a crisis.

༄

Thirteen-year-old Rosemary Sargent glared at her typewriter—her fingers wouldn't move, the keys didn't click. She peered at the worksheet on her desk and tried again—success, this time.

It was her first day back at Catford Central School in Lewisham in the southeast part of the city, just forty-eight hours after her father had died in their home. Most of the schools in London had been closed the day before, as the fog threatened to plague the city for yet another night. The younger children, who could walk to school and didn't need transportation, had returned on Monday. Little Sue complained to her mother about the fog that day—*why did she have to go, if she couldn't even see across the street?*

Now, the smoke was virtually gone, and Rosemary returned to her assigned desk, typing out busy work. Ms. Atkinson, her teacher, greeted her, and Rosemary handed her the brief note that Edna had written. "Her father has died." Ms. Atkinson looked down at Rosemary and said, "I'm sorry," before moving on to other students. Later, Ms. Atkinson typed out a letter to Edna.

Dear Mrs. Sargent,

I am writing to say how sorry I am to hear of your great loss.

*This must be such a time of difficulty and strain for you
that it may help to know how very calm and brave Rosemary has been in school yesterday and today. She is a lesson
to all of us!*

*Now that she is growing into such a capable girl, I am
sure you will find her a great comfort. The staff all join me
in sending their sympathy.*

Rosemary was praised for remaining stoic—and it was quite a
compliment. She was miserable. Her best friend, Joyce, plopped
down in the neighboring chair and greeted her with a warm
smile.

"Happy to be back at school?" she asked.

Rosemary concentrated on her typewriter. She didn't want to
talk about it, what had happened two days earlier—she'd chat
about anything else. But she couldn't lie, not to Joyce.

"My dad died Sunday."

Joyce quickly glanced at her, eyes wide—she let out a little
gasp. She waited for a longer explanation. Rosemary was de-
pleted. Her brown eyes were tired, red. They begged Joyce to
stop asking questions. Rosemary stayed quiet.

"Oh," said Joyce.

Rosemary looked down at the paper in the typewriter; her fingers moved. She heard the clicking of Joyce's typewriter. Nothing
more was said—that covered it. She might have seemed morose,
but she was actually relieved to be back at school. Rosemary
could no longer stand being trapped inside that house; her mother
was nagging her, constantly, about helping her with household
chores. Malcolm and David were confused. No one talked about
Albert's death. And everyone was lying to her younger sister, Sue.
"He's in hospital," the neighbors said. Edna Sargent couldn't tolerate another anxious child. It was easier this way.

One of the most astonishing things about this deadly fog was who it first alarmed—not politicians, reporters, or even doctors, but undertakers. Across London, funeral directors reported a surge in bodies, so many that the demand for caskets was insatiable. It became a logjam. And even when a family was lucky enough to purchase one, there were few burial spots left for them to claim. Undertakers walked around the backstreets, responding to calls from worried families who feared their friend or relative was dead in bed. Sometimes the police would break in, or perhaps neighbors would have a key. Undertakers removed multiple victims from the same home. Soon florists were alarmed, too. They couldn't stock funeral wreaths and flowers quickly enough. The demand was enormous. Something was wrong. But when the fog cleared, there were no bodies lying in the streets, as there had been during the Blitz. There weren't hundreds of dead people floating in the Thames, like during a massive flood. The dead were concealed inside homes, morgues, and hospitals. The backlog caused terrible delays. Albert Sargent had nowhere to go, so there he lay, in the parlor—for weeks.

"Hurry up," yelled Edna at her eldest child that morning.

As Rosemary opened the side door to walk to her bus stop, she averted her gaze from the front room. It was too hard to remember. She still refused to cry.

The practice wasn't so shocking, keeping her father there with them. It was a Victorian tradition to store a loved one's body in the parlor for the viewing and wake. It was often referred to as the "death room" and it had served as a place for funerary rituals about until about fifty years earlier, at the turn of the century. After the person died, the body was watched for several nights to make sure he was truly dead. That was the origin of the term "wake," the social gathering before a funeral. When "funeral parlors" gained popularity in the early 1900s, home parlors were renamed "living rooms."

Most modern British families didn't display a body in the front parlor anymore, but the outdated custom became a necessity in the Sargent household. They couldn't buy a gravesite for Albert. They called around to funeral parlors, but they were all stacked up. He had to stay with them, as long as necessary. It was difficult for Rosemary to imagine: the father she adored, who protected her, was lying there in a frigid room, covered in a sheet—all alone.

While Rosemary ate her lunch at school, the Sargents' neighbors were busy at home. The man next door had been a medical attendant in the army; he knew how to lay out a body—a somewhat gruesome task that involved washing the corpse, dressing it, and permanently closing the eyelids. The body's appearance had to be tidied: the hair brushed or the face shaved. Albert had had a falling-out with that neighbor and they hadn't spoken for several years, but Edna begged the man to help. They carried in a coffin, laid it on the floor, and he began to work.

"When I came home from school, he was in the coffin already and the room was locked," Rosemary remembered. The lid was closed, the door latched. She would never see his face again. That wooden box lay where their Christmas tree would typically stand, a spruce adorned with paper chains and glass bulbs. Not this year. The fog that frightened her, and then snatched away her father, had now blown away, but it left behind such sorrow in her family—and in that room.

"We weren't allowed to go in," said Rosemary. "I never liked it, it was always closed."

Only her mother had the key. Five-year-old Sue had no idea her father was hidden behind that door—waiting. But Rosemary knew.

The fog's exodus didn't provide the city's doctors with any relief. Their catastrophe was just beginning. The Emergency Bed Service warned that one out of every five patients would not have a hospital bed. That was certainly true for Middlesex Hospital in Westminster, where Dr. Donald Acheson struggled to save lives during his four-day-long shift. There were dying people crammed inside every room in the building now. Men and women, mostly elderly and all gasping for breath, took every spare bed.

"To make room I had to ask permission to cancel all routine admissions for the next week," Donald remembered. "But many people died in spite of everything we could do for them."

Donald had stopped sending the patients to specialty wards based on symptoms—there was no need. He knew what was killing them. The black mucus they were coughing up was his evidence. Deaths blamed on bronchitis increased by ten times from the previous week; deaths attributed to pneumonia increased four times. Donald was desperate—he placed patients wherever he could find a bed, or even some space. He was in the midst of the worst medical crisis of his generation—the deadliest health catastrophe since the influenza pandemic of 1918.

There were dramatic stories—an ambulance was lost in the fog on its way to the London Maternity Hospital with an expectant mother. The driver radioed that she had given birth in the vehicle. A milkman walked six miles through the fog, leading a heavy tanker to distribute milk to poor East End families. Less than a mile from his depot, he collapsed and died. There was suffering everywhere.

In his desperation for space, Donald placed patients in unconventional areas. Men were struggling with coughs in the maternity ward. Women were rolled into the dissection rooms. The sick lay side by side, with no regard to gender, age, or ailment. Their stomachs ached, their throats burned.

The lips of the dying were blue. Most were over the age of forty-five, and there was little doubt that many of them suffered from preexisting lung disease or heart disease. Heavy smoking and chronic exposure to pollution had already weakened their organs. Particulates and acids in the killer fog triggered massive inflammations. The dead had suffocated. Babies were dying, too—their fragile organs couldn't fight the powerful toxins in the air—but those numbers were much smaller. Ambulance drivers, desperate to save their patients, hopped out of their vehicles only to find the victims dead. The morticians soon ran out of space in the city's morgues—bodies were stacked up against walls; corpses were scattered on benches, tables, even the floor, uncovered with their gaze to the ceiling. They weren't even swaddled for burial yet; most mortuaries had already run out of shrouds.

The bodies would have to wait for their autopsies—if they received them at all. The practice wasn't the elaborate public spectacle it had been during the Victorian years, when physicians displayed their talents in pubs, just feet from pints of lager and bitters. There wasn't time for autopsies today. In Middlesex Hospital, Donald knew the chapel was needed—not for prayer, but for storing his dead patients. He ordered assistants to move teaching cadavers from the anatomy department to a different building. They carried the bodies down halls, just to make room for fog victims. Meanwhile, Donald scoured the ward for more oxygen tanks, in vain—they were all in use or empty. And the flood of patients wouldn't stop.

He was constantly filthy and sweaty, regardless of the fog. The coalman arrived at the merchant yard early each morning, grabbed a heavy shovel, and began scooping clumps and dust into his dirty leather sacks, heaving each of them atop his wooden cart with a grunt. Children gawked at his strength as he humped a hundredweight sack on his shoulder across the city; he was the embodiment of London's past. Along with the rag-and-bone men, the coalmen were among the last to use huge horses to drag along their wagons during deliveries. His face blackened as he checked addresses off his list; his nails were chipped and filled with soot. He secreted a chemical smell—not smoke, but unburned fuel. There were pale rings around his eyes where he rubbed away the dust. Housewives cringed as he trudged through their kitchens, knocking over gas lamps and dumping coal nuggets into their storage space.

Ethel Christie usually greeted the coalman in the hallway of 10 Rillington Place. He would shuffle over, hand her a slip of paper with her order number. She would glance down at the bill and sign her name. He would produce a receipt and then quickly shove the coal beneath the hallway stairs. The fog had faded, but the freezing wind was intolerable without a fire. Coal was critical.

That Tuesday, December 9, when the bitter fumes cleared, the sun appeared—and the residents who lived inside 10 Rillington Place finally ventured out. Ethel Christie, still ill from the fog, prepared to write a letter to her sister, Lily, in Sheffield. The two were close, along with their older brother, Henry. Ethel often wrote Lily of her life in London, and their troubled relationship with the upstairs neighbors. She'd had a great deal to report two years earlier, when her tightly circumscribed life had become abruptly more exciting. Scotland Yard detectives had finally uncovered those secrets inside the wash-house in her back garden.

Ethel's part in the drama involving the Evans case had begun on December 2, 1949, three days after Tim Evans first confessed to murdering his wife. Late that morning, Chief Inspector George Jennings had called on Ethel, demanding to conduct yet another search. He tromped through the small garden, kicking over plant pots and picking through rubbish. Still nothing. He pushed hard at the washhouse door—he couldn't open it. Jennings needed to get inside, so he returned to Ethel's door.

"What is this?" he asked Reg and Ethel, as they stepped outside.

"We have been using this place daily for the purpose of getting water for rinsing the slop pail, when emptying it in the lavatory which is situated next door," Ethel explained to officers. Reg also stored building materials inside, but it was available to all of the building's residents, if they had a device with which to open the broken lock.

Ethel retrieved a piece of metal from behind the back door, stuck it in the lock, and unlatched it. The door swung to the left and the officers began searching behind piles of old paint cans and brushes. There was no smell of death—but then again, the small building was so cold and dry, a suitable place to preserve a body. Reg knew that. He had stored two bodies there, briefly, five years earlier. He paced up and down the garden as the investigators stepped inside. He was holding the small of his back, grimacing like he was in pain.

A wood pile blocked the bottom of the sink. Using a torch, Jennings reached behind it and touched a large package. Officers dragged it out. It was a green tablecloth, wrapped around a blanket, tied tightly with a thick sash cord. A second discovery—behind the door, a much smaller package was partially concealed by pieces of timber. The investigators carefully unbound each item. Beryl and Geraldine Evans had finally been found. The investigators were accustomed to locating dead wives—this was such a violent area—but the body of a dead girl was disturbing. They called the pathologist.

It was late that night, almost ten o'clock, when officers surrounded Tim Evans as he sat inside the Criminal Investigation Department (CID) office at Notting Hill station. Detective Inspector James Neil Black removed Tim's handcuffs, ordered him a cup of tea. Black looked over at Inspector Jennings, stripped off his mackintosh, and took out a notebook as another officer opened a cupboard door. He dumped a slew of articles on the floor: Beryl's clothing, along with Geraldine's gown, some rope, wrappings, and a man's tie. Tim looked down—spotted a striped tie and picked it up. Jennings introduced himself.

"I am Chief Inspector Jennings in charge of this case. At 11:50 a.m. today I found the dead body of your wife, Beryl Evans, concealed in a washhouse at 10 Rillington Place, Notting Hill, also the body of your baby daughter Geraldine in the same outbuilding, and this clothing was found on them," said Jennings. "Later today I was present at Kensington Mortuary when it was established that the cause of death was strangulation in both cases. I have reason to believe that you were responsible for their deaths."

Tim looked him the inspector and simply replied, "Yes."

Inspector Black began to scribble quickly in his notebook as the Welshman told a new story, an explanation quite different from the first two confessions.

"She was incurring one debt after another and I could not stand it any longer," said Tim, "so I strangled her with a piece of rope and took her down to the flat below the same night whilst the old man was in hospital."

In this new confession—his third in two days—Tim seemed to absolve Reg from being an abortionist, a murderer, or even an accomplice.

"On Thursday evening after I came home from work I strangled my baby in our bedroom with my tie," said Tim, "and later that night I took her down into the washhouse after the Christies had gone to bed."

He was very matter-of-fact, very calm, as he confessed to two murders. Black stopped writing and asked Tim to sign the confession. As Tim picked up the pen, he looked up.

"It is a great relief to get it off my chest. I feel better already. I can tell you the cause that led up to it," he said.

Tim quietly wept as Inspector Black put his arm around his shoulder and told him to not upset himself. Tim described the motive; it seemed fairly straightforward—he had simply snapped. He and Beryl had often bickered over money, Tim explained. He gave her money for rent, furniture, and milk, but she frittered it away. A few days before she died, they had begun a fight that stretched over Sunday and Monday; he had threatened to smack her, she threw a milk bottle at his head, then he stormed off toward his favorite pub. He had returned that Tuesday evening from work, when the Christies said they were away from the flat. Beryl and Tim were alone in 10 Rillington Place. She confronted him over their dire finances. It would be their last disagreement—he was enraged.

"I hit her across the face with my flat hand. She then hit me back with her hand," Tim told detectives. "In a fit of temper I grabbed a piece of rope from a chair which I had brought home off my van and strangled her with it."

He then described carrying Beryl's body down the staircase to Mr. Kitchener's empty flat and dumping her there, which might have explained the thud heard by Reg and Ethel that night…if the Christies were to be believed. Tim said he had returned to his own flat to feed Geraldine, and later that night had brought down a green tablecloth from his kitchen table and a blanket to wrap Beryl.

"I then slipped downstairs and opened the back door, then went up and carried my wife's body down to the washhouse and placed it under the sink," he said. "I then blocked the front of the sink up with pieces of wood so that the body wouldn't be seen. I locked the washhouse door. I come in and shut the back door behind me. I then slipped back upstairs. The Christies who live on the ground floor were in bed."

The details in Tim's confession seemed to match the evidence, according to police. But a curious note—Tim never mentioned bringing a piece of metal to open the latch to the washroom to hide his wife's body. He might have forgotten that detail, though that seems unlikely—it would have been difficult to carry a body while fiddling with a broken lock. Someone else might have left the door ajar earlier, but if not, Tim would have been unable to open the door without an instrument. Investigators seemed to ignore that detail.

Tim said he had left Geraldine alone in their flat two days in a row, for eight hours each day, as he worked—but no one had reported hearing the toddler cry. It wasn't believable—it seemed to be another tall tale. Then on Thursday, he had been fired from his delivery job.

"I then went home, picked up my baby from her cot in the bedroom, picked up my tie and strangled her with it," he explained. "I then put the baby back in the cot and sat down in the kitchen and waited for Christies downstairs to go to bed. At about twelve o'clock that night I took the baby downstairs to the washhouse and hid her body behind some wood."

Detective Black finished scribbling in his notebook. He read the story aloud and Tim signed the confession. Investigators never asked Tim why he would kill his daughter—*why not just leave her with his mother, or even a stranger?* His confession was all they needed to make an arrest. It was just past eleven in the evening now—the Met detectives sat down together. It would be a long night, as they tried to untangle their suspect's convoluted and conflicting stories.

The next morning, Tim sat in his cell and watched officers as they filed in and out of the jail. He chatted—they watched. And then Tim struck up a conversation with a sergeant on station duty. They discussed mundane things—like football. This was Len Trevallion's job; he sat at the cell's entrance and eyed his prisoner.

"He seemed completely relaxed and unperturbed," Len recalled. "At no time did he proclaim his innocence."

Tim began offering up details about his case—his wife had squandered their money. She was pregnant again. And now both she and their daughter were dead. Len was detached—prisoners frequently tried to make conversation with him. They were mostly degenerates, he thought. Len looked at Tim and made a simple observation.

"Well, one can understand possibly something happening to your wife, but to your baby, that sounds a bit much," said Len.

Tim looked at Sergeant Trevallion.

"Well, it was the constant crying of the baby that got on my nerves," replied Tim. "I just had to strangle it, I just had to put an end to it, I just couldn't put up with its crying."

And with that, he had made yet another confession. When Len walked out of the cell a short time later and reported the admission a colleague, Len was told that Tim had already confessed: *No need to write it down.* There was no written record, no other witness to the confession. Tim later confided in a doctor, while he awaited trial in Brixton Prison. He told Dr. John Matheson, the principal medical officer, the same initial story he had told police—that he and Beryl had fought over money and he had strangled her—but he didn't mention Geraldine. Tim never again admitted to killing his daughter. There were so many stories to sort through—it seemed impossible to know the full truth.

Timothy Evans' trial date was set for January 11, 1950, a Wednesday, at Old Bailey Courthouse in Central London. The building was a celebrated landmark, constructed almost three hundred years earlier just two hundred yards northwest of St Paul's Cathedral. It hosted some of Britain's most high-profile cases—now Timothy Evans would beg for his life within its walls. Under British law, a suspect could be tried for only one murder at a time, so senior counsel Christmas Humphreys chose to put Tim in the dock for the strangulation of his daughter, not his wife. The prosecutor was concerned that the defense could paint Beryl as an unsympathetic victim, an offensive woman who provoked her husband. Humphreys reasoned that a young father who had killed his innocent daughter would repulse a jury.

There was no ballyhoo over the case in the press, just small mentions. The murders weren't salacious or high-profile—Tim and Beryl weren't an affluent couple from Westminster. He wasn't a frenzied serial killer. The victims weren't butchered. They were poor people, trying to survive in a Notting Hill slum. Newspapers largely ignored the story. "Alleged Murder of Wife" was the headline of a seventy-word *Times* article. Harry Procter, a reporter for the *Sunday Pictorial*, said reporters dubbed the murders "fish-and-chippy," dull and unglamorous. The press box was vacant for much of the trial.

During his opening statement, prosecutor Christmas Humphreys laid out a mostly circumstantial case. Tim Evans, the Crown contended, was a habitual liar. And a killer.

"You will bear in mind that he begins with a story most of which he abandons, and that he goes on to tell another story, which is a terrible accusation, if it is true, of the murder by a man downstairs of his wife," Humphreys told the jury, "and then he throws both these statements away and clearly confesses to the murder of his wife and child."

First, Humphreys presented the forensics—the jury learned how Beryl and Geraldine had died. They heard testimony from Dr. Donald Teare, the pathologist who had performed the autopsies. Geraldine and Beryl had both been strangled—the killer had looped a men's tie around Geraldine's neck, then tightened it with a bowknot. The murder weapon used to kill Beryl was missing, but the deep grooves it left in her flesh were still there. On the right side of her neck there was an abrasion three and a half inches long, tapering to the rear. Dr. Teare suspected she had been strangled from behind, likely with a rope—Tim's last confession to police mentioned a rope.

Beryl wore a dress, blouse, and jacket—her panties were missing, and her breasts, upper abdomen, thighs, and private parts were all exposed. The body was in a jackknifed position with her knees tucked under her chin—police said it was a classic method for packing up a body for convenient disposal. There were two large bruises on her left inner leg, one on the calf and one on the thigh, as if someone had tried to force her leg down during a struggle. And there were more disturbing details: As Beryl had told the Christies, she was indeed pregnant; she was sixteen weeks along with a healthy boy.

There was also considerable swelling on her right eye and mouth, so much inflammation that her lip actually touched the tip of her nose. It appeared come from one strong blow with the back of the hand, less than half an hour before she died. Whoever killed Beryl Evans had managed to keep her quiet before tying a rope around her neck from behind. It seemed unlikely that she would have allowed her killer to hit her shortly before her death—unless the killer was her abusive husband and they were arguing.

And there were more delicate details. Beryl had an old scar along with some bruising inside the posterior wall of the vagina; she had likely received them within a week of her death. Dr. Teare suggested the bruising had been caused either by rape or, more likely, a self-inflicted abortion attempt—but neither scenario likely happened the day she died. Beryl had been very clear that she wanted an abortion. The forensic evidence was so confusing: *Was she raped? If so, when? Did she try to abort her own child? Did someone else?* There were no reliable answers, but if there were, they might have changed the course of the case.

And then one of the most unfortunate mistakes in the investigation was revealed. Before Beryl's autopsy, Dr. Teare had asked Chief Inspector Jennings if he should take a vaginal swab sample, to test for semen. "No," he was told. Investigators were certain her husband was the killer. When Dr. Teare performed her autopsy, he made no note about seeing semen, but he wasn't specifically searching for it, either. There was no conclusive evidence that Beryl Evans had been sexually assaulted before her murder—if there had been, defense attorneys might have argued that Beryl had been raped and killed by someone other than her husband.

The jury then heard a litany of details about Tim's mental state that seemed damning to the defense. Dr. John Matheson, the principal medical officer at Brixton Prison's hospital ward, interviewed Tim after his arrest. Matheson's charge was to determine if Tim was fit to stand trial. Matheson conducted a slew of tests meant to test mental acuity—and he determined that Tim had an IQ of about 65 and the mental age of an eleven-year-old. He labeled Tim a "dullard," but blamed it on a lack of education, not an innate defect. Matheson then interviewed Tim about the murderers.

"Wife then got jealous of baby—rows—at first he ignored her but she kept it up and he got fed up with it," read the scribbles from Matheson's notes. "He came home from work, a row started on debt, he lost his temper and strangled her."

As Tim awaited trial, there were other visitors to Brixton Prison, people he trusted. On December 4, Tim's mother sat across from him, concerned about her son's mental health.

"I did not touch her, Mum, Christie did it," Tim insisted. "I didn't even know the baby was dead until the police brought me to Notting Hill. Christie told me the baby was at East Acton." Tim was repeating the second of his three confessions, now to his mother. His stories were becoming more jumbled.

John Reginald Christie, the Crown's star witness, spent two days on the stand. The prosecutor asked him about Thursday night, the day Geraldine was likely killed. Reg replied that Tim had claimed he'd resigned from his delivery job earlier in the day.

" 'If you can find anyone better to do the job, then get him,' " Reg recalled Tim saying. " 'I have got prospects of a job in Bristol and I may be going down at the weekend.' " In truth, Tim had been fired.

Reg described Tim as irate, upset, "really wild, as though he had had a terrific row." Then Reg saw his neighbor again late Friday night when Ethel left the hallway light on. Reg asked about Beryl.

"She has phoned me; she is all right. She is going to write you," he said. He told Reg he was going to sell his furniture the following week.

The first day of the trial ended with Reg's testimony. Prosecutor Humphreys began establishing his star witness's credibility with the jury. He had been a war policeman for four years. He had lost much of his voice during World War I, thanks to gas exposure, and he wasn't in good health now. He had stayed out of trouble for more than fifteen years. Reg was a pathetic, but sympathetic, character on the witness stand. The next day, January 12, 1950, Tim Evans' attorney launched an aggressive cross-examination.

"Could you keep your voice up?" snapped Malcolm Morris.

"I have a quiet voice," was Reg's meek reply. "It is the reaction of gas poisoning in the last war."

Morris attacked Reg's statements about the tie used to kill the little girl, accusing him of telling people that it was Tim's tie.

"I think I did say I had seen Mr. Evans wearing a striped tie, but I could not say whether this was the one or not," was Reg's reply.

Reg denied offering Beryl an abortion or carrying a body down a flight of stairs. He was in such pain from enteritis and fibrositis in his back that he could scarcely bend down.

"I went up to the doctor, so it would be impossible," said Reg.

And Reg claimed it was absurd to accuse him of carrying a body down several flights of stairs.

"I had to crawl out of bed, and if I wanted to pick up anything off the floor I had to get on my hands and knees to do it," he insisted. "Physically impossible!"

Tim Evans shouted, accusing Reg of the murders and proclaiming his own innocence. The witness took off his glasses and wept. Reg would later hiss, "What a wicked man he is." Reg denied each of Tim's accusations. He listened as Tim's defense attorney ticked off Reg's list of past offenses, including four convictions ranging from swiping postal orders to stealing a car. Then Malcolm Morris mentioned a violent attack on a girlfriend in 1929, when Reg had smashed a cricket bat over the woman's head. He admitted to them all.

Now both sides focused on witnesses who had been milling around 10 Rillington Place during the week of the murders. There were discrepancies over work done on the building's hallway, and Prosecutor Humphreys wanted to address them. The defense claimed the wooden planks in the hallway floor were being replaced the night Tim claimed to have killed his wife. If that were true, it would have been difficult for anyone to lug a body down the dark, rickety stairs, as Tim claimed, and out the back door without falling. That must have meant that Tim's confessions were false, according to the defense. Reg claimed the work began days after the murder—that meant Tim was the killer.

The workmen submitted timesheets supporting Tim's story, but later admitted that they didn't keep accurate records much of the time. They were little help to either side—and they likely confused the jury. Another odd point—the workmen were repairing the washhouse that Tuesday, the day Tim claimed Beryl died. The workers would have likely noticed two bodies hidden inside the small building. Beryl and Geraldine had not been moved into the washhouse, most likely, until Thursday—none of Tim's confessions fit that timeframe, including the one accusing Reg. The stories were perplexing, and none made sense.

After Reg concluded his testimony, a dowdy housewife was next on the witness list. Ethel Christie raised her hand, swore to tell the truth. She described Tim's fury at his boss on the night he claimed he killed Geraldine. And she repeated her story about that thud in the night that awoke them in early November.

"Do you remember one night in November being wakened up by a bump?" asked the prosecutor. "It was the 8th November," replied Ethel.

"Did you hear anything unusual after the bump which woke you up?"

"Well, just afterwards, I heard a movement upstairs as if furniture was being moved above," answered Ethel.

The Christies' recollection of that bump seemed suspicious, because they only mentioned the story to the police *after* Tim was arrested for the murders. It might have been an innocent omission, but still detectives should have been more wary. The prosecution then paraded in a host of police officers and witnesses, who all confirmed that Timothy Evans failed to tell consistent stories. Tim's aunt from Wales, Violet Lynch, sat in the witness chair—she confirmed that her nephew was upset when his mother's scathing letter was read aloud, accusing him of being a habitual liar. Hours later, he confessed to killing his wife at the police station.

The Crown rested, assured that it had made the case for Geraldine Evans' murder: A poorly educated, high-strung husband had lashed out when his sloppy, wasteful young wife kept picking fights. His daughter was collateral damage. Now it was the defense's turn, and Malcolm Morris called just one witness: Timothy Evans.

"Did you strangle your baby daughter Geraldine?" he asked Tim.

"No, Sir."

"Were you in any way responsible for her death?" Morris asked.

"No, Sir."

"Did you strangle your wife?"

"No, Sir."

Morris asked Tim about his final confession, the one he had offered after Inspector Black told him that Beryl and Geraldine had been found inside the washhouse—the confession wherein he took full responsibility. "Why?" asked Morris.

"Well, when I found out about my daughter being dead I

was upset and I did not care what happened to me then," Tim explained. "I thought if I did not make a statement the police would take me downstairs and start knocking me about."

His accusation was believable—police frequently used physical intimidation to strong-arm suspects. But Tim had never complained about mistreatment, except to his mother—he claimed they kept him up until five o'clock in the morning, but he never mentioned violence. Tim testified that, despite the details in his final confession, he kept no rope in the flat and he didn't own the tie used to kill Geraldine. Morris repeated Tim's last confession, the one in which he admitted to killing his wife and daughter. He asked Tim, point by point, if it was all a lie—"yes" was the reply.

"As I said before, I was upset and I do not think I knew what I was saying," he testified. Finally, Prosecutor Humphreys cross-examined Tim.

"That is your defence, that you pleaded guilty, that is what it comes to, and confessed to the murder of your wife and child because you were upset on learning that your daughter was dead?" barked Humphreys.

"Yes, Sir, because I had nothing else to live for," replied Tim.

"And therefore you make an allegation in terms through your counsel against a perfectly innocent man that he caused the murder," replied Humphreys. Of course, the prosecutor had no idea that the "perfectly innocent man" was, himself, a serial killer.

The Crown then rattled off all of Tim's lies—the fibs he had offered his employers, the Christies, his family members, and the police. Tim replied that he had lied to protect Reg, a neighbor he respected and trusted—though there was no evidence that the two men were close.

Finally, both sides gave their closing statements, as the jury prepared to take the case into their room to deliberate. The defense team claimed Reg had manipulated a naïve Timothy Evans. The prosecutor contended that a husband strangled his wife in a fit of rage, and did away with his daughter because she was an inconvenience. Christmas Humphreys scoffed at Reg's motives for killing Beryl and Geraldine—*what did he gain from their murders?* There was no robbery, no argument, and no conclusive evidence of a sexual assault.

"Even if Christie had been responsible for the woman's death, why should he two days later go up to that flat and strangle, unknown to this man, an innocent little baby lying there aged fourteen months?" That was a valid point—there seemed to be no obvious motive for Reg to be the killer—*at least, not yet.*

But defense attorney Malcolm Morris warned the jury that its only charge was to decide if Tim had killed his daughter, not his wife. To emphasize that, he offered a theory—he suggested that Beryl killed Geraldine herself, and then Tim killed Beryl. Therefore, Tim was innocent of killing his daughter and should be found "not guilty." In hindsight, that argument may have confused jurors more than anything.

On the third and final day of the trial, Judge Lewis issued the jury instructions, which included his summary of the evidence—a very biased summary. He called Tim a habitual liar. He questioned what motives Reg might have to kill Beryl and Geraldine, particularly because he was in such poor health. Judge Lewis said it would be a terrible thing if a person "should have it said of him because seventeen years ago he was in trouble with the police that he cannot be believed on his oath and is a practiced abortioner and a murderer."

The jury took just forty minutes to reach a decision—guilty. There was sobbing at the rear of the courtroom—Reg wiped his spectacles. It was so inappropriate, such a spectacle. Outside of the courtroom, Tim's mother spotted Reg and Ethel and shouted: "Murderer, murderer!"

"Don't you dare call my husband a murderer," snapped Ethel. "He is a good man." Reg wrapped an arm around his wife, then leaned over and kissed her.

"I didn't do it. Christie done it," was the last thing Tim said to his family. Timothy Evans was hanged on March 9, 1950—still proclaiming his innocence and Reg's guilt. Now, almost two years later, the case against Timothy Evans was buried in law files and he was interred, in disgrace, in a prison graveyard. On December 9, 1952, the horrible fog was finally retreating from London; Reg was able to breathe deeply. He was anxious to leave his flat, to have privacy, finally. His pathetic life was becoming too much to endure—something had to change.

That day, his wife would locate stationery to write her sister about the disgusting smoke, while Reg plotted something devious in the next room. Ethel Christie had so stalwartly defended her husband in court against their upstairs neighbor Timothy Evans. Now she had just days left to live.

❧

Meanwhile, at the end of his five-day police shift in December 1952, Stanley Critchon finally returned home to his wife, Maura, exhausted. She interrogated him about the fog—about the dead bodies, the thieves, and the "fog bandits" who robbed helpless Londoners. He didn't want to discuss it; he asked about her cough. "Better," she assured him.

By this time, Stanley was familiar with the stories from Metropolitan Police officers. The press claimed Sunday was "the worst crime night since the war" and a "crime orgy." The reality was a bit less dramatic. The fog had inhibited criminals as much as it hindered the police response. There were isolated incidents, but the newspapers' zealous descriptions of a "crime wave" were exaggerated.

"Thugs added terror to the fogs and other hazards when they bashed and robbed under its cover," wrote one reporter. "Crime soared as ghostly figures loomed out of the murk to cosh women and snatch their handbags. Bricks crashed into jewelers' windows and trays of gems vanished in the dark."

All true accounts, but they represented the minority of crimes during the fog. Still, they were frightening, if only because they were carried out in a dismal, creepy setting—like London during the Middle Ages. The newspapers ticked off the list of crimes: In the center of the city, someone knocked down and robbed a theater manager, while in the West End a policeman wrestled with a suspect over a loaded revolver. Bandits attacked a shopkeeper in southwest London and stole four hundred pounds. Firemen swung hurricane lanterns as they led their engines home, in hopes they would receive no calls. Two trains crashed into each other.

The stories were exhausting for Maura to hear—but as Stanley looked at her, he was more concerned about his wife's long-term health. Her asthma seemed to have subsided, but how would the smoke affect her later? Luckily, he had convinced her to avoid venturing out in the stuff, but her recovery was slow. He gazed at her in the light of their bedroom.

"Maybe I can get us a transfer out of London," Stanley suggested.

"Good," Maura replied. She looked over at him. "Wonder when this stuff will come back?"

CHAPTER SEVEN

Smothered

London had been reeking in a green-yellow fog.
—*Winston Churchill,*
A Traveller in War-Time, *1918*

The weather was so different today, Wednesday, December 10—the day after the fog blew away. It was warmer now, close to fifty degrees, and stormy. There were strong winds from the south that sucked up the rain and spewed it across the city— showers that pelted from above and every side. If the gusts had arrived just a few days earlier, they might have quickly whisked away the smog, so it would have had no chance to strengthen, to spread, and to kill. Wednesday's blustery weather was a bit jarring, as if each gust carried some mischief, looking for a place to settle.

Ethel Christie sat down to pen that letter to her sister, Lily, on the tablet she frequently used to write to family. She carefully wrote her return address, *10 Rillington Place*, on the top right corner of the first page. Her next pen strokes were important, so crucial that they would be mentioned in court one day. She pressed the black ink gently into the grey stationery to mark the date, "December 10th 1952." Then she began to write.

"I have not heard from you since I wrote to you in November," Ethel said. She fretted over an aunt who had not returned her notes; she asked Lily to visit the elderly woman, to make sure she was safe. Then Ethel began complaining about their upstairs neighbors—and the fog.

"I wish we could get out of here," Ethel griped. "It is awful with these 'people' here. How are you getting on now the winter has arrived? It was really dreadful here at the week-end with the fog & made us feel quite ill, but it is better to-day." Ethel never mentioned Reg's resignation, and she didn't disclose that they would be forced to ask for money from the Unemployment Exchange—two important events she would have certainly mentioned to her sister. Ethel was clearly oblivious. But Reg's colleagues at the British Roads Services knew he was now unemployed.

Ethel finished the letter, but she decided against posting it just yet. She frequently abandoned notes on the pad for days before finishing them. And there was a stack of beautiful Christmas cards that still needed attention. Ethel left the tablet on the table, went about her day; she was so naïve—and vulnerable. She trusted Reg implicitly, despite his alarming past.

John Reginald Halliday Christie was born on April 8, 1899, near Halifax, in northern England, in what he described as "a large dark house, which still stands on a bleak Yorkshire moor." He was raised with five sisters and a brother in a strict, working-class Victorian household. He considered his mother, Mary Hannah Christie, to be extraordinarily kind and loving. His father, Ernest Christie, was a strict taskmaster who drank little, but leveled a frightening punishment if he felt it was warranted. His son recalled his horrible temper—and how his mother had tried, in vain, to protect the children.

"I always lived in dread of my father," Reg recalled. "He was stern, strict and proud."

Ernest Christie insisted the children march with him to their Anglican church every Sunday, embarking on a five-mile trek wearing their formal dress.

"We had to hold our shoulders back, swing our arms, and walk like guardsmen," said Reg.

Ernest worked in a factory where he was well respected, especially for his aptitude in medicine and first aid, a trait that Reg aspired to later in life. But as much as he respected his father, he continued to fear him. Reg remembered a day when Ernest suspected him of stealing tomatoes—which the boy hated—and hit him. When his mother finally convinced Ernest that their son was innocent, Reg received a shilling as an apology.

As he aged, Reg settled into normal schoolboy activities. He became a Boy Scout and later an assistant Scoutmaster. He sang with his church choir and excelled at sports and academics, particularly mathematics. He tinkered with mechanical things, like clocks. He loved photography. But Reg was always a nervous, awkward person, even as a child. He was scared of the dark, and as an adult he was still easily spooked at night. He awoke frequently from bad dreams. And, most disturbingly, Reg had always been absolutely entranced by dead bodies.

"When I was eight I saw my first corpse. It was my grandfather," said Reg. "You would expect that for a little boy this would be a terrible experience. For me it was not. I was not frightened, worried, or perturbed in the slightest. I looked at the corpse with a strange pleasant thrill."

That image of his grandfather, lying stiff on a table in the family's parlor, was beguiling for the young boy—and foretelling. As he grew older, his social awkwardness hindered his relationships, especially with women, until he met Ethel Simpson.

It was a short courtship of just a few months, but Reg and Ethel wed on May 10, 1920, at a government office in Halifax. She was twenty-two and quite attractive; he was twenty-one and still painfully shy. Their union might have given him a sense of stability, but it also prompted some devious behavior that would follow him for decades. The Halifax Post Office hired him the year after the Christies married, but his supervisors quickly fired him after he was caught stealing postal orders—Reg spent three months in prison. Ethel remained with him, but soon there were more troubling accusations.

In 1923, after just three years of marriage, Reg left Ethel in Halifax and moved to London. He claimed she was drinking heavily and having an affair with her boss at an engineering company. The following year, Reg was convicted again of stealing: this time a bike, money, and cigarettes. He spent eight months doing hard labor. In 1929, Reg was staying with a married mother named Maud Cole along with her young son in a Battersea flat. He was living off her income and, when she pressured him to find employment, Reg became incensed, hit her on the back of the head with a wooden cricket bat, then pushed her out the door.

"It half stunned me. It was all the world like an explosion," said Cole. "Everything seemed to go black for a second."

She was left with a five-inch gash in her head. Reg claimed it had been an accident—he was just taking a practice swing. But the judge believed it to be attempted murder, and Reg spent five months in prison with hard labor. He couldn't seem to stay straight. In 1933, Reg was convicted of stealing a car and served three months in Wandsworth Prison. After more than ten years apart, Ethel came to see him. As he sat across from her, dressed in prison clothes, her intentions seemed more pragmatic than romantic.

"At the visit she said it was a question of divorce or coming together again. I asked her which she preferred and she said coming together again," Reg recalled. "After a couple of weeks we felt as if we had never been parted."

This time, Ethel seemed to be a steadying influence on Reg's troubled life. He worked as an electrician, a lorry driver, a dispatch clerk—his longest employment was as a War Reserve policeman during World War II, which was his post for four years, until 1943.

They had no children, though both claimed they hoped for some. Reg even mentioned that Ethel had volunteered to adopt little Geraldine Evans if Beryl ever walked away from the family. But they never became parents, except for two loyal pets. Since he was a child, Reg had adored animals, so the couple owned a young black cat that stalked birds in the back garden. And there was also that dog, the old brown Irish terrier that was blind in one eye—the one who liked to dig in his garden.

"Humans never seemed to understand me quite, but animals always did," Reg said. His dog was fifteen years old and Reg cared for her as a puppy. So this was the Christie family: Reg, Ethel, a cat and a dog—together for years.

"My wife and I were really happy together. Just the two of us, and the animals," said Reg. "We were contented."

Neighbors found Reg to be an exceptionally quirky man, but they had no idea of the contradictory nature of his public and private lives. They knew he was consumed with his camera and constantly flanked by his dog. He was an amateur photographer, who occasionally snapped photos of street parties, Ethel, and, apparently, prostitutes. He was also a teetotaler, who bristled at the implication that he ever visited public houses for a pint—he preferred tea. Yet witnesses said he chatted up women at pubs, with a beer in hand. He supported the Queens Park Rangers, the same football team that Timothy Evans gushed over during his long train ride with the police from Wales to London.

The Christies were not especially social; Reg didn't seem to have many friends. Ethel was close with her family, but Reg let fifteen years pass without speaking to any of his siblings. The couple had only each other. One neighbor recalled that Reg was "a very polite man who never talks to anyone very much." He generally kept to himself, so people labeled him as either affable or aloof.

"I am a quiet, humble man, who hates rows or trouble," explained Reg. "I love animals. I am fond of children. I come from a solid, respectable, old-fashioned type of Yorkshire family."

And so that Wednesday, Ethel's afternoon continued on, and her letter lay there, unassuming and undisturbed, for days — until Reg noticed it, picked it up, and made a small change.

∽

Two days after the end of the fog, the Ministry of Health needed information and data — very quickly. The press may not yet have realized that the city was in the middle of a health crisis, but medical experts knew. They needed to get ahead of the story before the media had an opportunity to alarm the public. So health officials began making phone calls to medical officers, coroners, and pathologists in more than two dozen boroughs across Greater London. *How many patients died over those five days?* they asked. *What were the causes? Were they fog-related?* The responses arrived within days — some just included the requested data; others also gave anecdotal evidence and personal stories. Lewisham in southeast London, where Rosemary Sargent went to school, had one of the highest mortality rates during the fog.

"My pathologists report that the great majority of these cases turned out to be deaths of elderly people from cardiac failure supervening on well-established emphysema and bronchitis," wrote Dr. William Heddy, the area's coroner. "The rush of cases occurred very suddenly."

A physician in Kensington explained that he was called to the homes of twelve very healthy, active patients. They all had bronchial spasms, along with rhonchi—low-pitched, rattling lung sounds that often resembled snoring. There was also wheezing. The medical officer of health for Walthamstow explained that during the fog, there were about seven hundred sickness claims, three times the normal number. The medical officer of health for Stepney disclosed that his borough's deaths had quadrupled.

"The total deaths of all ages for Stepney during recent normal weeks was 25," wrote Dr. F. R. O'Shiel. "The total deaths of all ages in fog-week was 83."

The medical officer of health for Wandsworth pulled his death records for those patients who had had a postmortem exam. Two experienced investigators found seventeen possible fog-related deaths, but it was difficult to declare a definitive cause. The medical officer suggested that the investigators eliminate other factors.

"They were instructed to look into the question of any possible infectious conditions in the household including upper respiratory infections, chronic ears, etc.," wrote Dr. Tudor Lewis. "As you will see the findings seem to be consistently negative." The fog was clearly to blame.

Within a week, the Ministry of Health wrote Dr. Lewis back, thanking him for his data on the "17 fog-deaths." That's how health officials began describing the victims.

"*Fog Deaths.* I have no doubt about it whatsoever," wrote Dr. Louis Beccle, the coroner from Romford in South Woodford,

Essex, northeast of London. "There was a sudden spectacular increase in cardio-respiratory deaths which although normally high at this time of the year was far and away above anything I had previously experienced and must be attributed to the fog with the assistance of the Coal Board's well-advertised 'Nutty Slack.'"

Dr. Beccle was furious; the fog had sickened him, too. He couldn't move for four days without pain from bronchial spasms and he suspected that the government's aggressive campaign of selling ration-free, dirty brown coal had made the fog even deadlier.

"This fog was a killer, and wiped out a great number of people who would have otherwise survived with their chronic bronchitis and emphysema, damaged hearts, etc.," wrote Dr. Beccle. "What are our wonderful scientists doing? In an age of jet propulsion, atomic energy…these wretched people can't solve the problem of a lousy fog!"

Each medical officer of health seemed to struggle with how to determine what a "fog death" would be—what if the patient was already sick? Most were already suffering from an illness, a respiratory problem, or a heart issue. What if no others in the household appeared sickened by the smoke? The investigation became so murky. Some medical officers also included lists of specific victims. In Battersea, sixty-nine-year-old Andrew Kingwell died of chronic bronchitis and emphysema. He had trouble breathing that Sunday night, and then died in his sleep the next day.

Eighty-year-old Edward Jones battled a cold for several days. On the first day of the fog, he ventured outside and, when he returned home, he refused to rest in bed, despite a horrible cough. He died in his sleep three days later. Sixty-seven-year-old John Spencer developed dyspnea—labored breathing—during the first day of the fog. He was dead in his chair within hours. A short time later, Spencer's wife was ill with pneumonia, a sickness doctors blamed on the shock of losing her husband. The notes about the victims seemed endless—the papers were typewritten, handwritten, and all very detailed. Each person had a medical history and a story about their death. But coroners still wouldn't connect the deaths with air pollution.

Their naïveté may seem stunning, but even doctors at the time didn't fully understand the risks of poor air quality. In the 1950s, public health statistics were only just starting to be retrievable for use in research. There were few computers in Britain, so data couldn't be calculated quickly. Finding a causative relationship between air pollution and elevated deaths would have been a daunting task. During the fog, Donald Acheson, like many other physicians, treated patients with a myriad of symptoms. Mucus hypersecretion was present in many victims, a telltale sign of asthma or cystic fibrosis. He assessed patients with heart problems. When patients were found dead or died in medical care, chief residents listed coronary heart disease, chronic bronchitis, or emphysema as cause of death on their death certificates.

"Acute respiratory failure due to smog would be the closest to the truth one would be likely to get," said Donald.

But that phrase wasn't listed on any death certificates. Doctors would later discover that bronchitis was the most common cause of death during the fog—the number of its victims increased tenfold from the week before the fog until after it finally blew away. British doctors knew this fog had done something to their patients, but they couldn't yet make the connection. And now America was concerned. A United States government department, the Federal Security Agency—later renamed the Health Department—was conducting an international air pollution study. The chairman sent a confidential letter to Dr. Albert

Parker, the director of Fuel Research at Britain's Department of Scientific and Industrial Research in London. In it, he referenced a newspaper report claiming the recent smog in England killed hundreds of people.

"It would be appreciated if you could supply us with information regarding these deaths and state whether they were attributed to the smog," wrote George Clayton, a senior sanitation engineer.

The Americans asked about the meteorological conditions, how long the event lasted, the causes of the deaths—the researchers also requested a map showing the areas where the dead people lived in relation to industry and other sources of pollution. The U.S. government was conducting an in-depth study, along with the Canadian government. Researchers in both countries wanted details about the contaminants in the atmosphere.

"Because of the recent air pollution disasters, we are attempting to obtain as much information as possible on the subject in endeavoring to prevent a recurrence of such disasters," wrote Mr. Clayton. The United States was working toward stopping air pollution—and it needed Britain's help.

The "recent air pollution disasters" included two deadly smog events, one in Europe and the other in America. The first was in December 1930, in the Meuse Valley in Belgium, one of the most industrialized areas of Europe at the time. For four days, an anticyclone—like the one in London—had trapped fog that combined with pollution from steel mills, coke ovens, foundries, and smelters. It created a potion as deadly as gas used during warfare, killing more than sixty people and sickening thousands more. The day after the fog lifted, the Belgian government launched a judicial inquiry by appointing a committee, which included experts in meteorology, toxicology, industrial chemistry, and pathology. The investigation led to the first scientific proof that air pollution caused death and disease.

After the findings were released in 1931, an editorial in the *British Medical Journal* warned that "the possibility of a similar incident happening in this country is a matter of great public health interest." The British government seemed to disregard the warning—the Meuse Valley smog happened more than twenty years before the 1952 London fog.

The second smog incident happened during the week of October 26, 1948, when a heavy fog settled over Donora, Pennsylvania. The cool night air combined with the warm waters of the nearby Monongahela River. The fog mixed with the hydrogen fluoride emissions from a nearby zinc plant, along with sulphur dioxide from steel smelting plants owned by the U.S. Steel Corporation. Those toxins joined the smoke and fumes from thousands of domestic coal-burning furnaces. Donora's smog lasted five days. Residents panicked when the air began to make them ill—and town officials acted quickly. Oxygen tents cared for victims in the community center, which was transformed into a hospital. A makeshift morgue was set up in the basement. Many people evacuated. Firefighters hauled heavy oxygen tanks to victims who couldn't leave their homes. Donora only had eight doctors, and they all raced from house to house, treating the sickest patients. The town hall became an emergency center. Drivers left their cars behind. Those who tried to navigate the streets drove with their wheels scraping along the curbs. It was all an eerie foreshadowing of scenes in 1952 London.

The thick, yellowish fog killed twenty people in Donora and sickened thousands more. Nearly eight hundred animals died. Autopsies later revealed that the victims' fluorine levels were within lethal range. The smog would have likely killed thousands more, if only the anticyclone had stayed longer.

The Donora disaster was credited with triggering the clean-air movement in the United States—and introduced Americans to a relatively new word: smog. Victims hammered U.S. Steel with lawsuits and the American government immediately launched an inquiry—investigators created a report, but researchers in the United States were still gathering information. The fog in London alarmed them.

But in Britain, the Ministry of Health was in the middle of its own crisis. As officials recorded organized data from its medical officers, the ministry also began soliciting information from the public. Ambulances were responding to an extra one hundred calls a day, weeks after the fog lifted. Patients filled the hospitals—still choking, coughing, and wheezing. *How did they die?* The Ministry of Health circulated a questionnaire called "Fatalities Possibly Associated With Fog." They asked the families of victims of "fog death" to fill them out.

"Did the illness worsen during or after the fog? If so what dates?"

"How long bedridden before death?"

"Do the relatives consider the fog contributed in any way to death? If so, how?"

The Ministry of Health began collecting their answers: names, ages, prior health history, and symptoms. There was a troubling trend. Victims were suffering from vomiting, chronic chest trouble, headaches, delirium, exhaustion, chronic coughing, and even pain after drinking water—such cruel ordeals, right before death. The Ministry of Health also compiled data about the levels and types of pollutants from the director of Fuel Research. He listed eleven districts that reported back information on the levels of suspended matter in the air.

"The maximum fog density is not known for six of the above

stations because the results were so high as to put the instruments off-scale," noted the internal memo. "The increase over normal was 10 times or more." The levels were too high to calculate in some places.

Health officials knew that immeasurable air pollution meant death for many Londoners. Just days earlier, more than eight million people were crammed into houses filled with smoke and fumes. There was no evidence of an influenza epidemic, so the excess deaths had to be blamed on the fog. And now the press was at last pursuing a promising story—mass deaths perpetrated by a mysterious fog.

The "Mystery Fog Illness" newspaper stories were becoming problematic for the Ministry of Health. The rumor was now spreading to all media—*Why did the fog make so many Londoners ill?* Health officials had still refused to release any specific figures, and the Ministry of Health officials were forced to reply.

"It was unusually dense and long-lasting and therefore unusually heavy in soot content, which is harmful to the respiratory tract," said the Ministry of Health spokesperson in the *New York Times*. "There was accompanying very cold weather which increased the susceptibility of aged bronchitis sufferers and also increased coal burning in London. It was nasty but not mysterious."

A few days after that article was published, Labour MP Tom Driberg asked Minister of Health Iain Macleod to provide firm statistics about how many people had died in Greater London as a result of the fog. Macleod said that not all of the figures were available, but he could say that more than two thousand people had died during the week ending Saturday, December 6—five hundred and nineteen more than during the same week last year. In two days, the fog had killed more than five hundred people, an astounding number. And the *Times* included that data, though it appeared in a tiny summary on page nine. Newspapers and Labour MPs slowly pressed Winston Churchill's cabinet for more details, particularly the minister of health. The queries were all focused on Iain Macleod because the number of deaths was so startling; the press was concerned with the effect of the fog, not the cause—for now. So Macleod would continue to squirm under questioning, on his own.

Then the government's own party began demanding answers. Tory MP Richard Fort, a former industrial chemist, and MP Herbert Williams, a Conservative with a science and engineering degree, asked the Ministry of Health to provide updated death numbers. Iain Macleod had to respond.

"The number of deaths from all causes in Greater London during the week ending 13th December was 4,703 compared with 1,852 in the corresponding week of 1951," he told Parliament. "The cold weather had already caused some increase, but a large part of these increases must be attributed to the fog."

There were 2,851 additional deaths. MPs were shocked—but there were even more disclosures. The Ministry of Health said that an informal inquiry of coroners' pathologists indicated that the increases in bodies varied from two to five times the expected number of autopsies. Macleod said there would be an investigation, which would include a study of lung chemistry in certain cases, an examination of pathology reports, and a chemical study of the fog and smoke.

"So far, informal reports from a variety of sources suggest that the duration and density of the smoke-laden fog could largely explain the dramatic increase in deaths," he said.

The next day a *Daily Mail* headline proclaimed, "Fog Week

Deaths Rose by 2,800." These numbers were startling, but they still caused no panic. The *Manchester Guardian* relegated that report to a brief of less than a hundred words in the middle of page eleven. The world's biggest lead story was buried. A city hardened by war still believed the fog was simply a prolonged peasouper, just another byproduct of living in London.

✑

A consensus was growing in Parliament: The Conservative government admitted that the fog had killed thousands of people. But despite a growing mound of evidence, lawmakers refused to blame pollution—and coal—for turning the clouds toxic.

MP Norman Dodds listened patiently. He watched the debates for weeks. His constituents complained to him, about the smoke and their illnesses. He was furious—it had burned his eyes, too, as he walked to Parliament on Monday and Tuesday. It seeped into his skin, made his path uncertain. He knew just how terribly the smog had affected the people he represented, and he knew the cause—coal. But no one in Parliament seemed to care. Norman needed a bit more evidence to prove the government was negligent—duplicitous, even. But more than evidence, he needed allies.

Those allies came from the National Smoke Abatement Society, the influential pressure group that had been fighting the government for decades. Founded in 1929, the NSAS was an independent coalition of politicians, medical officers, news reporters, sanitary inspectors, and other health professionals—even some powerhouse attorneys. The Society was funded through membership dues, donations, and, for many years, by the manufactured gas industry, which had a large stake in the decline of coal. The NSAS used its resources to order research, request documents, consult experts, and generally harass the government over air pollution. Its well-regarded quarterly subscription journal, *Smokeless Air*, was an annoyance to many Conservative ministers—it was frequently circulated among MPs, and then referenced during parliamentary debates. The National Society for Smoke Abatement was a reliable friend for clean-air advocates like Norman—and a vigorous opponent of Churchill's government.

NSAS committee members demanded to see London's death records for the past century. As they examined them, they were stunned. The numbers confirmed what everyone had suspected: there had been a huge spike in deaths following the December 1952 smog. In fact, since they had started keeping records, only four other times had the numbers of deaths been higher than in the week following the recent fog. The jump in deaths was alarming. The committee went to the press and demanded the government launch an official investigation "in view of the abnormal concentration of pollution in the atmosphere during the fog period and its exceptionally serious consequences."

The group insisted on a government inquiry, just like the one conducted in Donora, Pennsylvania, four years earlier. The NSAS would be Norman Dodds' ally. And he knew their main adversary would be Harold Macmillan, the minister of housing and local government. Air pollution fell under his purview, after all. Norman submitted a question to be read in front of everyone in the House of Commons.

"In view of the discomfort experienced by many millions of people as well as animals in the recent foggy conditions…there is enough evidence to justify more energetic research into the harmful constituents of the air in towns." Norman asked what action the government would propose to reduce smog.

Norman looked across the aisle at the Tories. Harold Macmillan was missing. In his place sat his junior minister, a bright but brash forty-five-year-old named Ernest Marples. When Winston Churchill had offered Macmillan the Ministry of Housing position a year earlier, Macmillan had been crestfallen—he had hoped to be appointed minister of defense. Housing just wasn't in his scope.

"On the whole it seems impossible to refuse," Macmillan wrote in his diary in October, 1951, "but, oh dear, it is not my cup of tea...I really haven't a clue how to set about the job."

Luckily, Macmillan knew how to select a strong team, like self-made businessman Marples, who often stepped in for him during sessions in Parliament. They were both incredibly wealthy men—yet their styles were different, so complementary. Macmillan was measured, efficient, but lacked spark. Marples exuded confidence and radiated passion—but needed to be toned down at times. Today, however, the junior minister was appropriately docile as he dismissed Norman Dodds and his pointed question.

"Arrangements have already been made to encourage the use of improved types of domestic appliances designed to burn smokeless fuel," replied Marples glibly.

But the appliances weren't the problem—there wasn't enough smokeless fuel to burn in them, something the government refused to admit. The country was yoked to coal—and not just any coal. The British were dependent on the cheap, polluting "nutty slack" coal dust. In fact, in December 1952 the government was *still* enthusiastically promoting it, despite the horrible smog.

Norman was livid—the deadly fog would be his next crusade. And he would need America's help.

But soon there would be another story that would draw the

media's attention away from the drab details of a London fog. It was much more salacious—a disgusting, revolting criminal who would soon sell millions of newspapers.

⌘

The weather was wintry on Sunday, December 14—a thin layer of sleet covered the ground. The Christies lay in bed early that morning, around eight fifteen. The house at 10 Rillington Place was quiet, almost peaceful, for once. The fog had disappeared just four days earlier. The carpet of grey smoke no longer cloaked those secrets in the garden.

Reg glanced at his wife—she was so tranquil, lying still. Her face was pale. A stocking was tied around her neck, leaving deep indentations beneath it. There was a makeshift diaper beneath her, between her legs. He was alone, finally—the house was his. He could leave and return whenever it suited him, with no explanation—bring anyone around he liked. But now his mind was so muddled. He needed to hide her, but he couldn't concentrate. It seemed too hard to figure out. He left her in bed for two or three days, but he couldn't bear sleeping next to her. He laid down some blankets and slept on the floor. His mind wasn't working right—he didn't know where to keep her.

"Then I remembered some loose floorboards in the front room," he recalled. "I had to move a table and some chairs to roll the lino back about halfway."

There were deep depressions under the floor of the Christies' parlor—just enough space to store a body. He returned to Ethel, now rigid in their bed, and tried to move her. This would be a cumbersome chore. At just under five foot four, Ethel wasn't tall, but she was heavy. And Reg's back still wasn't right. He tried to carry her, but she was too bulky. He placed a pillowcase over her head and slipped her gold wedding ring off her finger. Then Reg picked up a pair of scissors and looked down at her. He snipped off some of her pubic hairs, caught them in his fingers, and put them aside—a final keepsake from his wife. He wrapped a flowered cotton dress around her and a silk dress over that, then slowly rolled her in a flannelette blanket.

"I had to sort of half carry her and half drag her and put her in that depression and cover her up with earth," recalled Reg. "I thought that was the best way to lay her to rest."

He replaced the flooring, moved back the table and chair. And now he plotted.

The next day Reg picked up the writing tablet, the one Ethel had used to write a letter to her sister, Lily, five days earlier. Her note, perfectly composed, was still there. He glanced at the date: "December 10th 1952." He took a pen, black with a thin point, and carefully placed two small marks at the top of the zero—one horizontal and one vertical. "December 15th 1952," it now read.

The woman lying beneath her own parlor floor was alive, as far as her sister would believe. But he thought his sister-in-law might need more convincing. Reg included a small note, written in the upper left-hand corner of his wife's letter.

"Ethel had no envelopes, so I posted this for her from work. Reg." He mailed it that day. Ethel's family might leave him alone now, at least for a while. But his wife honored little customs, especially around the holidays. He needed to give those some attention.

"Dear Lil, Ethel has got me to write her cards for her as her rheumatism in her fingers is not so good just now," Reg wrote. "Doctor says it's the weather and she will be O.K. in 2 or 3 days. I am rubbing them for her. As soon as Ethel can write (perhaps by <u>Saturday</u>) she is going to send a letter. Hope you like the present she selected for you, Reg." A disgusting lie.

He gathered together the parcel, placing the stationery inside. At the top of his letter, he included a note meant to be comforting, even underlining the first line.

"<u>Don't Worry She is OK.</u> I shall cook X-mas dinner. Reg."

He filled out a Christmas card, addressed to Ethel's brother Harry Waddington in Sheffield. It was a scene from a Victorian winter: A woman in a flowing dress and bonnet holds the arm of a man in dress tails and a top hat as they walk along the road of a picturesque town.

"Christmas Greetings—with all kind wishes for the best of health and good luck," it said. At the bottom of the card, he wrote: "From Ethel and Reg."

There were so many things to do. Ethel's murder was a new impulse for Reg, with a different motive from the killings before. He had murdered the other women because he wanted them to comply—he had charmed them, raped them, and then killed them. But his wife's murder was so different—he didn't poison her with coal gas. He didn't rape her. But he did strangle her. And Ethel wasn't unconscious. The abrasions on her neck showed she was strangled from the front. Ethel Christie, eyes wide open, watched her husband of more than thirty years as he twisted and squeezed the stocking tighter—then he killed her.

"After she had gone," Reg would later say, "the way was clear for me to fulfill my destiny."

CHAPTER EIGHT

Hearth and Home

Once upon a time—of all the good days in the year, on Christmas Eve—old Scrooge sat busy in his counting-house. It was cold, bleak, biting weather: foggy withal...[t]he fog came pouring in at every chink and keyhole, and was so dense without, that although the court was of the narrowest, the houses opposite were mere phantoms.

—*Charles Dickens,* A Christmas Carol, *1843*

With the flick of a switch, they brightened—hundreds of little lights in the darkness of an early Saturday evening, December 20. The green leaves gleamed, and white luminescence chased off the silhouettes of its dark branches. The Christmas tree in Trafalgar Square was so delightfully radiant, spilling light onto thousands of revelers below. The spruce's reveal marked the start of the city's most joyous time of year. Children chased pigeons around the Charing Cross Underground station as Londoners filed out. Carolers sang "Silent Night" and "O Come, All Ye Faithful," as they strolled near the lion statues. The square's two fountains glowed with lights.

From atop his column, Admiral Horatio Nelson studied the tree from above. For the past five years, Norway had donated a sixty-foot spruce for the grand ceremony, a token of gratitude for British support during World War II. The tree was a symbol of perseverance and unity, of kindness toward each other even during difficult times. And the beginning of the month had been so taxing for Londoners. Christmas was a reflective time filled with faith, family, and peace—and traditions.

Earlier in the week, Londoners rushed from their offices to make last-minute purchases on Oxford Street. In Leadenhall Market, the Christmas turkeys hung in rows. White heather and lilac lay on display, waiting for wives on the hunt for table decorations. Bins were stuffed full of nuts and oranges. Vendors peddled large and sturdy Christmas spruces in Covent Garden for twenty-eight shillings. Visitors toured Regent Street in the West End for a glimpse of its famous Christmas lights. Commuters packed the new diesel buses, determined to make it home before sundown. And there seemed to be much to celebrate— the country had a new queen. Queen Elizabeth II's first Christmas speech was warm and inspiring.

"We must keep alive that courageous spirit of adventure that is the finest quality of youth," said Queen Elizabeth, "and by youth I do not just mean those who are young in years; I mean too all those who are young in heart, no matter how old they may be."

The newspapers were filled with copy about toy sales, Boxing Day plans, and weather predictions. The stories about the deadly fog were now gone, abandoned for the holidays. And there was a different type of ceremony in London this year, one common in every district. Families prayed in churches, cooked wonderful meals—and dressed in black. There were funerals across the city during the holidays—thousands of them. The families of the fog's victims spent their holidays planning memorial services, selecting caskets, and buying burial plots. Perhaps they would move forward with holiday celebrations this year; they might put up a tree in the parlor, hang stockings on the mantel, and buy a goose, but their dinners would certainly be more solemn. For the people who lost someone to the fog, the holiday season brought little joy—their Christmases would never feel the same.

◦⁄∘

More than two weeks after he died, Albert Sargent finally found a resting place. The family's parlor, his crypt for all that time, was now empty. It seemed so much larger without his casket. The room was cleared—the door left unlocked. It was still an unsettling place for Rosemary, as it would be for as long as she lived there.

Albert's funeral was scheduled for three days before Christmas, a time when the children and their father would typically make holiday paper chains for the parlor's hearth. The Christmas tree would glisten with colorful lights and cheap tinsel—boxes wrapped with paper adorned with snowmen and reindeer would lie underneath. Not this Christmas. Her mother contacted relatives about the memorial service. As Rosemary watched her mother scribble down information, she thought about what it might be like to see her father's burial, to watch him being lowered into the ground.

She approached her mother carefully—Edna Sargent seemed so fragile now. Any innocent query might send her into fits of anger. They still refused to speak about his death; none of the children talked about it. It just wasn't proper. And little five-year-old Sue still didn't realize her father was dead. "He's in hospital still," her mother insisted. Before she left for school the morning of the services, Rosemary screwed up the courage to talk with Edna.

"Can I go to the funeral?" she asked.

"No, children aren't allowed at funerals, Rosemary," was her mother's terse response.

She and her siblings would have to stay home. In the Edwardian and Victorian years, children weren't permitted at such sad events; they stayed away and grieved on their own, mostly in silence. Rosemary was indignant. Why couldn't she say good-bye to her own father? She had tried to save his life—she braved that horrid fog for two hours, tripping her way to the doctor's office for that pill, arguing with her neurotic mother along the way, only to arrive home to her father's body. She was entitled to be there, but her mother was incredibly stubborn.

That afternoon, Albert Sargent was placed in a grave in a cemetery in Catford—he and Edna were to be buried next to each other. But for now, his wife had to raise their four children without him. When Rosemary returned home from school that day, she weaved through the crowd of relatives crammed into her house as they returned from the funeral. She complained like mad to her Uncle Arthur, her father's youngest brother. She was bitter and furious over Edna's callousness. He gazed at her— tried, in vain, to temper her anger.

"It's better that you don't go," he said, sweetly.

"Why?" Rosemary wanted to know.

He gave her an earnest look—he wanted his niece to understand why her mother had made a sensible decision. Arthur and Albert Sargent had lost their own mother decades earlier; Uncle Arthur was around Rosemary's age, almost fourteen, while Albert was eighteen. The boys' father had allowed them to go to their mother's funeral services.

"You know, I can still remember the color of the carpet on the carriage that we went to the funeral in," he said gently. "Everything about it will be too vivid."

Rosemary looked back at him—her uncle had lost his mother

almost forty years earlier and he still remembered those tiny details, like the pattern and shade of blue carpet. He recalled every traumatic moment of that day. Rosemary stopped her grumbling.

She watched her mother move about the house, preparing for the holidays. She hung the Christmas stockings on the mantel of the fireplace near the kitchen.

Slowly, Edna began assuming Albert's chores—she picked the vegetables in the back garden. She glanced over the pile of bills. She carried the nutty slack inside with a scooper for their fires. It seemed like such a heavy burden for a mother, now alone and obviously worried.

Edna *was* worried. She was afraid she would need to sell the house—her family had little savings. Edna had no job, no education. She was like the millions of widows left alone after World War II. While she fretted about finances, she struggled with physical problems, too. Edna's gums were aching—her teeth throbbed. When she visited the dentist, he told her that the shock of her husband's death had killed the roots. They would all need to be pulled and replaced with false teeth. Her dentist offered a sobering observation: if the shock had been more severe, it could have killed her.

On Christmas Day, many children in London awoke to the smell of roasted turkey or cockerel, boiled vegetables, and, if their mothers had gathered enough rationed ingredients for baking, a medley of sweet pies. But Rosemary's house was hushed that morning. It made her so uneasy—*what would Christmas be like without him?* Clearly, Edna would forgo her traditional holiday dinner, but *where would they go?* She hoped to see her mother's family—three uncles and an aunt who doted on the children and sympathized with their sister. But that's not where they spent Christmas.

Her mother was so beloved at their Methodist church; she had such a close-knit family—and now they were visitors eating Christmas dinner in a stranger's home. But her mother had moved about in a haze for weeks. She was immersed in depression; she wasn't thinking rationally. And she was furious, especially toward God for taking her husband. Edna, Rosemary, David, Malcolm, and Sue walked to the nearby home of one of the women in the church, someone the children barely knew. Rosemary was so confused—*why were they there?* A peculiar woman in an unfamiliar house hosted her family during their most sacred holiday.

Edna was a devout Methodist, and now she disavowed church. She forced her children to go, alone, on Sunday afternoons and evenings, but she refused to join them. And this Christmas, Edna refused to celebrate with close friends or family. It was all too painful. Their celebrations would remind her too much of him.

On Christmas Day, all five Sargents sat near the fire, close to the kitchen—the kids opened the presents, bought long ago by their parents. Rosemary fingered the rabbit fur–lined gloves and silently admired them. She peered at her stocking suspended above the hearth in the living room, just over the glowing orange coals—such a strange place to find it. There was no tree, no tinsel, and no paper chains nearby. Those Christmas memories belonged in the parlor, the cold room that now served as her father's empty tomb.

❧

The parlor. It was such a horrid place to keep a body. The parlor was meant to welcome guests, host sing-alongs—even the occasional impromptu dance. Now it was a crypt, a room to be avoided inside 10 Rillington Place. And there was that faint smell, slowly building—it wasn't quite overwhelming, not yet, but it soon would be. The parlor worried John Reginald Christie.

He was feeling adrift without his wife. Ethel had tended to so many things—she paid most of their bills. She did their grocery shopping and purchased their coal. She dropped off laundry. In fact, two days before her death she had left some items at Maxwell Laundries in Kensington, including pillowslips and a bedsheet. It was the last time she'd been seen. Though it seemed that no one missed her much—yet. Except, perhaps, the milkman. He still delivered a pint to the Christies' doorstep every day—two pints on Sundays—then rapped on the door each Saturday, expecting his four shillings, four pence. No response today. The Christies rarely said more than "hello" to the milkman, anyway.

Reg began making plans. Without his job, he knew he didn't have enough money to pay rent, so he began selling his furniture. He peddled it to the same man who had purchased Timothy Evans' furniture three years earlier.

"I kept my kitchen table, two chairs, some crockery, and cutlery," Reg said. "These were just enough for my immediate needs because I was going away." Reg was ready to leave 10 Rillington Place—he just wasn't quite sure when or how.

In the meantime, he saved money. He looked at Ethel's gold wristwatch and her precious twenty-two-carat gold wedding ring, the one he had placed on her finger more than thirty years ago. He shoved them in his pocket and took them to a jeweler in Shepherd's Bush—the man handed him fifty shillings.

Rosina Swan lived at 9 Rillington Place, right next door—she had befriended the Christies when they first moved there about fifteen years earlier. She was one of Ethel's closest friends, a confidante. Mrs. Christie often escaped the harassment of the neighbors by visiting Swan for tea. They gossiped and talked about their husbands. Ethel rarely complained about Reg, but his fascination for young women vexed her. The year before he killed Ethel, Reg had invited home a young woman he met at a café. Ethel was home and it was Guy Fawkes Night—a popular celebration that usually culminated with fireworks and a bonfire; Reg suggested the three of them watch fireworks together— the girl might have felt safe, if Ethel were there. It was another testament to his occasional charm.

But then Reg urged Ethel to go to the kitchen to prepare dinner. Ethel suspected that Reg wanted to be alone with the girl— the kitchen was tucked in the back of the flat behind the building's main staircase, fairly secluded. Ethel refused to leave and argued with Reg.

"Mrs. Christie told me she was upset about this woman coming to visit her husband because she was rather young," Rosina Swan remembered.

After that night, the girl came around several more times, until Ethel chased her off. Reg's wife knew he was capable of womanizing—after all, he had lived with at least one woman when they were separated, the one he had whacked over the head with a cricket bat. But it's doubtful that Ethel knew just how wicked Reg was when she was away. Neighbors had watched as different young women entered 10 Rillington Place over the years, whenever Ethel was away visiting family in Sheffield. They had often wondered what was happening inside that flat. Reg seemed like a devoted husband, if a bit odd. Indeed, aside from that strange story about the persistent young woman, Swan thought the Christies were an affectionate couple. They had gone through so much together, most notably the Timothy Evans trial.

Rosina Swan had also been a police witness in that case, as well—the one who saw two figures wrestling near the window of the Evanses' top-floor flat. Swan said it appeared as if the woman was trying to get away. Someone across the street said she thought the man was trying to push her out of the window. The Crown used her statements in court. Now, two years later, Swan was curious about her friend Ethel. She hadn't seen her since the week the fog lifted, when she came over to Swan's to watch a television program. Swan questioned Reg when they greeted each other on the street a few days after Ethel's murder.

"You are just the person I want to see," said Reg. "I have got a job at Sheffield."

That was the same lie he had told his supervisor, George Burrow. He insisted his wife had left the day before, to prepare for his arrival. Swan was miffed—*why wouldn't Ethel say goodbye to her closest friend?* Reg hastily explained that Ethel had knocked on her door, but no one had answered. His wife would be in touch soon, he was certain. A few days later, Reg called Swan over to the small wall separating their back garden. He flashed a piece of paper, then pulled it to his face.

"It's a telegram from Ethel," he said, "saying 'arrived safely, love to Rosie.'"

Reg added with his strange laugh: "I will have to choke her off for sending love to you and not me."

He offered various lies to explain Ethel's disappearance. He told one neighbor she had gone to Birmingham to have a "woman's operation." To another, he claimed Ethel was up north, nursing her sick sister. He told the owner of Peter's Snack Bar, a café he frequented, that Ethel was indeed in Birmingham and he was accepting a job in the road haulage business. The owner of that restaurant had been leery of Reg for the past year. Margaret Sergison had watched him bring a girl, about eighteen years old, into the café three or four times a week in 1951, the year before Ethel died. She noted that they chatted and then left together—always in the daytime. The girl didn't seem to be a prostitute; she was too well dressed for that. But if she lived in Notting Hill, she was likely to be working class. Sergison did notice that one time, Reg came into the café wearing broken glasses, mended with adhesive tape. There were scratches on his face. Soon, the teenager stopped coming in. Reg asked that, if she ever did return, she be given any food she wished—he would pay the bill.

Christmas Day was certainly unusual for Reg. Each holiday season, Ethel's seventy-seven-year-old aunt, Emily Legg, invited them to her home in Sheffield for celebrations. They accepted the offer every year—until this Christmas. Ms. Legg's invitation went unanswered; with his new freedom, Reg made his own plans. He was invited to his neighbor's house next door, where they exchanged gifts and watched television. He left a box of handkerchiefs for Rosina Swan, addressed to "Mrs. Swan" from "Ethel and Reg." Swan thought that was so bizarre; Ethel would have never referred to her as "Mrs. Swan." She and her husband invited him inside, but he wasn't good company, especially this Christmas.

"He appeared to be all nerves," Swan remarked to her husband. Reg told the Swans that he expected to leave London by the end of January to be reunited with Ethel in Sheffield. He continued to cover up her murder, and for months, Reg held a ritual early in the morning—one, he hoped, that would help protect his secrets from his snooping neighbors.

"I noticed that he was disinfecting the place," said Lena Louise Brown, who lived in the building. "He was sprinkling disinfectant all over the passage that leads from the front door. He told me one morning that somebody had thrown dirty water down the drain."

The residents watched as Reg sprayed Jeyes Fluid in his parlor, the passageways on the ground floor, in the building's outdoor drainpipes—and in the back garden. The smell of Jeyes was foul and sharp, like iodine splashed on the floor of an old hospital. It drowned any other *unpleasant* odor that might be wafting up from the floorboards. The neighbors thought he was overreacting; sure, the place was shabby, but Jeyes was such an extreme response to dirty water.

Disturbing episodes seemed to haunt 10 Rillington Place— the murder of a woman and her young daughter, violent arguments on the top floor, police prying up drain lids in the dark, and strange noises in the garden at night. But Reg went unnoticed. The bespectacled former policeman, with his balding head and raspy voice, faded quietly into the scenery of Notting Hill. John Reginald Christie was simply another peculiar man, one of many found in every community—the eccentric neighbor who would seldom spark a light in his front parlor. Night after night, he would sit in that room, near his old bay window, alone in the dark—watching.

∐

The weather that Christmas Day was beautiful, with more than five hours' worth of sunshine in London. Meteorologists at Kew Observatory noted that it was the sunniest Christmas Day in more than forty years. With the temperature at a crisp forty-nine degrees, Londoners shed their overcoats and strolled around Hyde Park, then many made their way to Christmas services. More than two thousand people filled St Paul's Cathedral; twice that number attended High Mass at Westminster Cathedral. Thousands of servicemen and -women were reunited with their families, home for the holidays from Korea. It was glorious weather; it practically begged Londoners to spend the holiday outdoors—then it quickly drove them back inside.

The rain began to the west in Ireland, then it traveled southeast to Wales and western England. The next day, Boxing Day, was wet. Then came the fog and the cold—and the smoke. Housewives stoked their open-grate coal fires—sparks burst and tons of soot wafted up their chimneys. It seemed to be happening again. Two days after Christmas, as Londoners prepared their New Year celebrations, they found themselves groping their way through yet another choking fog.

"Acrid, white clouds swirled through the streets and seeped into houses gay with Christmas season decorations," wrote the *New York Times*. "The smoke-heavy mist brought hardship to aged persons and those suffering from heart and respiratory ailments."

The streets were clogged once again with fumes and mist— visibility was limited to just ten yards. The fog moored ships on the Thames, canceled football and rugby matches, and grounded flights. The roads were icy and wet. Delayed trains marooned some holiday visitors in the murk. And it was so painful to breathe, just like the last fog. Houses and trees were barely visible in the haze. "It was the second 'peasouper' of the month, making this December rough even by London standards," concluded the *New York Times*. That was an understatement. There seemed to be little interest from the press, despite the Ministry of Health's revelations about elevated deaths from the first fog.

But there was a debate brewing in the media—the *Times*' "Letters to the Editor" section was hosting a row over the killer fog and how to stop it from returning. The crux of the argument was the government's secret—there wasn't enough smokeless fuel to abandon coal. The debate began with a letter from Dame Caroline Haslett, an electrical engineer who was heavily involved in educating women about careers in science. She was frequently the "first woman" or the "only woman" on science committees. Dame Caroline was concerned how the fog added to the workload of housewives—and how electricity could help.

"I was paying a heavy price to my neighbours' indulgence in 'nutty slack' or some similar form of solid fuel," wrote Dame Caroline. "A coal fire by any other name would smell as foully and would blacken my reputation as a good housewife, for clothes, linen, hangings were all equally begrimed."

Her real point was that all Londoners should consider changing from coal to electricity.

"My all-electric house commits no nuisance to my fellow citizens of London," she said. "Would that my neighbours could say the same to me."

Her suggestion was idealistic, and not at all realistic. Most Londoners could never afford to convert their heating sources from coal fireplaces to electricity, or even gas. Many could barely afford their grocery bills. The *Times* printed an acerbic reply.

"It is a blessed thing perhaps to feel so secure in virtue as Dame Caroline Haslett does in her all-electric house," wrote one reader. "Those of us, however, who live under the rain of grits from Lots Road and Battersea power stations may ask ourselves whence she derives her satisfaction."

Then advocates of the coal industry weighed in, focusing on Dame Caroline's claim that her all-electric house did no harm to her neighbors.

"It may not do so directly," wrote Eric Bellingham, the director-general of the Coal Utilisation Council, "but may I quote from the last report of the Director of Fuel Research?

'The heaviest pollution is centred round the (electricity) generating stations.'"

Generating electricity came at its own cost. And the same was true for gas production—in 1952, it was estimated that two-thirds of gas sold by the North Thames Gas Board came from plants that emitted large amounts of smoke. All fuel was dirty. Other readers chimed in, arguing that while an all-electric community would noticeably reduce the smudge in London, the real culprits were motor vehicles and oil-burning plants. Finally, Parliament entered the debate, by way of one lone MP. Conservative Arnold Gridley wrote the editor, saying that all of this quibbling was useless. Gas and electricity, though idyllic solutions, were just too expensive. Converting an old-fashioned fireplace to burn gas would cost between ten and twenty pounds, multiplied by more than eight million Londoners—it was an inconceivable cost for the still-struggling Crown. Coal-burning fireplaces could be converted to burn solid smokeless fuels, like clean-burning coke or anthracite, for a fraction of that cost, making it appear to be a better alternative. The problem, Gridley contended, was that there simply wasn't enough smokeless fuel to be had in post-war London.

"Because of the great shortage of smokeless fuel—a situation which the National Coal Board admits cannot be remedied in the foreseeable future," wrote MP Gridley, "the majority of these continuous burning appliances are having to burn bituminous coal."

And that was the crux of the country's energy problem: There wasn't enough smokeless fuel available—and Churchill's apathetic government wasn't working toward a solution. The country was financially exhausted—smokeless fuels were scarce, gas and electricity were expensive, and coal was deadly. As the final fog of 1952 slowly floated away, Londoners looked toward a new year and a beautiful coronation for their new queen. And smoke abatement champions, like MP Norman Dodds, readied for a vicious fight.

∽

In late December, the bells of Big Ben rang as the clock struck two thirty, usually signaling the start of Parliament. But the rows of seats inside the House of Commons were now empty. The politicians were on holiday—any talk of pollution reform would have to wait. The Great Smog made its last appearance on Parliament's Order Paper—the list of the day's agenda—on December 19, the final session before the break.

Norman Dodds quietly read through the written responses from Parliament at home during the holidays. There would be little he could do about the fog during Christmas, so he concentrated on being with his family. His wife, Eva, managed their home in Dartford like a well-organized business—chores for the children were mandatory, the menus were structured, the sewing was always quickly completed, and the two boys were well-mannered—much of the time.

Thirteen-year-old Alan and twelve-year-old Brian were rambunctious kids, adept at sports and music. But their parents expected a certain amount of propriety, even when they were teenagers. Norman lectured them about the responsibilities of being a public servant and avoiding personal controversy. Their parents taught them discipline.

"They quickly learned to be independent," remembered Eva Dodds, "though they always knew that both Norman and I, at any time and no matter how busy we were, always had time for their problems."

The humble exterior to 10 Rillington Place in Notting Hill, London, and the unassuming man who lived inside, John Reginald Christie. No one knew the horrors that lay behind this façade.
The National Archives of the UK

During five days in December 1952, a choking smog took ahold of London, turning day into night and causing an estimated 12,000 deaths—a number that the government did its best to cover up.
TopFoto/The Image Works

A high pressure weather system trapped pollution from factories, vehicles, and coal-burning fireplaces. Sulphur dioxide, carbon monoxide, carbon dioxide, and smoke particles poisoned Londoners for more than 100 hours.

Rosemary Sargent (right) and her family during happier times, before her father succumbed to the suffocating smog that attacked his already weak lungs.
Courtesy of Rosemary Sargent Merritt

Albert Sargent died at age 42 after walking home from his job at a bus terminal in Camberwell Green during the first day of the smog.

Stanley Crichton was a beat cop trying to keep order during the tumultuous dark days. *Courtesy of Stanley Crichton*

The fog caused chaos on the city's roads. This was one of two coaches that crashed head-on in southwest London on Croydon Road, injuring eleven people. *TopFoto/The Image Works*

Ethel Christie

Hectorina MacLennan

Rita Nelson

In the weeks and months that followed the fog, more victims joined those who were already interred at 10 Rillington Place, including his wife, Ethel, as well as Hectorina MacLennan, Kathleen Maloney, Ruth Fuerst, Muriel Eady, and Rita Nelson.
The National Archives of the UK

Ethel Christie in the floorboards

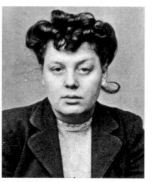

Kathleen Maloney

Ruth Fuerst, Muriel Eady

One of the enduring mysteries is
Christie's role in a murder that
occurred just upstairs from him a few
years earlier—that of his neighbor,
Beryl Evans, and her baby, Geraldine.
Beryl's husband, Tim, was tried and
executed for the crime. Above, left—
the washhouse in the garden where
Beryl and Geraldine were found.

TopFoto/The Image Works

In the aftermath of the smog and the Christie case, three men battled to shape the future of the UK. Labour MP Norman Dodds (above, with Margaret Thatcher) argued with the Tories in Parliament, demanding a law to control air pollution.

Minister of Housing Harold Macmillan (right, with Prime Minister Winston Churchill) was Dodds' prime target; Macmillan stalled the progress of clean air legislation.

Dr. Donald Acheson (below) tried to save the lives of smog victims in Middlesex Hospital in Westminster.

TopFoto/The Image Works

Newcastle University Library

In his youth, Norman was athletic—he had competed in road walking events in Newcastle. Then he developed a love for dance, and he started a ballroom dancing school in London. "If you're dancing on the floor, you're not at the bar," he would say. He rarely drank, though it was difficult for a popular politician to avoid alcohol at social events.

Norman was completely devoted to Eva. He courted her when she was a teacher, just out of training college. By the time she met Norman at age twenty-one, she had completed six more years of education than he. Eva was raised in a middle-class household in Peckham, attended the prestigious Mary Datchelor School and graduated when she was eighteen. She was quite bright and ambitious. She volunteered with the Labour Cooperative Party, which was how they met—he was her senior by nine years; he admired her intelligence and beauty.

During World War II, Norman volunteered for the Home Guard, a defense organization in the British Army—he served in East London during the Blitz. In 1942, he joined the Royal Air Force and served there for three years. After the war ended, Norman ran for Parliament and easily won his seat. Eva would have been happy to stay home and tend to the house, but Norman was concerned.

"One evening, my husband gave me a serious talking-to," Eva said. "He said I was in danger of becoming a 'cabbage.'"

Norman encouraged her to travel and find her own career path, a progressive suggestion for a traditional British husband. He believed that educated women should hone their talents. So Eva became active again in the Socialist party, which sometimes called her away to conferences for several days.

"He was always willing to help," said Eva. "My husband would cope with the children, the shopping, and the household chores, with the greatest goodwill."

They were a modish couple, Norman in his pinstripe suits, Eva in her stylish dresses—both superbly hatted, especially on Sundays when the Doddses attended services at their Protestant church. Norman was invariably dapper, even when on the pitch as the President of the Dartford Football Club. Friends joked that they were always dashing, as if they were headed to the genteel Royal Ascot horse races.

Eva sometimes thumbed through Norman's pictures and the newspaper clippings she kept that showed his devotion to his constituents. There was one of him wielding a spade alongside a gang of other people. "We'll do it and I'll do it with you," seemed to be his belief. And that would become indisputable in the coming year.

Just after Christmas, outside the walls of Parliament, Norman called the United States Embassy in London with a special request. He wanted a copy of the report from the US investigation into the smog that killed twenty people in Donora, Pennsylvania, in 1948. Now Norman planned to use the American report as a weapon in Parliament—he and other MPs were banding together to prepare for a full-scale attack against London's air pollution. He would also use the press, one of his most potent accomplices.

"Publicity is the lifeblood of a back-bench MP," said Norman. "You have to get into the papers."

"Donora Report to Aid Britain in Smog Fight," proclaimed the headline in the *New York Times* from December 28, 1952.

"A United States embassy spokesman in London said today that the Donora report would be sent to Labourite Member of Parliament Norman Dodds, who asked for it in preparing an all-out campaign against London's smogs."

Norman told reporters that there had been thousands of

deaths in London—the fog was a murderer, and the government was callous.

"A number of MPs of all parties feel, like myself, that the effects of the fog have not been treated seriously enough," said Norman. "In 1948, though only a few people died in the Pennsylvania smog, the United States Government carried out a full-scale inquiry." He was only partially right.

Like the British government, American lawmakers had hoped their own smog crisis would disappear, too. In 1948, there was an incredible amount of reticence to investigate what actually caused those deaths and illnesses during the fog in Donora, Pennsylvania. U.S. Steel employed the majority of the town, including most of the members of the local government. If the mills were closed, Donora could be financially devastated. But after pressure from outside groups, the U.S. Public Health Service launched an official investigation. Pathologists studied the bodies of the twenty victims—their blood contained fluoride up to twenty-five times the normal amount. The department's scientists conducted air sampling and weather monitoring. Nurses blanketed the town with questionnaires about symptoms. The results of the U.S. government's extensive investigation: inclusive. The Public Health Service's report said that "no single substance" was responsible for the Donora fog. Researchers refused to lay the blame on U.S. Steel's zinc mill and its fluoride emissions. It would not conclusively connect the deaths with the polluted air—and the British government was likely to take the same position.

The report from America might not have been scathing, but Norman could still use it to threaten MPs—Parliament rarely felt comfortable being a step behind the United States. He was slowly collecting evidence and recruiting allies from both parties—he was ready to challenge the prime minister's cabinet.

Norman Dodds would soon accuse the British government of malfeasance and demand to know why it was refusing to investigate a mass murder. And his mark was a Tory minister, the one who had represented Churchill during debates over controlling air pollution—the minister of housing and local government, Harold Macmillan.

CHAPTER NINE

Squeezed

The day, in the highest and brightest quarters of the town, was damp, dark, cold and gloomy. In that low and marshy spot, the fog filled every nook and corner with a thick dense cloud. Every object was obscured at one or two yards' distance. The warning lights and fires upon the river were powerless beneath this pall...

— *Charles Dickens*,
The Old Curiosity Shop, *1841*

It was January 1953 when he eyed the man from across the road, strolling toward the bakery. The store sat on St Mark's Road just off Ladbroke Grove in Notting Hill. Len Trevallion watched him. The Met sergeant enjoyed tracking criminals, even the pickpockets who worked so deftly near the Underground entrances. The suspicious man slipped inside the bakery too hurriedly to be a paying customer. Within seconds, the door flung open and he dashed out, carrying a tin of biscuits under his arm.

Len sprinted after the thief, pumping his arms — he was patrolling alone, in plainclothes, with no partner, no gun, and no radio. It didn't matter. The crook turned the corner and scurried into a nasty building on the left, at the end of a cul-de-sac. The sign read Rillington Place. Len knew the block — he was the head of Notting Hill station's vice squad. The thirty-eight-year-old led a unit of five plainclothes policemen who targeted illegal drinking club owners, abortionists, bookmakers, and brothel-keepers. Len and his investigators arrested quite a lot of prostitutes. There were loads on that particular street.

Len ran through the open door of the tenement labeled "10" and scrambled upstairs, into a flat; he found his suspect cowering under a bed. Len cuffed him, walked him down the stairs and out the door toward Notting Hill station. Once he had jailed the thief, he returned to 10 Rillington Place. Len walked inside the building and rapped on the door of the ground-floor apartment. A balding, middle-aged man answered. Len recognized John Reginald Christie—after all, he had been the Crown's star witness in the murder trial of Timothy Evans. It was difficult to forget Christie—the former War Reserve policeman with a weak voice, the one who had sobbed when the verdict was read.

Len himself had played a small role in that murder case, too. He was the sergeant assigned to observe Timothy Evans in his jail cell, the one who had heard the Welshman say, "Well, it was the constant crying of the baby that got on my nerves. I just had to strangle it, I just had to put an end to it, I just couldn't put up with its crying."

Christie looked at Len and invited him into the front parlor—he didn't seem at all nervous. Most Notting Hill residents weren't eager to allow an officer inside their flats; they were always hiding things, like drugs, weapons—perhaps bodies. He introduced himself as Reg, and they chatted about the just-arrested man, one of Reg's upstairs neighbors who caused him such aggravation. Len paused. There was a strong smell in the room. It was awful. He thought he could ignore the stench, but the noxious odor pervaded everything.

Len Trevallion was a cop's cop—a World War II hero who had flown bomber planes across Europe and watched friends die. Now he chased criminals in a London slum. He was certainly used to foul surroundings, but this scent was vile. He turned to the man.

"What a rotten stink that is," said Len. "Can't you do something about it?"

"Well, it's all these coloured people and their strange cooking," Reg explained. "It makes a terrible smell."

It was a bizarre explanation, but Len didn't have proof that the stench came from anywhere else. He shook the man's hand, stepped out of the parlor into the hallway, and walked out.

Reg shut the door behind him, and turned the lock. The cop had left and he was alone again—in a way. Ethel was still there, under the floorboards of her own parlor, concealed. The disinfectant couldn't disguise the smell of her rotting skin; the chilly air inside the flat wouldn't stop her from decaying. And two women still lay hidden in his garden. It would be months before Sergeant Len Trevallion learned that Reg's dead wife was below the wood planks that creaked beneath his shoes. Even more upsetting was that Reg would be the one to tell him.

❦

Meanwhile, in Parliament, workers packed up the myriad of holiday decorations and stored them for the season. It was back to work for the government. Christmas might have served as a pleasant distraction from the fog crisis, but now Churchill's MPs would feel real pressure, and not just from newspapers and opposition politicians—but from the rising number of bodies.

Shortly after the fog subsided in December, Minister of Health Iain Macleod had reported to Parliament that there were more than three thousand additional deaths in Britain due to the weather event—an astounding number, one that should have sparked a panic. And a few weeks later, the government's critics were gifted with more ammunition. The London County Council issued its annual medical report, asserting that the December smog was more deadly than the infamous 1866 cholera epidemic that had killed 5,596 people in London.

The government's ministries scrambled to coordinate information. On New Year's Day—when most politicians were toasting 1953—Harold Macmillan's office was planning a preemptive strike against the attack of antipollution fighters, like MP Norman Dodds. The Ministry of Housing sent a memo to the Ministry of Health, requesting data—and empathy.

"We have also been under fire," admitted S. G. G. Wilkinson, Macmillan's assistant secretary.

The Ministry of Housing wanted to know if the victims were already sick *before* the fog enveloped London—*what if they were likely to die anyway?* Macmillan's ministry wanted to know how sick the victims were "due to cold and damp, quite independently of fog."

That could be the key to making the story go away in the press—to discover that most of the dead would have died anyway because of the cold, wet temperatures. Macmillan had been a politician for two decades now—he knew it was crucial that the Conservative government present a united front to Parliament, and to all Londoners. But that would prove difficult. No one seemed to want to admit blame, take responsibility, or spend money to prevent it from happening again—at least not yet.

The weather grew colder in late January. Norman Dodds walked into the House of Commons, placed his name card in its slot, and watched the minister of health on the other side of the aisle. In mid-December, Iain Macleod had said there were a little more than three thousand additional deaths. Now, nearly a month later, Norman suspected the actual number was much higher. On January 3, the highly respected *British Medical Journal* had suggested that the fog, now referred to as "smog," had murdered more than five thousand Londoners—a stunning revelation, and a starkly higher number. And information was still coming in—none of it good for Churchill's government.

Norman was demanding that an updated number be officially announced in Parliament—and now the minister of health was uncomfortable. Winston Churchill had appointed Iain Macleod to the post about eight months earlier, after watching him humiliate a Labour opponent during a debate in Parliament over health care. Macleod was a passionate spokesperson in the Commons, though he must have appreciated irony in his job as minister of health. Macleod was not a particular paragon of health or clean air himself—he had once famously announced at a press conference: "It must be regarded as established that there is a relationship between smoking and cancer of the lung." He was chain-smoking during his speech.

Now Macleod was under immense pressure, especially from within his own party. Norman made the written request, and the health minister was forced to make a startling admission in Parliament: there had been more than *six thousand* additional deaths between the start of the fog and the end of December—not three thousand as had been previously reported.

"A large part of the increase in Greater London can be attributed to fog," admitted Macleod.

His announcement sent a shock wave through Churchill's ministries—the death toll was incredibly high. The government's chief medical statistician, W. P. D. Logan, immediately demanded Macleod retract that claim.

The fog "was a catastrophe of the first magnitude in which, *for a few days*, death-rates attained a level that has been exceeded only rarely during the past hundred years," said W. P. D. Logan.

The key phrases were "for a few days" and "only rarely." Privately, Logan insisted the cutoff date for "fog deaths" be moved back from December 31 to December 20. It was distressing for Macleod, who was still a fledgling MP, having joined Parliament just three years earlier. Now Macleod and his Ministry of Health panicked.

"The Minister of Health is anxious to find out the actual number of deaths which might rightly be attributable to fog during the period 5th–20th December," read a confidential memo sent to Wembley Hospital in Middlesex.

Logan soon successfully lobbied the cabinet to have the period of "fog deaths" shortened by almost two weeks. Anyone who had died *after* December 20 would not be considered a victim of the fog. He announced the new death toll for the smog: more than four thousand dead, two thousand less than the Ministry of Health's estimate. Logan listed off the numbers of dead per day: four hundred in the first twenty-four hours, six hundred on the next day, nine hundred on Sunday, and another nine hundred on Monday. On the final day, when the fog lifted, nearly eight hundred people died. More than four hundred died by the following week.

By shortening the window of time, the government was essentially covering up thousands of dead victims. But people were starting to pay attention. The National Smoke Abatement Society members read the newspapers—they sensed the Ministry of Health was scrambling, hoping to spin a deadly disaster into a tragic, but fleeting incident. It was time to squeeze Iain Macleod and the Health Ministry.

The NSAS insisted on a meeting, demanded to know what Churchill's government would do next. Macleod didn't attend, but he sent four representatives. In mid-January, the society's secretary, Arnold Marsh, sat across from the group inside the Ministry of Health building in Mayfair. A medical officer outlined the nature of several studies, including research on meteorology, coroners' reports, pathologists' analyses, information from the Ministry of National Insurance, and hospital admissions. And that was just a partial list. Marsh seemed impressed—but he wondered if there were any independent studies being done, outside the influence of the government. *No*, was the reply. The Tories had control over the deadly fog investigation.

❦

The metal presses of Fleet Street roared that January, churning out tabloids and broadsheets, all declaring that the December fog had killed thousands of Londoners. The highly reported conclusions from the *British Medical Journal* and the London County Council seemed to enrapture journalists. The media began its aggressive reporting. The fog from December had brought in pollution that was the worst in recorded history for London. Scientists couldn't blame the bitter winter—the Emergency Bed Service revealed that the majority of its patients came in for respiratory diseases, not hypothermia. The number of hospitalized people in London increased by *73 percent* from the same period in the previous year.

"A smoky atmosphere is a dangerous killer of the old and sickly," reported the *Manchester Guardian.* "London Fog Deaths: Investigations in Progress," read the *Times* headline.

"Clamor Rises in London for Smog Relief," said the *Washington Post.* "Newspapers, Members of Parliament and private citizens joined in the demands. Prime Minister Churchill's government has already said it is treating the smog as 'a problem of the very greatest urgency.'" Perhaps the government was working toward a solution, a way to prevent the next deadly fog. The press reported that the country was planning to build the world's first nuclear power station, a huge plant that would generate electricity on an industrial scale—a replacement for coal. Calder Hall would be constructed at Sellafield in Cumbria, North West England, within four years.

"There is no reason why nuclear reactors should not before very long provide a useful additional source of industrial power," assured Duncan Sandys, Winston Churchill's dapper minister of supply.

But the minister's boasting was a bit misleading—he didn't mention the plant's classified assignment, one hidden from most MPs. The government didn't commission a thirty-five-million-pound nuclear reactor simply to generate electricity for industry. In fact, it was never intended to reduce the country's dependency on coal, and it wasn't going to solve any fuel problems. Calder Hall station was codenamed "PIPPA," for Pressurized Pile Producing Power and Plutonium. The power station would soon secretly produce weapons-grade plutonium for Britain's nuclear program. Clean, cheap electricity was an illusion.

∽

January was a difficult month for the minister of health. Members assailed Iain Macleod in Parliament over and over again—they hurled at him phrases like "man-made atmospheric filth," "appalling and unnecessary loss of life," and "mass extermination." Macleod stayed calm, a steadying force on the side of a castigated Conservative government.

"My department has been looking into this matter as a problem of the very greatest urgency," he typically replied.

MPs peppered Macleod with questions about how the fog was to blame for heart and lung diseases—he didn't have answers, which was very discouraging for an orator who always prepared for a debate. Away from Parliament and the press, the health minister was clearly frustrated with the ceaseless badgering over the fog.

"Really, you know," said Macleod, during a public speech in January, "anyone would think fog had only started in London since I became Minister." He was receiving calls from the press, requests from other ministries for information, and now the National Smoke Abatement Society was asking for money to keep its offices open. But the society was a horrible nuisance to the government—members planted questions to be asked by Labour MPs, meant to pressure the Tories. The government didn't appreciate being harassed. Macleod's answer to the grant request was unabashedly "no." And then he warned Harold Macmillan that the NSAS might come to the Ministry of Housing, asking for money.

"I fear that they may now approach you," wrote the Health Ministry secretary, in a confidential memo.

Critics from all parties refused to absolve the government. The fog concerned a number of departments, and there was a severe lack of coordination and, even worse, a lack of initiative—Labour accused Churchill's ministers of negligence. Yet some Labourites also advocated in Parliament for coal, even pushed for rations to be lifted.

One Labour MP said: "We in the United Kingdom have a desperate need for more coal. If we do not get more coal there may be no national survival." Without the dirty fuel, millions would be left cold this winter. It was an impossible position. Labour's allegations against the Conservatives were at least partly motivated by politics, that was certain, but even a number of Tories were stunned by the government's callousness. The accusations would only become more boisterous—they would echo inside every room in the Palace of Westminster.

⌒♊⌒

Albert Sargent's funeral service had been held a few days earlier, and Rosemary's mother was horribly depressed. Not only was her husband of fifteen years dead, she was now left alone with four children and without income. She had no education—she was a full-time mother who needed to become fully employed, quickly.

Edna visited the National Assistance Board, looking for financial help from the government; she was frightened that she would lose her home of more than twenty years, and that she and her children would become homeless. She needed reassurance that her family would still thrive, despite Albert's death. Agents at the NAB gave her a suggestion that was little comfort: Edna should sell her home and live off the proceeds as long as possible. What would happen then wasn't their concern.

The National Assistance Board, in its (meager) defense, was under tremendous financial pressure. It had been created four years earlier to provide relief for residents suffering from poverty in postwar Britain, but its applications had increased dramatically in the past year. Two hundred thousand more people were receiving weekly assistance in 1952 than the previous year. The NAB was now spending over one hundred million pounds a year. More than one million women were drawing assistance. The agent told Edna Sargent that she should return when she had no money—there were families far worse off than hers. She was devastated.

Then Edna became concerned for the children's schooling.

Rosemary's brother David went to a public school near her school in Catford. "Public" education in England was similar to "private" in America—a public school in Britain was selective and required tuition. It was not easy for many Londoners to afford public school for their children. Now that Albert's income was gone, Rosemary's family couldn't pay David's modest tuition; he would likely have to attend state school—one run by the British government and a much less desirable option. Edna was panicked. She asked for a meeting with David's headmaster at Alleyn's School.

"Your son is a grand boy," Mr. Pritchard assured her.

The school didn't want to lose him—so the headmaster offered David a scholarship, which would cover the tuition. Rosemary could tell her mother was relieved. Education was so important to their family. Edna was determined that all of her children go as far as they could in school. And more good news arose from that meeting with the headmaster—Edna was given a job. He knew of a public school in Catford that needed some help in the cafeteria. Edna was a brilliant baker—she made wonderful cakes and pastries and she really enjoyed working in the kitchen. So her baking skills were put to good use. She began working at St Dunstan's less than a week after her husband was buried.

Within a month, the Sargent household was transformed from one of relative comfort and stability to a house filled with grief and a good deal of stress. Edna fretted over money; she worried about coping with all four children alone. She nagged every child at home who caught her eye.

Rosemary couldn't concentrate at school—it was all too much pressure. Her grades began to slip, at the worst time. The General Education O-level certificate exam wasn't far off. She had to pass it to move on to a grammar school, and an education that might steer her away from secretarial work. Her mother warned her that if she didn't stay sharp, she would need to leave school at sixteen, like many other British children. If Albert were still alive, then public school tuition would be assured, but now—her future was uncertain. Still, Rosemary dreamed of being a teacher.

~

Labour MP Norman Dodds sat across the aisle from the Conservative minister of housing in Parliament on a brisk winter afternoon. It was January 27, and Big Ben struck two thirty. Norman waited patiently, quietly rehearsing his statement, ready to leap up when the Speaker of the House of Commons called out his name. Harold Macmillan sat on the green bench just to the right of the Speaker—where the "frontbenchers" all sat. It was an area reserved for cabinet members who would be pelted with questions from Members of Parliament, a daily practice abhorred by most politicians. But Macmillan was typically well prepared—it wasn't easy to ambush him. The fifty-eight-year-old minister of housing was one of Winston Churchill's most promising protégés, a rising star in the Conservative cabinet of sixteen ministers. But now, like Iain Macleod a few weeks earlier, it was Macmillan's turn to have a difficult day.

The minister of housing had been a fixture in Parliament for more than twenty years, starting as a backbencher who soon accepted posts from Winston Churchill. The prime minister admired his acumen and patriotism, but Macmillan wasn't particularly popular with other MPs, thanks to years of self-doubt, punctuated with occasional bouts of elitism. When Labour took over in 1945, Macmillan was dismayed.

"I hate uneducated people having power," he wrote, "but I like to think that the poor will be rendered happy."

Macmillan served with distinction in the British army during World War I, fighting on the front lines in France. He was wounded three times—the most severe injury came as he led a platoon during the Battle of the Somme in 1916. He was shot, and lay in a trench for ten hours trying to avoid German detection.

After the war he entered politics, sitting in the House of Commons beginning in 1924. In 1940, he joined Churchill's wartime administration. The prime minister appointed Macmillan parliamentary secretary to the Ministry of Supply—the department that coordinated the supply of equipment to the British armed forces. Macmillan also traveled to North Africa and the Mediterranean, representing the British government. And while his profile in Parliament slowly grew, so did his social circle. Macmillan married Lady Dorothy Cavendish, the daughter of the 9th Duke of Devonshire, joining one of the most deeply rooted Conservative aristocratic families in England. After World War II, Conservative ministers took notice of the newly cocksure MP.

"He has grown in stature during the war more than anyone," said Bruce Lockhart, a British diplomat and author. "He was always clever, but was shy and diffident, had a clammy handshake and was more like a wet fish than a man. Now he is full of confidence and is not only not afraid to speak but jumps in and speaks brilliantly."

But of course, not everyone appreciated Macmillan's bravado. Opposition MPs resented his dramatic, oratorical style of delivering speeches.

"He would put his hands on the lapels of his coat and turn to the backbenchers behind him for approval and support," said Emrys Hughes, a Labour MP. "He would raise and lower his voice and speak as if he were on the stage. His polished phrases reeked of midnight oil."

With the Conservative victory in 1951, Prime Minister Winston Churchill appointed Macmillan minister of housing, entrusting him to fulfill the party's promise after the Blitz to build three hundred thousand houses a year—a herculean task, but Macmillan was well on his way to achieving Churchill's goal. It was his primary concern, despite the fog crisis last month. After spending weeks hurling accusations at Macmillan, Norman Dodds wanted to trap him. He needed the minister of housing to admit that the Tory government was culpable in more than six thousand deaths.

The contrast between the two men was unmistakable—their backgrounds diverged at childhood. The housing minister had been reared in a privileged home in London at the turn of the century, the grandson of a wealthy publisher. Macmillan's American mother controlled his education through home-schooling; he had learned multiple languages, including French, Latin, and Greek.

Norman was raised in Dunston, a small mining town on the banks of the river Tyne in northeastern England. As a boy, Norman spent most weekends in Northumberland with his grandmother, a widow with a penchant for feeding and caring for just about anyone who walked off the road and knocked on her door.

"Twice a week, she would bake tea-cakes for the people of the road who called upon her," recalled Norman.

When he was there, Norman watched the downtrodden strangers, "flotsam and jetsam," as he described them. There were some odd characters—at least, they were odd to a nine-year-old, but he was fascinated with them all, especially the Romany gypsies. Those folks enthusiastically predicted his grandmother's future in the tea leaves at the bottom of her cup.

"The experience left me with a lasting impression, indeed conviction, that the most unlikely human material can generally respond to kindness and understanding," Norman said.

Norman's father was a miner. There was little money, and when the time came to make a decision about public education, his family couldn't afford it—so he left school at fourteen, and began working for the Labour Party. In 1945, he was encouraged to run, and when Labour MPs captured a large majority for the first time in party history, Norman was elected to Parliament. He had only been challenged twice since then, both by the same candidate. But his opponent was quite remarkable.

She was a beautiful and quick-witted twenty-five-year-old politician named Margaret Roberts, soon to be Margaret Thatcher. Norman admired the young woman's charisma, and he respected her ideas. Thatcher knew she would be outnumbered at the polls. Norman was a popular politician in the blue-collar area of Dartford, a commuter town for Greater London with almost eighty thousand residents. Norman guessed he would handily win this election, but he prodded Thatcher to keep with the campaign by challenging her to public events. They confronted each other at debates in packed halls—both holding their own.

"I was lucky to have an opponent like Norman Dodds," Margaret Thatcher said. "A genuine and extremely chivalrous Socialist of the old school. He knew that he was going to win, and he was a big enough man to give an ambitious young woman with totally different opinions a chance."

Off the campaign trail and inside the Commons, Norman was a fighter. He boasted of being an advocate for the disenfranchised. He sat on a board that raised money for disabled veterans, and during his maiden speech in 1945, he encouraged the British government to provide food for children in German refugee camps. He served on a committee for the minister of pensions and campaigned for patients in mental health facilities, particularly women. And he fought for the land rights of disenfranchised Gypsies, the same kind he had met at his grandmother's home.

Norman drew inspiration from his childhood, especially from his grandmother—she had treated everyone, rich and poor, with respect, and he wanted to do the same. So he argued with the Tories over issues that mattered to his constituents. He argued very loudly for votes—and for media attention. He was just a backbencher, but Norman managed to rankle Harold Macmillan, one of the most powerful men in Europe.

Today, the men sat on opposite aisles, as always—one hoping to avoid a confrontation, the other waiting to expose a derelict minister. Macmillan was concluding his reply to an innocuous question about crumbling pathways in public parks when the Speaker summoned Norman.

The MP stood, looked at Macmillan, and asked about "the last occasion on which an inter-departmental committee inquired into the cause and effects of fog? And what action has since been taken to combat the worst features of this type of weather?"

A cacophony of noise erupted from heckling MPs. Macmillan stood up, faced his opponent and abruptly replied: "So far as I know, no inter-departmental committee has investigated the weather conditions which cause fog; I believe they are generally well understood."

Norman had predicted Macmillan would dismiss that question, so he fired back: "Does the Minister not appreciate that last month, in Greater London alone, there were literally more people choked to death by air pollution than were killed on the roads in the country in 1952?" Macmillan might have ventured a reply, but Norman barely paused.

"Why is a public inquiry not being held, seeing that inquiries are held into air and rail disasters which do not affect so many people?" Norman barked. "Is consideration being given or will it be given to initiating a much more thorough investigation, on the lines of that conducted by the American government in 1948? Has the right honorable gentleman seen the report?"

Norman held up the research from the United States. "It begins with: 'The whole nation was shocked when 20 people died as the result of fog in the last week in October, 1948, in the town of Donora, Pennsylvania.'"

Norman thrust the American report at the Tory bench. Macmillan refused to answer—Norman sat down and waited for his fellow MPs to take over. Now the Labour Party would begin its organized assault on Harold Macmillan. Six different MPs unloaded questions on the housing minister within minutes. They demanded answers about the economic waste of bad fuel, about smokeless fuel, about the deaths of thousands of Londoners. Macmillan deflected each question—he refused to be pinned down.

Soon, Conservative MPs began heckling the Labourites with screams of "speech," accusing the opposition of preaching. One MP managed to eke out a question before being shouted down by Macmillan's supporters.

"Is the Minister aware that the increased use of these modern appliances, which burn all night, using fuels like nutty slack, have during his tenure of office added another 250,000 fog-producing and air-polluting flues in this country?" demanded Colonel Marcus Lipton. "What is he doing about this?"

Macmillan appeared fed up with the whole mess. He calmly ignored the question and requested that the Speaker move on. Macmillan had once been a renowned debater and student politician at Oxford University—he knew how to reduce an opponent quickly. The minister's response infuriated Norman.

Labour's strike against the minister of housing went well—they had never expected him to answer their questions truthfully. But Macmillan's blatant stonewalling was maddening. Glaring at the housing minister, Norman stood and declared, "owing to the amazing display of apathy, I give notice that I shall raise the matter on the adjournment."

Norman and his cadre of MPs believed that Macmillan's blasé response was proof that the cabinet was overwhelmed. The fog was smothering them—air pollution was too difficult to reduce and too expensive to eradicate. Norman Dodds refused to allow the fog to slip back outside, through the walls of Parliament. He forced it to stay—where it would curse the House of Commons for months.

○‿◞

On a frigid night in early January of 1953, a coal fire warmed Kathleen Maloney and her friend Catherine Struthers inside the Westminster Arms. They sat by its hearth in the seedy pub in Paddington, a favorite spot of Kathleen's when she required a strong drink and some comfort. She needed both quite often these days.

Kathleen was a prostitute from Southampton, homeless, often drunk, and constantly running into scrapes with the police. Her life had dragged on this way for years, and the stress of it showed. She looked far older than her twenty-six years, with dyed blonde hair and sullen, dark eyes. Kathleen had earned a long police record over her short life, mostly for being drunk and disorderly, selling sex, and assaulting police officers. She had been barred from several of her favorite pubs for boorish behavior, which included obnoxious singing, all fueled by too much red wine—"jolly jump up," Kathleen called it. She was an occasional vagrant—if she couldn't find a customer, she sometimes slept in ladies' public toilets.

"She had no place to live and went home at night with any man she could find," said an acquaintance.

"She was always drunk," claimed another. "She was a prostitute and usually picked sailors and Americans as her clients."

Kathleen was in and out of prison—her family in Plymouth wanted nothing to do with her. She had five children, all of whom were being raised by other people. She had been orphaned when she was three, and had been raised by nuns in a Catholic convent. As an adult, her behavior was embarrassing—and Kathleen knew it. So it wasn't surprising, on that cold January night at the Westminster Arms, that Kathleen Maloney was already intoxicated when the door swung open and a middle-aged man walked in; he asked to sit by the girls and buy them some drinks. Kathleen recognized him—and she didn't hesitate to invite him over.

She and her friend Maureen had met him in early December, in fact just days before the deadly fog. They had both been "on the game," both looking for clients. They recognized the man from the neighborhood. He focused on them quickly, followed them to two different pubs on that cold day. He seemed so nice and polite, very different from the men who normally kept them company. Kathleen frequently entertained American soldiers or Irish navvies who slipped her two pounds for a night in a bed-and-breakfast in Sussex Gardens; their clients were brash and rough—unkempt. Fred, as he called himself, was amiable, though her friend thought he was a bit strange-looking.

"He wore horn-rimmed glasses," remembered Maureen Riggs. "He had thinnish lips and he was sort of licking his lips when he was talking."

He had seemed so happy to see them. He asked the pair if they wanted to earn money taking nude pictures at a rented room he called his "photo studio." He was so fond of cameras. They agreed, and he led them to a room off Marylebone Lane. They walked through the door and stared at the floodlights hanging from the ceiling and the camera sitting on a stand.

"I was naked. Kay sat on a chair and watched," said Maureen. Then Kathleen took pictures of Reg and Maureen, without clothes, simulating sexual acts. It was so strange, but he seemed very pleased. He said he would develop the photos immediately—*they'll be fantastic.* He handed the women a pound each, then demanded they leave. Within days, John Reginald Christie would become trapped in that fog with his frumpy wife, with only those photos as a keepsake for his devious fantasies. That photo shoot taunted Reg.

So it wasn't alarming to Kathleen Maloney when, on that cold January day in 1953—a month after the photo shoot—she came across Reg at a fish-and-chips shop and he kindly offered her a place for the night. His wife had just died, he told her. He even gave her some of Ethel's clothes. Kathleen was relieved to see Reg—it was chilly, she had nowhere to sleep, and this kind (if curious) man was a useful solution. She wanted to meet another friend, Catherine Struthers, later that night at the Westminster Arms; *would Reg like to join them?* He assented, and the trio chatted and drank for about an hour before Kathleen put on her black coat to leave with Reg.

"She then asked the man to give her two shillings," said Struthers. "He did this, and she handed it to me for a drink."

It was Kathleen's final, kind gesture toward a loyal friend.

She was quite tipsy now—she had consumed the equivalent of thirteen ounces of liquor. It was incredible she could even walk. She stumbled to the number 27 bus stop, bound for Notting Hill. Her companion kept her steady. The rest of the night was blurry—the scenes were scattered.

Reg led her inside the dirty flat, back to the secluded kitchen; he sat her in a deck chair—she was so befuddled, she didn't know what was happening. There was a cord behind her shoulder, hanging from the back of the chair, and then a strong smell—vile coal gas. The cord wrapped around her neck. He was on top of her, taking off her clothes. Between the gas and the spirits from the pub, Kathleen was helpless—then dead. He left her lying in the chair, stiff, with the cord around her neck. He walked behind her to the parlor. He must have fallen asleep.

He returned to her the next morning, stepped around her prone body, and put some water on the stove for tea. Studying the scene for a moment, Reg pulled the boards off the cupboard and peered inside the alcove. It was dark, it smelled musty. There was plenty of room; it would do fine.

When Kathleen vanished from the pubs on Praed Street, no one seemed to care. No missing person reports were filed. No relatives frantically phoned the police. And now she was squeezed inside that small, acrid-smelling coal cupboard, with old bricks trapping her. She lay in the dark upside down—a pillowcase over her face, a blanket around her body, a cord tied around her neck, and her feet bound by a sock, tied in a reef knot. Her mouth was covered.

And it was terrifying because she wasn't alone. She and the other one were crammed together, so closely that their heads touched on the hard ground, their feet pointed toward the ceiling—like two pieces of timber stacked inside a woodshed.

Kathleen's companion was twenty-five-year-old Rita Nelson, a pretty blonde Irish girl with lively brown eyes from Belfast. She had also been living out a sad story, filled with prostitution convictions and nights fueled by alcohol. But her life had some bright spots. Rita visited frequently with her sister, who also lived in London. She had a stable place to live.

Like Kathleen, Rita was a mother; she had a two-year-old named George who lived in Northern Ireland. And now she was six months pregnant. Her life might have worked out eventually—but then she met John Reginald Christie one afternoon in mid-January, likely within weeks of Kathleen Maloney's murder. Rita chatted with her girlfriend as they sat in a café in Notting Hill Gate. The place was so crowded; it was difficult to find a seat. Someone slid out a chair across the table from them—a tall, balding man wearing glasses. There was nowhere else to sit. They ignored him and continued their conversation as he quietly watched them, and listened.

Rita hoped to move out of her rented room. It was furnished, and the landlady was kind. Rita was a good tenant—she paid her rent a week in advance. But she and her friend wanted a change.

Then Rita made the first of two terrible mistakes. She turned to the stranger, the man across the table, and asked for a cigarette. He handed it to her and admitted he was eavesdropping. He introduced himself, and said he had room in his flat in Notting Hill—he would likely be moving out soon. *Would they like to see it?*

He seemed sincere, or they wouldn't have agreed to go. They had no idea that he had tried this with numerous other women—he offered them a place to stay, to lure them home. But ignorant of the danger he posed, the pair arranged to visit him later that evening.

Rita's second mistake was that she arrived alone.

She looked sweet in her blue cardigan and pretty dress, standing outside his door. He offered her something to drink—whisky or port, if she wanted some. She accepted and walked around the flat, sipping from the glass and inspecting the three rooms. She stepped through the parlor, with the uneven boards. She looked at the gas stove in the kitchen, just feet from the coal cupboard, now newly covered with wallpaper. The flat was quite dirty, but it would do.

"She said it would help her and her friend," he remembered.

What happened next must have been so clouded for Rita. She was sprawled out in his deck chair in the kitchen. And there was that strong, pungent smell, like gas—she blacked out. Something tightened around her throat. A bone in her neck cracked. He violated her as she lay dying.

The kitchen could be quite cold in the winter, but the warmth of the fire would help. They were both so cramped inside there, hiding together in the small coal cupboard—it was only four feet wide and less than six feet deep. They lay there silent, breathless, waiting to be discovered. The women were so similar, though this was their first encounter. They had so many things in common—unpleasant things. Their fates had converged, thanks to him. He was the reason they met here. Now Rita was lost in the darkness, next to Kathleen. Together they were entombed in a coal cupboard, hidden deep inside the home of a monster. And he still wasn't finished.

CHAPTER TEN

Buried

I leant upon a coppice gate
When Frost was spectre-grey,
And Winter's dregs made desolate
The weakening eye of day.
The tangled bine-stems scored the sky
Like strings of broken lyres,
And all mankind that haunted nigh
Had sought their household fires.

—*Thomas Hardy, "The Darkling Thrush," 1900*

There was no warning—no way to save themselves, really. The weather doomed them that day; the air was heavy and wet, and their homes offered no protection. It was a national disaster, mass panic—but it wasn't another deadly fog. This time, it was the Atlantic Ocean that was causing such suffering and hardship. The damage was more sudden, more dramatic...but as devastating as it was, it still wasn't as deadly as the fog, even if the government wouldn't admit it yet.

Still, the way they died was terrible. On January 31, 1953, as the North Sea churned with spring tides, a deep depression in the Atlantic spawned massive gale winds. The weather system pushed north over Scotland, and raced southeast down the coast of England. Winds whirled over England, up to 126 miles per hour. While these gale-force winds were pummeling the coast, the North Sea was also at high tide—a calamitous and deeply unfortunate confluence of events. The gusts, combined with the Atlantic Ocean's waves and the low pressure, caused an unprecedented storm surge, with water levels almost nineteen feet above sea level. Tidal waves slammed into eastern coastal towns in England, as well as parts of Scotland, Belgium, and the Netherlands. The flood damage was devastating.

The water poured through doors and top-floor windows of homes and businesses in Lincolnshire, Norfolk, Suffolk, and Essex. It spilled into the windows of cars, trapping people inside. The waves and wind smashed through weak seawalls, causing a wall of water to rush inland, and killing three hundred and seven people in England. An additional nineteen died in Scotland, twenty-eight in Belgium, and an astonishing eighteen hundred in the Netherlands—half the country was just a few feet above sea level, leaving it vulnerable to massive floods. Queen Elizabeth II rushed to the English coast, offering condolences on behalf of the royal family.

But the deaths were only the beginning of the frustration. The area was devastated, and the British government evacuated more than thirty thousand people. The flood deluged power stations, railways, and gasworks, severely damaging the essential infrastructure of the entire region. It was Britain's worst natural disaster in the twentieth century. And it came with a tremendous cost for the already struggling nation—about fifty million pounds, a crippling debt for a bankrupt government.

The storm damage was calamitous, the result of bad fortune and poor planning. MPs spewed vitriol in the House of Commons—distress and concern masked as contempt. The government, including the previous Labour cabinet, had neglected to set up a proper storm warning system. The wooden, prefabricated postwar buildings, built under the supervision of the Ministry of Housing just a few years before, had crumbled in the waves. Film footage running nightly on television showed scenes of frightened mothers and children crammed into emergency shelters. Day after day, editors stuffed newspapers with stories topped with headlines like: "Flood Havoc in Holland," "Death Toll Mounting," and "Cost of Flood Disaster."

It was crucial that the public see the government reacting quickly and decisively during such a public calamity; it was a stark contrast to Parliament's reaction to the fog, almost two months before. Winston Churchill's cabinet quickly prioritized which rebuilding projects would be fully funded. On March 14, minister of housing Harold Macmillan sent the group a confidential memo, insisting that future flood prevention was the first concern.

"Every necessary expenditure by local authorities on the restoration of coast protection works to their pre-flood condition should be reimbursed in full," wrote Macmillan. "I am sure that the House will not tolerate anything less." The will was there, but the coffers were empty, and getting the money to these projects and people was going to be a challenge.

The first week of February was filled with debates in Parliament, many of them antagonistic. And the bickering exacerbated the already testy relationship between Harold Macmillan and Labour MP Norman Dodds. Their resentment intensified with Macmillan's controversial decision to cancel the requisition of twenty empty houses for flood victims in Erith, in southeast London. Macmillan was absent from the session that day because he was touring the flood damage on the coast—moving slowly from town to town, mostly being carried in a "Duck," an amphibious American military vehicle.

"It was very hard to make out just what was the extent of the Great Flood," Macmillan wrote in his diary. "But it was clear that it was a terrible calamity."

Macmillan's key spokesman, Ernest Marples, took his place in Parliament. Norman rose to ask the parliamentary secretary a question, which quickly evolved into an interrogation.

"Does the right honorable gentleman appreciate that there are *hundreds* of people—men, women, and children—in church halls and that this type of accommodation is not suitable for more than twenty-four or forty-eight hours?" demanded Norman. His fellow Labour MPs screamed "Shame!" toward Marples before he had even had a chance to respond.

"We ask that without further delay these twenty houses, which are now empty, will be used," said Norman.

It was a small point in the overall scheme of the disaster, but it was symbolic. And Norman enjoyed winning a few symbolic victories—they showed tenacity, especially when they were wins against unpopular ministers. Norman knew that, to get things done in a bureaucracy, a politician needed to move public opinion first—and then lawmakers would likely follow.

Marples, bracing for a long, arduous session, calmly explained that the housing minister's decision was a practical one. He hadn't canceled the requisitioning of the homes, insisted Marples, because he had never given his permission to begin with.

"The short-term problem is to get these unfortunate people into furnished accommodation," explained Marples, "because when a person is wet through and has lost his possessions he does not want an unfurnished house." It was a good point, and, as usual, Marples made it eloquently. Norman wasn't an expert debater, but he was determined—and he had supporters behind him.

"Answer the question!" yelled scores of Labour MPs. Marples faced the jeers and stayed composed—at least in the House of Commons. That evening, Marples made an urgent call to Harold Macmillan, who was in Hunstanton, a seaside town in Norfolk, England, still touring flood damage.

"I got a telephone call (the telephone had just been repaired) about a row in the House of Commons in my absence," Harold Macmillan wrote in his diary. "Poor Marples had (it seems) a rough time...which was caused by Mr. Dodds."

Macmillan was convinced that Labour was turning a natural disaster into a political scrap. And he blamed Norman, who was quickly becoming more than just an occasional bother.

"The Socialists are still trying to make capital out of the disaster, of course," Macmillan mused.

Norman's designation as a provocateur for Labour was one of his most important roles in Parliament. It clearly vexed the Conservatives, particularly Macmillan. Much of the arguing over the flood, the fog, and just about any subject was created for political strategy. And despite the hostility in Parliament, the government did act swiftly in the flood's aftermath. There were studies on strengthening coastal defenses, and proposals to build storm-surge barriers on the River Thames and the River Hull. The government quickly offered funds to help rebuild and relocate families. Norman agreed with the decisions—that was also one of his duties, to help promote unity in Parliament during a national catastrophe.

But when the debates shifted to air pollution, he was happily a pest. The cabinet's speedy reaction to the East Coast floods nagged at Norman. The government was adept at crisis management, yet there had been no rapid response after the fog last December. Both disasters had resulted in tremendous loss of life, but the death tolls were so different. The flood had killed fewer than four hundred in Britain, while the fog had murdered thousands. *Who cared for* those *victims?* The government had been passive over air pollution—and now Norman was ready to awaken Conservative lawmakers.

With the emergence of this new disaster, the fog quickly vanished from the Order Papers in Parliament and faded from the newspaper headlines. Certainly the media was partly to blame. Footage of despondent, homeless survivors, wading through their homes and collecting ruined belongings, was broadcast across the city—the visuals were indelible. Norman knew why the fog didn't receive the same attention: film of Londoners hacking and feeling their way through clouds of smoke evoked little empathy. All Britons endured fogs; they had for centuries. The East Coast floods, an unparalleled natural disaster, were threatening to usurp December's fog as the country's leading tragedy. Norman refused to let that happen.

⁊

They lay in the dark, just the two of them, for weeks. It was dusty and cold in that old coal cupboard. Soon after they died, the smell had become putrid. Then, on March 6, there was a bit of light. Someone ripped down part of the wall and opened the door to their hiding place—perhaps a suspicious investigator. Maybe the police would finally catch him, and unveil his depravity.

But it was only the man again. He stood in the darkness of the entryway, dragging along another companion to keep them company. He didn't even bother shrouding this one—she was still wearing her blue bra and black stockings, her hands tied with a white handkerchief. He heaved her toward the opening— he wasn't strong enough to carry her. He tossed her on the ground. She slumped, her back facing him, like a tattered rag doll discarded by an ungrateful child. Her head drooped. A deep, dark indentation circled her neck. He began sealing all three of them back up again, behind the wall.

The woman was twenty-seven-year-old Hectorina MacLennan, a Scottish girl born in Glasgow. Like Kathleen and Rita, she had illegitimate children—two of them were living with her parents in Scotland. Ina, as she was called, had had a complicated life even before she met the stranger. She bounced between two men, one married and the other in prison. It was a familiar story—a vulnerable woman, unstable and overwhelmed with life in London, struggling just to stay safe.

In early 1953, Ina met him in front of a cinema in Hammersmith—a tall, slender man who offered to sublet his flat in Notting Hill. Ina visited the nasty place, towing along her boyfriend. The stranger seemed irked.

"I told you not to tell anyone," he snapped at her. "I don't want a lot of people making inquiries about the flat." He reluctantly served them tea, and then offered to let them stay for a few nights. Ina and the stranger slept near each other in his kitchen, in two chairs, while her boyfriend lay on a mattress in the back bedroom. *It would be inappropriate for you two to sleep in the same bed,* he told them. *My wife, Ethel, might walk in and become upset.* Little did they know they were sleeping just feet away from Ethel, still tucked under the floorboards. The man gained Ina's trust, slowly. The couple even left some personal items there, intending to return later.

Then Ina blundered, a small misstep, just like his other victims. That Friday, she arrived at his flat alone. His method and tools were nearly infallible by now—the deck chair, the coal gas pumped through a rubber tube, the ligature, and the disposal. She had scratches on her back, from being dragged. Before evening arrived that Friday, Hectorina MacLennan became yet another package, stuffed inside the coal cupboard. He didn't have time to wrap her in blankets or a pillowcase. Unfortunately, Ina arrived with some inconveniences.

Unlike the others, she was missed. That same day, just hours after he killed her, there was a quick knock at his door. It was her boyfriend, demanding to know if Ina had kept her appointment at the flat. He had waited for her at a café for nearly three hours, he complained. *Come in and look around*, the man replied. The boyfriend moved from room to room, through the parlor and into the kitchen. He stood so close to her, just feet away. He was confused, then perturbed. The stranger offered to help him search in Shepherd's Bush, just a few blocks away. The door closed, the lock turned. And now the three women were abandoned once again.

$$\infty$$

The British government's swift reaction to the January floods that destroyed homes and lives in parts of Northern Europe was justified, of course. The cause of the tragedy was evident and the remedy was clear. But there was no such consensus in the months after the December 1952 fog. Agreement on just what had caused the fog—and how to prevent it in the future—was in danger of getting locked up in politics, bureaucracy, and government inaction. The government hoped the public's ambivalence about air pollution would continue. Norman Dodds watched as each week passed and a new disaster took the fog's rightful spot on the front pages of the country's newspapers. There was always another crisis, another big story—the threat of the fog would virtually recede in collective memory. The moment to act for change would be lost. At least, until the next cold snap. But

Norman was determined to force Parliament to focus on air pollution.

By early spring, inside the government buildings on Whitehall the Tory ministers were sorting through a blizzard of reports about the fog, hoping to answer two substantial questions: the first was whether the fog was even responsible for thousands of deaths—*was there definitive proof?* And the second: *which component of the fog had proved to be so deadly?*

The opposition, led by Norman, arrived at Parliament daily, armed with accusations. MPs demanded an independent inquiry, headed by independent experts who didn't have a stake in the results. But Churchill's ministers took their time to coalesce— they sparred over the government's message. *Was coal the real killer?*

The General Register Office, the department in charge of collecting statistics on victims, offered some advice. A researcher suggested a way for the Ministry of Health to redirect the blame away from home fireplaces, packed with the government's cheap coal.

"It may be very important to establish, if it *can* be established, whether the deaths can fairly be charged to some more specialized sources than the domestic fires," wrote a GRO officer to a doctor with the Ministry of Health. *Other causes? Like what?* The officer suggested that perhaps the government might find something else to blame for the fog—a cause that might be less *expensive* to correct. Again, the Ministry of Health restricted its purview to the impact of the fog on the health of Londoners, not the source of the pollution.

But the Labour Party continued to hammer Conservative MPs publicly. By early spring, they were targeting the majority of Churchill's ministers in Parliament, during a barrage of aggressive questioning. The minister of fuel and power was pummeled day after day over cheap, dusty nutty slack—even members of his own party demanded detailed answers. By February of 1953, the government released more than one million tons of the fuel for sale to the public—and Britons bought nearly 20 percent of the stock within three months. Nutty slack was dirty, it burned poorly, and MPs griped to the fuel and power minister that it was too costly (in more ways than one) for the price his countrymen were paying for the stuff.

"Is the Minister aware that to charge more than 5 shillings a hundredweight for this rubbish is bare-faced robbery?" asked Labour MP Willie Hamilton. "Can he indicate the co-relation between the derationing of this nutty slack and the increase in fogs in the London area?"

Geoffrey Lloyd avoided both questions, and then promptly promoted the cheap fuel.

"I am myself a user of nutty slack," contended Lloyd, "and in my opinion it is useful, particularly in this cold weather, to eke out supplies of ordinary coal."

The National Smoke Abatement Society, the government's intrepid antagonist, set out to discover the true cost of using this "cheap" fuel. The government had rejected the society's request for funding earlier in the month; so, in response, the members published a scathing survey of the fog in the Society's popular quarterly journal, *Smokeless Air*. In it there were details about pollution levels, meteorological conditions, medical reports, and financial predictions. The fog would cost London millions of pounds—there would be massive bills, thanks to grounded planes, extra police, overworked hospital staff, and lost wages for most industries, which were shut down for five days. The report was circulated throughout Parliament. Now, MPs demanded that the minister of fuel and power respond to the Society's accusations, particularly its sharp attack on nutty slack.

"Does the right honourable gentleman still maintain that the use of nutty slack, which seems to produce smoke without fire, is having no effect whatsoever on the pollution of the air over our great towns and cities?" asked a Labour MP pointedly.

The government still defended nutty slack, albeit less fiercely, claiming it was the "best the government could offer right now"—a slightly less full-throated voice of support than they had offered just a few weeks before.

"Of course, it is the fact that coal, even good coal, produces smoke, and it is a matter of degree," Minister of Fuel and Power Geoffrey Lloyd replied, "but it also produces warmth, which is very much required at the present time." He added: "This particular coal has needlessly got a bad reputation in regard to that particular fog."

Each session, Norman Dodds and his smoke abatement supporters castigated the Conservative government. One Tory demanded to know why three million tons of good-quality coal was reserved for large industry, rather than domestic fireplaces. A Labour MP questioned whether housing minister Harold Macmillan had reviewed America's report on the Donora, Pennsylvania, smog—the one requested by Norman Dodds.

"The results of the Donora report have been studied and are being borne in mind," replied Macmillan's parliamentary secretary, in a clipped and (some felt) dismissive voice. The minister of housing was working quickly to complete the prime minister's deadline of building three hundred thousand houses per year. Macmillan realized that his future in politics could depend on the project's success. The prime minister vowed that Britons would soon have new homes.

"Churchill says it is a gamble—make or mar my political career," wrote Macmillan in his diary in October 1951. "But every humble home will bless my name, if I succeed." The minister of housing was focused on his main task, a very important one: building new houses for a country still climbing out of rubble.

In the spring, Churchill's entire cabinet was asked essentially the same question most days: *What is the government doing about air pollution?* The answer was consistently ambiguous: *We're conducting research and gathering committees, but both take time to reach conclusions.* Internally, the ministries now settled on a message: "Investigations are continuing."

The minister of fuel and power, the MP charged with monitoring the main sources of pollution, was especially vulnerable to public accusations. So, to allay his anxiety, he called a meeting with the Ministry of Health and the Ministry of Housing.

"The Minister was greatly concerned at the suggestions that the marketing of 'nutty slack' was associated with a fog producing an abnormally high death rate," read the minutes of the February 24 meeting. "In fact, the distribution of this fuel had not begun at the time of the fog."

That was patently false—the government had begun marketing nutty slack about two weeks *before* the start of the fog. And the coal dust went on sale December 1, four days before the anticyclone arrived in London.

The ministers then discussed diesel exhaust from vehicles, like the new double-decker buses, and whether it might have also contributed to the deadly fog. *No*, said a doctor with the Ministry of Health: although the exhaust sometimes contained a high content of finely divided carbon, there was as yet no evidence to suggest that the latter had carcinogenic properties. That was also false.

A few weeks later, on March 28, the Ministry of Housing sent a confidential note to Minister of Health Iain Macleod.

"There is now an urgent need for a comprehensive review of the problem, covering effects, causes and cure, and that this might best be undertaken by an interdepartmental committee," read the memo. "The setting up of such a committee would help to allay public disquiet about the dangers of the fog, and the publication of its report would make it clear to the general public just what could and could not be done to eliminate pollution."

The minister of health quickly refused to be on the new committee—in fact, he requested that Harold Macmillan omit his name from the announcement. Once again, Iain Macleod was drawing a line—the health minister would not be pulled into a public row involving the cause of the smog. And he refused to be rushed, even in the House of Commons.

Near the end of March, Parliament slogged through a debate that dragged on for more than five hours; MPs revived arguments over how East Coast flood victims would be compensated— and the strain between Norman Dodds and the housing minister intensified. Norman and Macmillan each pontificated in thirty-minute segments, trading barbs in polite terms, constrained by the formal rules of Parliament. But as the contest escalated, each man seemed to agitate the other more. The content of the debate wasn't as important as *how* they debated.

"Unless much more is done to correct those things which have not been done properly, there will be many more of these debates," snapped Norman.

Macmillan countered with gibes about the Labour MP's "character and tone of his attacks upon us ever since this matter started." The dispute finally concluded, amid clapping and taunts, with the House of Commons ultimately supporting the prime minister's plan to distribute funds. But Harold Macmillan had the final word, and he lambasted Norman Dodds.

"I feel myself that since this debate started, there have been opposite me a number of Balaams," declared Macmillan— referring to the wicked prophet in the Bible. "They came to curse, but they stayed to bless. On that Biblical note, I stated earlier that I might even get a blessing from the honourable member for Dartford before I had finished."

Norman stood up. "I always give credit where credit is due." But he was far from sincere. Norman and Macmillan's relationship was periodically argumentative and sporadically cordial but, thanks to the fog, it had devolved into combative. And it would soon become bitter.

Despite the bickering and boasting in Parliament, there was now urgency for both sides—cold weather was less than six months away, and so was, to be certain, another sickening fog. But the media's attention seemed to have shifted to other stories: the flood, the budget, and, soon enough, a serial killer murdering women in London.

⌒♾️⌒

There were just a few, at first—a handful of lurkers who were curious about the framed note tacked to a screen of corrugated iron. It was March 24, right before lunchtime. They glanced at the pair of royal guards, then squinted at the small type, printed on official royal stationery—then they strolled away. A second framed note arrived two hours later, and more Londoners took notice this time. There were hundreds now, concerned faces reading the bulletin outside of Marlborough House, the mansion in Westminster that was home to Queen Elizabeth's grandmother, Queen Mary.

"During the past hours Queen Mary's condition has become more grave. There has been a serious weakening of the heart action which gives rise to increasing anxiety," read the notice.

Later that night, Prime Minister Winston Churchill stood up after the final vote for the evening of Parliament.

"I beg to move 'That this House do now adjourn,'" he said with a strained voice. "I have with great regret to make the announcement that Queen Mary has died."

Queen Mary, the mother of King George VI, had passed away in her sleep at the age of eighty-five. In the House of Commons, MPs bowed their heads. Labour leader Clement Attlee replied, "I am sure the whole House will join in that expression of sorrow."

Despite the feuds imbued with self-promotion, most politicians cherished the royal family. Hundreds now gathered before Marlborough House to read the final notice and lament the queen's death. A line of photographers loitered near the gate, waited for details. Women and children wept—men gripped their hats. They all pushed to the front, just to get a glimpse of the letter.

Queen Mary was a beloved figure, for epitomizing poise and grace under the weight of public scrutiny.

"She discharged the duties of her high station with a dignity which was truly queenly," read her obituary in the *Times*, "and which yet won for her the warm-hearted admiration of the populace."

She had outlived her husband and three of her six children. She had survived two wars with regal nobility. She had watched with concern as one son ascended the throne, and then abdicated to marry an American divorcée. She oversaw her second son's reign of more than fifteen years, only to witness his death in 1952. And she had been readying for her granddaughter Elizabeth to be crowned queen in a few short months. But she was not to live to see Elizabeth's coronation. British flags were lowered to half-mast while newspaper vendors peddled papers with headlines reading, "Death of Queen Mary." It was such a somber occasion for a country anticipating the crowning of

Queen Elizabeth II, scheduled for the summer. Queen Mary had told her family that, in the event of her death, her granddaughter's coronation celebration in June was not to be postponed. It was just three months away.

❧

By March of 1953, life was arduous for John Reginald Christie. He was nearly destitute—and his landlord, Charles Brown, was demanding rent. Reg was three months delinquent. His milk and coal bills were overdue, too. He had drained the couple's bank accounts, even forging Ethel's signature. He allowed his life insurance policy to lapse—there was no one alive to collect the proceeds, anyway. Reg had no more furniture to sell, no jewelry to pawn. His government assistance had run out—he really needed those two pounds a week. Of course, none of that deterred him from prowling Notting Hill, searching for women. He tried to lure them to his flat, those girls he chatted with at local cafés. If he was able to entice them inside, they were quickly frightened off. Reg was soon labeled "the creepy man with the strange laugh." His luck was waning—it was time to leave. Reg had his beloved Irish terrier, afflicted with old age, euthanized.

He met a couple, the Reillys, who were interested in subletting his flat. Reg requested three months' rent in advance, about eight pounds; he even had them sign a lease. During their tour of the flat, Reg pointed to the newly whitewashed area where the coal cupboard stood. "Those repairs I did myself," he said. Mrs. Reilly sniffed.

"I noticed a peculiar smell in the place," she later said. "We tried to open the cupboard in the kitchen, but found that we could not. So we left it."

His agreement with the Reillys was illegal—Reg knew his

landlord would never allow them to stay. It didn't matter. He handed Mr. Reilly the keys and shoved some papers, clothes, and trinkets into a borrowed brown suitcase. He stepped into the hallway, shut the door, and turned the key one last time. On March 20, 1953, John Reginald Christie disappeared from the doorway of 10 Rillington Place.

～～

Rosemary Sargent's younger sister Sue was slipping on her Brownie uniform, carefully pulling up the brown knee-length socks, gripping the trademark woolen beret. Rosemary helped her straighten the tunic dress, adorned with badges and patch pockets. When they finished, Sue looked at her older sister and asked a simple question.

"Where's Dad?"

Their father had passed away months earlier, but there were still no discussions about his death, the nasty fog, or the vacant parlor.

Rosemary was surprised, then confused.

"I told you—he died," she replied.

Sue's eyes widened. "No, I thought he was in hospital."

The little girl said a friend down the road had walked over to her earlier in the day and declared: "Your dad is dead."

Sue didn't believe her, but she was confused. She remembered staying at Mrs. Hatham's house, with her best friend, for so many days after the fog lifted.

"Didn't you think it was strange that you stayed there so long?" asked Rosemary, gently.

"No, I just thought he was in hospital," replied Sue. She began to cry.

After their father died, Sue slept with their mother every

night; Edna wanted the little girl to keep her company. The six-year-old loathed not having her own room, and now she was sleeping in the bed where her father had once lain. Rosemary pitied her little sister, but there was nothing she could do.

⌒⌒

Beresford Brown stared at the wall, trying to sort out the project. It was March 24 and he wanted to hang a wireless set in the small kitchen, so he could listen to music while he cooked. The wall needed to be solid, or the metal brackets would pop right out. He tapped and listened. The top section sounded promising, but as Brown moved his knuckles down the wall, the sound began to thump like a hollow log.

"There must be a cellar of some sort on the corner of the kitchen," Brown thought.

He started peeling off the wallpaper, peering inside a six-inch hole in the door. "It was a cellar." But he couldn't quite see inside. He went to his own flat upstairs to search for a flashlight.

Beresford Brown stood in the flat that had belonged to John Reginald Christie—the strange man on the ground floor who had complained constantly. None of the residents of 10 Rillington Place had seemed disappointed to watch him pack up his sorry suitcase and leave four days earlier. The landlord, however, was livid that Reg had tried to illegally sublet his flat. Charles Brown evicted the Reillys just days after they moved in.

A few days later, Charles' wife chatted with Beresford Brown, another Rillington Place resident who had lived above Reg for a few months, and gave him permission to use Reg's kitchen while the apartment was empty. So here Brown stood, peering into the once-hidden cellar in the ground-floor flat. He flicked on his flashlight. He stuck his hand inside the hole and looked down.

The flashlight illuminated the cupboard—the light bounced off Ina's pale skin. She glowed.

∾

Everything happened very quickly after that. Within hours, 10 Rillington Place was swarming with Metropolitan police processing the scene and peering into every dusty corner of the small, dilapidated flat. A police photographer snapped pictures; he was the same officer who had taken photos of Beryl and Geraldine Evans after investigators discovered them in the washhouse three years before. Cops stood in front of the building, protecting the entrance from gawkers. CID, the Met's criminal investigation department, sent a team of detectives to gather evidence.

Those three women inside that coal cupboard stayed crammed in there for hours, while police jotted down notes. Then, one by one, they were pulled out and laid on the kitchen floor. Reg's alcove provided almost perfect conditions for preservation. It was cool and dry with a bit of airflow. Investigators waited for the pathologist. Once he had finished prodding them, they were shoved into body bags. Then detectives, with their lit pipes still gripped between their teeth, carried them through the front door and into a horde of news photographers.

The cameras were close to the police van, just a few feet away. A wave of neighbors nudged forward, and then two more bodies followed behind. Reporters scribbled notes, called out questions. The press was frenzied—journalists begged for any tidbits. *What happened? Are there more?* Later that night, Chief Inspector Albert Griffin carefully stepped through the parlor. It was cramped and dark, so empty. It was hard to imagine that anyone could live in that flat—there were papers, rubbish lying all over, ash and dirt. Griffin scanned the walls, looking for fresh wallpaper in the parlor—nothing there, really, but a portrait of Reg, dressed in his policeman's uniform. The fireplace was empty. He glanced down and noticed something odd— loose floorboards.

"I lifted the floorboards and noticed that the earth under the floor had been disturbed," said Griffin. "I later made a further examination and discovered another body which was completely buried in the earth two feet six inches below the floor."

There were more photographs, more measurements, and plenty of notes. Police took samples of the dirt and coal ashes. Ethel Christie lay there, wrapped tightly like a mummy. She had been secluded under those floorboards for more than three months, and she would have to wait in that hole for twelve more hours, while young police constables stepped around her. Griffin looked out the kitchen window, the one overlooking the back garden—Reg's private plot.

Three days later, officers from Notting Hill station arrived to dig. Their sergeant stood inside in the flat, watching them as they thrust shovels into the ground. That was his job, to ensure that his officers were properly digging through the dirt, identifying important pieces of evidence during a sort of grid search. They dropped various bits into boxes, categorized them— squinted at every tiny item. News photographers stood atop nearby buildings, clicking their shutters, capturing scenes of investigators sorting through mounds of evidence.

Police easily unearthed the remains of Ruth Fuerst and Muriel Eady in the small garden. They were barely covered with dirt. But they were so degraded that they came out in pieces—chunks of bone, an assortment of teeth, clumps of hair mixed with weeds, shards of newspaper, and chipped flowerpots. The dis-

covery of the teeth was important. Pathologists eventually identified Ruth by her metal crown, one they determined had been
made either in Germany or a country close by—Ruth was in
fact Austrian. Their flesh had rotted long ago, but the officers
found a skull, shattered into almost one hundred pieces. They
used sifters to sort out the rubbish. There were bones everywhere, not just human. The garden contained skeletons of codfish, chickens, turkeys, rabbits, rats, cats, dogs—even sheep and
cattle. And investigators finally noticed that femur bone propping up the fence: Muriel's leg, which had been hidden in plain
sight for years. The officers divided the garden into sections, to
keep the locations straight. The sergeant left his officers, walked
into the home, and strolled through the flat. He stood in the parlor and stared at the hole in the floor. He remembered that day
in January, when he had shaken the man's hand.

"What a rotten stink that is," the policeman had complained.

"Well, it's all these coloured people and their strange cooking," the man had replied. "It makes a terrible smell."

Len Trevallion now realized he had stood over Ethel Christie
that day—he had been just inches above her. The sergeant
walked out of the parlor. He moved toward the kitchen and
looked over at the hole in the wall, where the women had been
entombed. He now realized he had been casually chatting with
a freak, a depraved serial killer who preyed on the most vulnerable, the weakest, and discarded them with little care and no
conscience.

Len peered out the window toward the garden, tried to concentrate on the digging. But he spotted something—a shiny box.
It lay atop a pile of rubbish. His officers, exhausted from their
digging, didn't seem to notice it amid the mounds of junk. He
swung open the back door, walked over, and bent down. He
recognized the label. It was a small Gold Leaf tobacco tin, cop

per colored. Len held it in his palm, then carefully pried open the lid. He stared down. Crammed inside were dozens of tiny pieces of hair—pubic hair.

꧁꧂

What came next was terrible anxiety, spreading across the city—provoked by salacious newspaper reports. "Three Women Found Dead in Flat," read the headline of the *Times.* The story was published before the discovery of Ethel Christie's body was reported to the press.

"The police were anxious to trace John Reginald Christie, a road haulage clerk, who might be able to assist in the inquiry," read the report. "Aged 55, height, 5ft. 9in., slim build, dark hair thin on top, clean shaven, sallow complexion, long nose, wearing horn-rimmed spectacles, dentures top and bottom, walks with military bearing." At the bottom of the story was an important paragraph—information that would change so much about British law.

"In December, 1949, Mrs. Beryl Evans, aged 19, and her daughter Geraldine, aged 14 months, were found strangled in an outhouse at the same address. In March, 1950, Mrs. Evans' husband, Timothy John Evans, aged 25, a lorry driver, was hanged for the murder of his child." *Was there ... could there be ... a connection?*

But that story would have to wait—there was a killer stalking London. The daily headlines were so alarming: "Nationwide Search for Tenant of Murder Flat," said the *Daily Telegraph.* "Murder Unlimited," read another. Papers around the world printed lengthy pieces. "Police Hunting for 'Man with Inane Laugh' " read the *Sydney Morning Herald.*

The media nicknamed Reg "the Notting Hill Killer" and

"Jack the Strangler." And some newspapers simply stoked fears with headlines like "Search for Moon-Mad Killer." It claimed that Scotland Yard detectives were desperate to arrest Reg in the next forty-eight hours, before the full moon would trigger another killing spree.

"A new examination of the mutilated bodies suggests he is mentally deranged and addicted to uncontrollable passion," claimed one paper. Reg never mutilated the bodies—pathologists would later conclude that he never even hit the women. The press craved a lewd story, but as the first bodies were being removed, journalists weren't particularly interested in the facts.

Now hundreds of Met officers fanned out all over London in one of the largest manhunts in British history. Scotland Yard sent an express message to police departments, ordering all districts to search for Reg.

"I have to inform you that Hotels and Boarding Houses in this town have been visited in an attempt to trace John Reginald Halliday Christie, so far without success," Brighton's chief constable replied. "Search has been made of the Missing Persons files here."

And families of missing girls sent messages, begging police to investigate their cases. The police collected hundreds of telegrams, letters, and phone calls—all from people claiming to have spotted John Reginald Christie. Officers stored bags of notes, and some might have included legitimate leads. But others were simply so absurd, they were amusing. There was a lengthy letter from about a clairvoyant who claimed to have visions of the victims. The writer referenced quotes from the woman, pulled from a newspaper story.

"The first was that of a young girl sitting at a table," the clairvoyant said in the article, "a man was leaning over her."

A man from Amsterdam claimed he could track down Reg

using a color system based on the women's names, if only the police could send him a list of possible locations where their suspect might be. Police chased down leads, including one concerning note found in a garden in Milton Common, about an hour from London by bus: "Any person who finds this communicate with New Scotland Yard. I am a prisoner in 10 Rillington Place, London."

Another letter read: "You will never get me. I am leaving England, good-bye, Staring Eyes." The signature referenced an unflattering description of Reg at cafés—served as a nickname, of sorts, like Jack the Ripper.

Most of the information made no sense and, as the search dragged on for a week, the public's anxiety peaked. Londoners stared at copies of newspapers, with Reg's picture on the cover. He was spotted everywhere—on subway platforms, in cafés and hotels all over the city and even across the country; the police had a hard time keeping up. One woman claimed he was a crossing guard in Notting Hill.

"I cannot remember his face very well," she said, "but I remember his hands. I remember his thumb."

The families of the victims arrived at Kensington Mortuary and identified each of their bodies—including Ethel's brother, Henry Waddington. Rita Nelson's sister looked at her corpse— they had not communicated for three months. Hectorina MacLennan's two brothers identified her body. No family arrived for Kathleen Maloney, so a male acquaintance confirmed her identity for police. It was such a painful process. The angst even spilled into the House of Commons, during a debate over reform of the British press. Frustrated MPs wanted to limit the rights of journalists.

"How is the public to deal with the sordid, squalid and revolting accounts of the Christie case which have monopolised pages and pages of our evening and daily press in the last few weeks?" asked an exasperated Labour MP.

Met officers guarded 10 Rillington Place, as the terrible address took on the dark glamour of infamy. Miscreants were stealing bricks from the building and selling them as souvenirs. The outside of the flat served as a photo opportunity for tourists. Hundreds of people stood on the sidewalk, staring at the "Murder House." Beresford Brown, the man who had discovered the bodies, received a threatening anonymous letter warning him to leave London. The other tenants abandoned the building—no one wanted to live in the "House of Horrors."

Five days after the search began for Reg, the *New York Times* reported "the discovery of what seemed to be the bones of a sixth woman victim added horror tonight to London's gruesome crime sensation—the Notting Hill house of murder." Police had finally found Muriel Eady, Reg's second victim. Ruth Fuerst had been discovered first.

Once again, December's deadly fog was nowhere in the newspapers. A serial killer on the run now overshadowed a mass murderer that had slaughtered thousands.

⚭

He was so exhausted—and he was ready to return home, back to 10 Rillington Place. After leaving his flat on March 20, Reg wandered to King's Cross—and just stood there, on the street. He stopped a man walking by and asked if he could recommend cheap accommodations. The man suggested Rowton House, once described as a "workingman's hotel" where a laborer could get a bed with clean sheets, a nice washroom, and access to a large dining hall. When Reg visited, poor pensioners slept there because it offered nicer quarters than other institutional facilities. The National Assistance Board referred many people with a small budget.

He walked inside the large corner building and requested a room. When the manager asked for his details, he replied: *John Reginald Christie, 10 Rillington Place*, then provided his identity card number. He carried papers with him—his marriage certificate, his St John's Ambulance badge, two ration books, and his Queens Park Rangers Football Club badge. He didn't lie—he wasn't trying to hide anything. He didn't seem to have the energy for dishonesty. Before leaving Rillington Place, he had gathered some meager items, but things that were special to him. Inside the case were photographs and extra pairs of spectacles, along with a woman's scarf and gloves.

The manager looked him over and agreed to give him a bed for a week. Reg stayed quietly at Rowton House for four days, and then walked out with no notice. He was restless. He wandered the city for three more days, toting along his brown suitcase. He sat in cafés, puffed on his cigarettes as he walked. Reg soon found himself in East Ham in Newham, miles away from Rowton House. He was almost out of money—he asked directions back to Kensington. As he changed routes, he stopped.

"I stood at a crossroad, and all of a sudden I realized a policeman had held the traffic up and had beckoned me to go across," he remembered. "I did not want to go across, but I went across and thanked him as I passed."

He slept on the streets, like a filthy vagrant. Yet he still approached women, hoping to rendezvous with one. No luck. He just couldn't help himself, like a drug addict searching for another high. Reg was desperate now, and incredibly fretful. Whenever he went to a café to eat, the diners were talking about him. He heard "Christie," followed by discussions about the murders. It somehow didn't panic him—he would take off his hat and listen. Even though every policeman in the city was searching for him, no one seemed to notice that he was right there—sitting nearby. Reg was invisible, as he had been for much of his life.

"I just finished in the ordinary way, and had a smoke and finished tea," Reg said, "and I just got up in the ordinary manner and went out."

He walked by a newspaper stand—"Will the Killer Strike Again?" was the headline, in large print. Reg glanced down and continued on. It was nine o'clock Tuesday morning, March 31— one week after Beresford Brown had discovered his secrets in the kitchen. Reg walked along the Lower Richmond Road facing the Thames, near Putney Bridge. He stopped and leaned against the embankment wall.

His arms braced against the concrete as he stared down at the bargemen while they loaded a vehicle—they looked up at him. He stayed silent and sullen.

"He looked tired and sallow and appeared as if he had not washed for some time," said one of the workers. "His face was grimy and he looked as though he had been sleeping out of doors."

Reg could imagine the scene at his home—detectives with shovels and crowbars, disassembling 10 Rillington Place, looking for more victims. He knew he was being closely watched— not by the bargemen, but by a tall, thin police constable, staring at him from a few yards away. It wouldn't be difficult to recognize him, given the incredibly detailed descriptions in the press. Every newspaper printed his picture. The constable walked over to him—Reg stayed still. He was too weary to run, and *why should he?*

"What are you doing, looking for work?" asked PC Thomas Ledger.

"Yes, but my unemployment cards haven't come through," Reg replied.

"Where do you come from?" asked Ledger.

"Paddington."

"What is your name?" asked PC Ledger.

"John Waddington." Waddington was the last name of Ethel's brother, Henry.

"What is your address?"

"35 Westbourne Grove," he replied.

"Have you anything on you to prove your identity?"

"Nothing at all," said Reg.

PC Ledger looked him over.

"Take off your hat."

By this time, several more constables had joined Ledger. They looked at every detail of his face.

"I asked the man if he would accompany me to Putney Police Station as I believed him to be John Christie who could help with certain inquiries," said PC Ledger.

Reg climbed inside the police van, then tossed his wallet at the constable with his identity card inside. And just like that, it was over. Later, when police searched Reg's pockets, they discovered a curious *News of the World* clipping from the winter of 1950. It had the headline "Second Murder Charge Against Young Husband," detailing Reg's testimony against Timothy Evans. The Welshman had been nothing more than a rotten corpse in a prison graveyard for two years—a degenerate killer who had slaughtered his wife and daughter, at least as far as the public was concerned. But soon, Tim Evans and his case would be roused.

CHAPTER ELEVEN

Illumination

A thin grey fog hung over the city, and the streets
were very cold; for summer was in England.
   —*Rudyard Kipling*, The Light That Failed, *1890*

Harry Procter was a Fleet Street provocateur. Part sleuth and
part hack, he humiliated rival journalists as he scooped them
on the latest crime stories in London. Procter boasted that he
would do anything in pursuit of a story; he claimed he had once
ripped a phone from a wall to prevent a rival from making a call.
His editors at the *Sunday Pictorial* revered him, because when
Harry Procter typed up a lurid crime piece, the tabloid's circulation soared.

"Sex, scandal, surprise, sensation, exposure, murder," Procter
would say. "And as many pictures of half-dressed, big-bosomed
damsels in distress as possible."

He was extolled by the public as part of an exclusive club
on Fleet Street, nicknamed the "Murder Gang." They were
star journalists, like Procter, who cultivated sensitive sources,
those elusive to other reporters—informants in Scotland Yard,

the courts, and Parliament. They were all men, dressed in nice suits and trilby hats, with cigarettes dangling from their mouths. Procter, with a pen in hand, talked to sources daily— occasionally running his hand through his dark brown hair, combed in a kind of short, mop-top style. What the Murder Gang lacked in humility, they made up for with ingenuity. They spent evenings typing up salacious stories, then chasing them with shots of whisky and pints of bitter at the King & Keys pub.

At age thirty-six, Procter was already an old-timer on Fleet Street. When he was sixteen, he had become a cub reporter at the *Armley and Wortley News*. Two years later, he was hired at a larger paper in North Yorkshire. He had spent the next four years hopping from paper to paper until he finally arrived on Fleet Street at the *Daily Mirror*. Now, almost fifteen years later, Procter's impact on the *Sunday Pictorial* was indelible.

Crime reporters were luminaries in London; it was such a renowned career that the press had created the Crime Reporters Association in 1945. It had a dual purpose: It was an organized group that could pressure Scotland Yard for better access to information. And it also distinguished its members from less professional writers. Now Harry Procter and the Murder Gang were onto the next big crime story—the biggest in years. When police captured John Reginald Christie at the end of March, a throng descended—there were spectators lurking near his flat, stalking the police stations where he was held, and sitting outside the Old Bailey court—Reg had thousands of gawkers. They approached fanaticism, fixated on a sex-crazed lunatic who stashed bodies around his home. Officers erected barricades for crowd control in front of 10 Rillington Place. Police were posted at his front door. Spectators showed up at Notting Hill police station a few days later to watch Reg being transferred to court for arraignment. He covered his face with a newspaper as photographers poised on roofs snapped pictures. As watchers crammed together outside the court, women lifted children on their shoulders to give them a better view.

The crowd parted to allow Reg's car to pass as he returned to jail for the evening. He dipped down to the floor of the vehicle to avoid the jeers. The public and the press tracked his every move. Newspapers printed new stories in every edition, each with more lurid details than the last. Reg's story could have been a plot from a Victorian penny dreadful—a cheap booklet that fictionalized lewd and bloody crimes, advertised to nineteenth-century London's working class. Reg might have appeared as a killer in *The String of Pearls: A Romance* slaughtering victims alongside Sweeney Todd, the "Demon Barber of Fleet Street."

"The Skeleton Mystery," said a *Daily Express* headline. "Mad Strangler," read another. Reg's trial would become a tabloid obsession, the same sort of case George Orwell chastised in his 1946 essay "Decline of the English Murder."

"Your pipe is drawing sweetly, the sofa cushions are soft underneath you, the fire is well alight, the air is warm and stagnant," wrote Orwell. "In these blissful circumstances, what is it that you want to read about? Naturally, about a murder."

When Harry Procter arrived at 10 Rillington Place in March, when the bodies were first discovered, the building seemed familiar. He remembered he had visited there before, three years earlier, reporting for a rival paper on another murder. In 1949, Reg himself had answered the door when Procter knocked.

"He smiled, a sickeningly, silly smile, and he gave me an unforgettably repulsive handshake, damp and limp," said Procter. "He told me his version of the Evanses' murders, the same version he told the police."

Procter had watched Reg's testimony in the Evans case from the press box, still feeling uneasy about the smarmy neighbor. The two had met again after the verdict, in the hallway of the court—another disturbing encounter.

"He appeared to be very upset because Evans had told the jury he believed Christie to be the real killer," recalled Procter. " 'What a wicked man he is,' rasped Christie."

Now, three years later, Harry Procter stared at John Reginald Christie once again, this time as he waited in the court's dock—the same place where Tim Evans had sat. Reg noticed the reporter and turned toward him.

"He smiled at me as a proud son might smile at his parents on speech day," said Procter. "While details of his atrocious crimes were being read out he was busy writing me notes."

Reg nauseated Harry Procter. The reporter truly believed Christie had killed Beryl and Geraldine Evans, and that Timothy Evans had been wrongly executed for the crime. But Reg and Harry were cohorts now—the celebrated newshound of Fleet Street's Murder Gang had made the serial killer a sickening offer.

❧

MP Norman Dodds tapped on his typewriter slowly, to make sure the words weren't smudged by excitable strikes. It was cold outside, especially for a day in early May. The whole project was taking a while; organizing his thoughts wasn't the problem, it was keeping his contempt tempered.

The issue of the fog was quietly dying in Parliament, drowning under stories about floods, war, and John Reginald Christie, the Notting Hill serial killer. Fog hadn't been on the Order Papers for weeks. Norman thought it was time to resurrect it, immediately. He told Housing Minister Harold Macmillan's secretary to expect a lengthy statement on Friday, May 8, in Parliament. It would be vicious.

"You may have seen that Mr. Norman Dodds, M.P., is going to raise the question of air pollution on the Motion for the Adjournment on Friday of this week," wrote the Ministry of Housing's assistant secretary to the health minister, Iain Macleod. "He tells us that he is going to deal in particular with the bad fog in London last December and that he hopes to get a more comprehensive statement of the Government's intentions than has been made so far. I would be grateful if you would let me have your comments on the draft as soon as possible."

The pressure on the Ministry of Housing was enormous now—there needed to be a cohesive plan, quickly. Health experts at the Ministry of Health agreed to help. They sat down with pencils and marked up Housing's planned speech in Parliament in less than two days. The government didn't deny that the fog was terrible—and deadly. But rather, the Conservatives planned to show that nutty slack—cheap coal—was not the only cause. The fog was, they claimed, an enduring and central tenet of London life itself...and it had been for hundreds of years.

The Ministry of Housing's speech was punctuated with dramatic references to John Evelyn, the seventeenth-century English diarist, who described "that hellish and dismal cloud of sea coal which is perpetually over this august and opulent city of London." Harold Macmillan's department admitted that the cost of smog to the nation was enormous, up to 150 million pounds, almost 190 million U.S. dollars. But Housing insisted that it was "futile to think that air pollution can be abolished overnight, and one must face the technical, economic and administrative difficulties."

The speech then listed off the research conducted through each department, including the Ministry of Health.

"They have been studying the causes of the deaths," read the draft. "It has not yet been possible to establish which particular element or elements in the fog were responsible."

There was a curious statement, written as if it were fact, but one that was clearly wrong. It was about the pollution levels recorded during the fog: "The available records of atmospheric pollution in London during the fog have been carefully examined, *but showed no abnormal concentration of sulphur dioxide or any other element which, according to our present knowledge, would account for the high rates of mortality and illness,*" read the speech. "We do not therefore know as yet which particular element we should concentrate on eliminating."

The claim that there was no data available was false. Five days after the fog blew away, pollution measurement machines spit out the amount of levels of sulphur dioxide and smoke, and those results had made their way into a report—one that had been sent to the Ministry of Health itself. The damning text read: "Sulphur Dioxide was also estimated and whereas the normal November concentration of this gas is between 0.05 and 0.15 parts per million, the concentration rose during the recent fog to between 0.16 and 0.72 ppm," according to the confidential memo. "These values are roughly between 2 and 3 times the 1948 figures." November 1948 had been another terrible, choking fog, one that killed close to eight hundred people. But these December 1952 pollution numbers were many times worse than had been recorded.

That report was the smoking gun. For months, the government had known about the incredibly high levels of sulphur dioxide and smoke in the fog, but now the Ministry of Housing was publicly denying it—the real information was hidden inside a government file.

Few outside the Ministries of Housing and Health knew about this damning report in the spring of 1953, however. Norman Dodds certainly didn't know...though he suspected. And he knew the time to mobilize was now. That's what his speech to Parliament on May 8 was designed to do. It would take more than thirty minutes to deliver. He typed nearly three thousand words, sculpting phrases that married hard facts with shades of frustration and disgust. The speech was so elaborate and dramatic that it nearly demanded a response from the Tory government. At times, he would sound less like a politician and more like a minister, sermonizing from the pulpit to a devout congregation. The synthesis of five months of apathy, acrimony, lies, and pressure would soon spill onto the House of Commons floor. And Norman Dodds would be the catalyst.

෴

John Reginald Christie sat in his cell, looked at the doorway as the officer walked over and plunked the metal tray on the table. Beef and potato stew was often on the menu—a nice treat for a man who hadn't eaten a proper meal for days. His notoriety was only growing now that he'd been located and he turned out to be a rather unprepossessing middle-aged man. Londoners were mystified by him, this mild-mannered fellow sitting like a blandly benign evil spirit in a jail cell under the city. While the reality of Reg was not particularly intimidating, a reader wouldn't know it when she glanced over the lurid tales in the newspapers. Journalists were comparing him to the escaped prisoner Selden, from Sir Arthur Conan Doyle's *The Hound of the Baskervilles.* In the novel, the killer is painted as a frightful, violent monster skulking about a moor in Devonshire. Doyle's escaped killer was spared from the gallows because the courts ruled that he was insane. Reg would use the same defense.

The guard slid the chair over, sat down, and watched his prisoner closely. Investigators with the CID, the Crime Investigation Department, were building a case for Crown prosecutors—sifting through evidence, interviewing witnesses. Reg's defense team readied its defense. And Britain's most well-known, most reviled killer rested in his cell, deep in the cellar of the Notting Hill police station.

The Met's uniformed officers often doubled as jail guards, supervising a prisoner during mealtime to thwart suicide attempts; a suspect, convinced he was destined to spend his remaining years in prison, might be tempted to smash a glass or shatter a plate, then use the shards to do himself in. When the guard sat down, he looked over at Reg and saw his face brighten, just a bit. The suspect had quickly recognized Sergeant Len Trevallion. *You were in my flat months ago, about the biscuit thief.* There was a familiarity, some sort of kinship between two police officers—at least, that was Reg's view.

Len considered him another despicable Notting Hill criminal—just like Timothy Evans three years earlier. But the sergeant listened to Reg, carefully. There, in the relative privacy of the Notting Hill jail cell, the prisoner unspooled a tale that he suspected would captivate Len. The bottom-floor flat of 10 Rillington Place was actually a backstreet abortion center for local prostitutes, he told the officer.

"It was Ethel who performed the abortions," recalled Len, "with Christie acting as an anesthetist and assistant, when necessary."

Reg claimed that over the years, the couple had performed many abortions—Ethel considered it a public service to prevent unwanted children. That was why he had devised his unique method of sedating the women with gas in the deck chair, said Reg. Ethel would then treat the "patients," and they would recover in the parlor while she cleaned up in the kitchen. Ethel botched some of these abortions and the girls died—accidentally.

Len listened to his story while the prisoner picked at the food. Reg didn't admit that he had raped them, even though the pathologist confirmed there was evidence he had. He never acknowledged that they were strangled, either, or that, crucially, pathologists found no evidence of attempted abortions on any of the women's bodies. Only Rita Nelson had been pregnant, six months along with a boy. Beryl Evans' murder had not yet been connected to Reg. Police also found no medical tools in the flat that would have suggested that abortions were performed. Len didn't bother pressing him for details—the Crown prosecutors were gathering their own information for trial. Reg continued chatting, and he recounted the day he killed his wife. According to his story, Ethel walked into the parlor and saw him molesting one of her abortion patients.

"Horrified, she threatened to report him to the police," recalled Len. "Christie said that at this point he had finally realized the enormity of what he had been doing and had been deeply ashamed."

Reg claimed that he had tried to convince Ethel to change her mind, that she was an accomplice to illegal abortions. But she was so disgusted with him, he said, that she refused to listen. He strangled her that morning. Reg then claimed that the three women, hidden in his coal cupboard, were prostitutes who had knocked on his door, requesting abortions.

"He had no wish to put Ethel's family through any further distress," said Len, "and would therefore not be blaming her for the abortions or the deaths. She was dead and, if his defence failed, he also soon would be dead. There was nothing to be gained by introducing such details unnecessarily."

Reg was nearly self-congratulatory as he described his circumstances to the sergeant. Len seemed like a fitting confidant for Reg. He was a police officer, but not a member of CID—he wasn't part of the investigation team analyzing the case. And Len had no reason to caution Reg of his rights; none of his story was admissible in court. He was free to say whatever he wished, for whatever reason. It was such a strange story, though. Reg sat back and looked at Len. He reminded the sergeant about their visit in his parlor months earlier, when the officer had stood above Ethel Christie. Reg remembered Len's concern about the rotten smell as he walked among the dirt and trash of his parlor.

Reg grinned.

"Now you know what it really was."

⁓

Norman Dodds sat patiently on the bench, eyeing his watch's hands as they ticked. He gripped his speech and watched the other MPs as they argued during lengthy debates over a bill that would establish a council to oversee the British press. There was also a row over a bill that would give separated or divorced women more financial autonomy. For Norman, his speech about the fog was the Big Moment of the day...but to the rest of the MPs, it was just one item on a long list of bureaucratic to-dos. Finally, Norman had his turn.

He was exhausted and resentful, when the Speaker finally called on him. He stood, and looked across the aisle. After all that buildup, Harold Macmillan wasn't there. In his place once again was his parliamentary secretary, Ernest Marples. A disappointment for Norman, yes—especially because he'd given notice to the Ministry of Housing ahead of time about this agenda item. But he was undeterred. Norman's opening line, an improvisation, seemed to set the tone.

"We certainly have had a very busy day and we have certainly seen some very shabby tricks," he began, referring to some of the other issues upon which the two parties had sparred throughout the session. "Fortunately for me, the rules of the House are such that I shall now be able to have my say."

Norman described the public consternation over the fog's heavy death toll.

"This alarm has been greatly increased by the amazing, at least outward, apathy of the Government," said Norman. "Most people who have deep feelings about this just cannot understand why there has not been a public inquiry after thousands of people were choked to death during the December fogs."

He repeated the numbers released by the government: More than six thousand more deaths in Greater London in December 1952 than the previous year—and the Ministry of Health agreed that the cause was air pollution, he said. *What would it take for the government to take action?* More attention had been paid to ordinary road accidents, which had numbered fewer during the whole of that year than had been killed in just four days by the fog. There were public inquiries over rail and air disasters that had killed less than one hundred people. The recent East Coast floods, with less than 350 British victims, drew a rapid response from the government—not so with this fog. Then he reminded Parliament of the exasperated reply from the minister of health, Iain Macleod, during a public speech in January.

"'Really, you know,' he said, 'anyone would think fog had only started in London since I became Minister,'" repeated Norman.

Then he added his own comment. "This was an entirely different fog from most. It is true that there was a higher death roll than at the peak of the cholera epidemic of 1866."

Norman rattled off a litany of numbers: twenty-five thousand extra claims for sickness benefits; nearly one million people were affected in some degree by the fog, but still the government refused to act.

"If much more is being done than is known to the general public, there is so much interest in this matter that this is the time to give the details," said Norman. Then he read a letter aloud, written by a Dartford constituent.

"May I offer my praise for your stand for the end of this disgraceful complacency, and indifference to the shocking pollution of our air?" asked the writer. "The deaths caused by the recent fog, though awful, were nothing compared with the thousands whose lungs were damaged to a lesser extent, perhaps to prove fatal at a later date."

Norman praised the National Smoke Abatement Society and denounced the minister of health for not offering it funding. He then heaped accolades on the American government for launching an investigation into its own fog crisis; he read an excerpt from the report on Donora, Pennsylvania.

" 'The whole nation was shocked when 20 persons died and several thousands more became ill during the smog that enveloped the town of Donora, Pennsylvania, during the last week in October, 1948,' " read Norman, before pausing and replying. "America usually does things in a bigger way than we do, but I wonder what they are thinking about 6,000 English people dying in Greater London alone."

Norman's message was that the Conservative government must prevent the next deadly fog, or air pollution might become the city's next bubonic plague.

"It might even be worse next time," warned Norman. "We may even once again in the London streets hear the cry, 'Bring out your dead.' Six thousand deaths is a high figure, and, what is probably equally important, many more have suffered very badly."

He finally listed off four suggestions: conduct a study on the causes of air pollution, make changes to the chemical processes that likely caused the smog, make improvements in combustion to eliminate smoke emissions, and create an alert system so that vulnerable people could perhaps leave town or better protect themselves during adverse weather. He finally suggested a permanent committee of "suitable persons shall be set up to make recommendations and to see that they are carried out."

That was a formidable list of demands, particularly for a struggling government. But Harold Macmillan's Ministry of Housing had a ready response.

"I would reply that the Government have decided to appoint a committee under an independent chairman, to undertake a comprehensive review of the causes and effects of air pollution, and to consider what further preventive measures are practicable," said Marples. "I want the honourable gentleman to understand that Her Majesty's government are taking seriously their obligations in respect of air pollution."

There it was—the final request in Norman's list of demands, an independent body that would study the causes and then propose real solutions. He was pleased, but not with Marples' snide tone.

"I hope that the honourable gentleman and the House, especially the three Socialist honourable Members present, will be satisfied with that announcement," said Marples, "but I think the public will be delighted to know that this is happening."

Norman enjoyed seeing the Tories squirm. And there was

that one concession: a committee. It wasn't sweeping change—but then, the Tories weren't about sweeping change, at least concerning smog. The government wasn't moving very quickly, but at least there might now be progress. Perhaps this new committee would finally provide some findings and offer tangible solutions, a way for Britain to finally move away from coal. But this step was really only a stopgap—Norman had to keep the pressure on. Winter was coming.

⁓

It was five-thirty in the morning, still dark in the borough of Kensington on Monday, May 18. The sun would rise soon, as the mist began to fall. A haze thickened into a mild fog. Thirty police constables patrolled inside the cemetery on Gunnersbury Lane; they stood near barricades, ready to discourage the crowd, angling to spot the gravedigger pushing his shovel into the hard dirt. The Metropolitan police press office warned journalists to stay away; still, a mob of reporters and photographers lined the nearby Bath Road embankment, just above the cemetery, as the coffin was lifted from five feet beneath the ground. The telescopic-lens cameras clicked, capturing the scene through the trees.

The elm coffin was the top one, in a common grave shared by five others. After almost three years, Beryl Evans and her daughter, Geraldine, were exhumed—soon to become two more pieces of evidence unearthed for the murder trial of John Reginald Christie. A menagerie of experts stood at the grave. Three pathologists and three Met investigators loomed near the hole, ready to claim the bodies. A psychiatrist, hired by Reg's defense team, watched nearby. They looked at the metal plate on the coffin: "Beryl Evans, aged 19 years" and "Jeraldine of 14 months"—Geraldine's name was misspelled, a final insult. The lid was lifted slightly; the putrid gases seeped out. Geraldine lay atop her mother—both rested on wet brown sawdust. A white mold had spawned stalactites inside the lid. It wasn't difficult to identify the bodies. Exhumations were not that unusual, but they were typically quiet affairs. This was so different—it was the cause célèbre in London. But there was also something else. The gravedigger wasn't there at the request of the Crown prosecutors, as might be expected. The exhumation was at the behest of Reg's defense attorney—he insisted on inviting Beryl and Geraldine Evans to his murder trial.

∝

Almost two weeks after Norman attacked the Ministry of Housing in Parliament, he was set to pressure Harold Macmillan, who was finally making an appearance in the House. Norman demanded to know who was on the new committee and their qualifications. "No sir," was Macmillan's response.

"Will the right honourable gentleman give some indication of how long that might be, in view of the fact that it took five months to decide to set up the committee?" asked Norman.

"It takes quite a time to get the people that one needs," replied Macmillan. "It is better to wait a little to try to get the right people."

A Labour MP glanced at Norman and then turned to the housing minister.

"In view of the fact that the Minister has stated that he needs active and qualified people for this committee, will he consider the qualifications of my honourable friend the Member for Dartford (Mr. Dodds)?"

Norman was startled. He wanted nothing to do with a committee championed by Harold Macmillan.

"I decline," said Norman.

"I will bear that in mind," Macmillan smugly replied.

❧

The rain outside slid down her aunt's window, gently pelting it—it wasn't distracting. Not that anything could really distract her right now. Rosemary Sargent stared at the television in the parlor. Even on a black-and-white set, Queen Elizabeth II was magnificent—a thirteen-year-old girl's deity. Rosemary adored her nobility, her elegance, and her femininity. She and David leaned in toward the set; they watched closely on Tuesday, June 2, as the queen sat, hands in her lap, tucked inside the horse-drawn carriage. Rosemary could close her eyes and imagine the colors the commentators were describing: Elizabeth's sparkling dress with a stunning red-and-gold train. The crown's cap, royal purple, was adorned with countless jewels.

Rosemary and her eldest brother sat side by side in the parlor in Sydenham, South London. They had taken the half-hour bus ride together just to watch Queen Elizabeth's coronation at their aunt's home. Their father's sister was seriously ill; she lay in the back room of the house. *Be quiet,* she and David were warned. The Sargents didn't own a television, so this was a special treat. They were a real royalist family—the monarchs were idolized in their house. Rosemary and David grinned at the scenes on the TV, the people clapping, the women crying.

An estimated three million people crowded the streets of London, praying for just a glimpse of the twenty-seven-year-old queen as she and her husband travelled the five-mile procession route from Buckingham Palace to Westminster Abbey.

Journalists, dressed in natty attire and fully hatted, stood atop the scaffolding stands along the route. Reporters slipped away to the nearby refreshment stands for a cup of coffee, and then laced it with brandy. The lavish crowning ceremony contained traditions that dated back a millennium. More than eight thousand dignitaries and guests were graced with an invitation; hundreds of millions listened on radio, and more than twenty million watched the proceedings on live television. Rosemary leaned forward to hear the quiet voice of the BBC commentator.

"She goes to take her stand near King Edward's chair and there the Archbishop of Canterbury will present her for recognition. And the queen will turn to her people to the east, and to the south, and to the west and to the north and each time the people cry out their willingness and joy to do her service. God Save Queen Elizabeth."

Rosemary and David were hushed during the most important part. More than a year after her own father's death, Elizabeth finally held the four symbols of authority—the royal ring of sapphire and rubies, the rod of mercy, the orb, and the scepter. Then the moment came, the one that made millions of little girls gasp. The Archbishop of Canterbury placed St Edward's Crown on her head. She was Queen Elizabeth II. "God Save the Queen," the crowd yelled as gun salutes discharged into the rain. She stepped into her gilded carriage and gently waved as she returned to her home. After the parade, Elizabeth stood with her family on the Buckingham Palace balcony and greeted the crowd as jet planes of the Royal Air Force flew across the Mall in tight formation. Fireworks lit the sky. There were loads of street parties, including in Rosemary's neighborhood in Bromley. The teenager danced and sang, blew horns with delight. But of course, there was always a pall over their celebrations.

Her father, Albert, had been dead for six months now. It was still agonizing for Rosemary, still distressing. She was flustered in school, anxious; her grades were abysmal. Her mother was working in the school's cafeteria, but they still had little money. There were so many reminders of him, simple ones like the family's sewing machine. Her father used to sit at their table, with material in his lap, as he cranked the handle to move the needle along. Albert never made garments, but he hemmed curtains and sheets. After the war, most London families couldn't afford to buy those items ready-made, so altering material had been Albert's job. That sewing machine, the door to the parlor, even her hairbrush—they all reminded Rosemary of her father. She glanced again at the royal family, beaming on the balcony. She empathized with the queen—another young woman forced to continue life without her father.

Queen Elizabeth's coronation marked a new beginning for Britain—after the ordeal of the war, it was a time of hope, a period of progress and achievement, heralding a "new Elizabethan age." But once the exuberance waned, Rosemary knew the pain would remain. Albert Sargent's death devastated his family and, while Rosemary tried to have hope, it seemed futile, in a way. She would not become a teacher. She would never go to college. But she would always yearn to hear his knock again. And she would always despise that fog.

CHAPTER TWELVE

Infamous

Unreal City,
Under the brown fog of a winter dawn,
A crowd flowed over London Bridge, so many,
I had not thought death had undone so many.

—*T. S. Eliot, "The Waste Land," 1922*

In March 1953, Reg had sat across from a chief inspector at Notting Hill police station, just hours after his arrest on the embankment. He was fatigued, penniless, and pitiful. The police demanded an explanation. Reg knew that, by now, investigators had discovered Ethel, along with the three corpses in the kitchen. He knew that his two graves in the garden were bare. The "Murder House of Notting Hill" was now free—the bodies were gone.

Tell us about your wife, Chief Inspector Albert Griffin demanded. Reg began to weep.

"I will tell you as much as I can remember," he assured them, with a feeble voice. He began to unfurl the first of three confessions—three confessions, just as his neighbor Timothy Evans had offered a little more than three years earlier.

Reg explained that he suffered from fibrositis and enteritis—he was in constant discomfort. And then in late 1952, Ethel's mental health deteriorated. They both blamed their degenerate neighbors, the immigrants from the West Indies who inflicted such angst. By last December, Ethel was miserable; she rarely ventured from their flat. And she was taking loads of medication for anxiety and insomnia, said Reg. Then he awoke in bed around eight fifteen the morning of December 14. Ethel was shaking.

"I sat up and saw that she appeared to be convulsive, her face was blue and she was choking," said Reg. "I did what I could to try and restore breathing but it was hopeless."

It was too late to call an ambulance, he thought. He couldn't stand seeing her struggle for air—he glanced at the side of the bed.

"I got a stocking and tied it round her neck to put her to sleep," said Reg. "Then I got out of bed and saw a small bottle and a cup half full of water on a small table near the bed."

Reg snatched up the bottle and read the label. Inside were phenobarbitone tablets, an addictive medicine that his doctor prescribed to help with sleep. Reg shook out two pills—there used to be twenty-five. Ethel must have swallowed the rest, he thought. Investigators recorded the statement—and watched Reg closely as he described the cover-up. He detailed how he had slid Ethel underneath the floorboards, then sold her wedding ring and his furniture. Investigators were skeptical—it didn't seem to make sense, to strangle a woman who was overdosing, instead of calling for help. They would wait for the pathologist to give them more information. If he found phenobarbitone in her body, then perhaps Reg *was* being truthful.

Still in the interrogation room, Reg described meeting each of his final victims, the three women hidden behind cheap wallpaper in the kitchen alcove. They were all tramps that entered his flat, either by invitation or force, he said. They harassed him and then demanded money for sex. *They refused to leave,* he said. He fought back, and killed each of them in self-defense. Reg never mentioned his deck chair in the kitchen, the rubber tube connected to the gas tap, or the rope. No confession of rape. Ruth Fuerst and Muriel Eady, buried in the back garden, were illusions. And he didn't say a word about Beryl and Geraldine Evans. Reg listened as police recited his statement. He nodded and signed the paper. They led him back to his cell. Outside Notting Hill police station, a crowd swelled to more than one hundred, pushing one another, hoping for a glimpse of the famous John Reginald Christie. Only thirteen members of the public were allowed into the small courtroom.

"A queue began to form at 9 A.M. for seats in the public gallery. Windows of a row of houses overlooking the Courtyard were packed with residents," wrote the *Sydney Morning Herald.* "He was wearing horn-rimmed spectacles and looked drawn and pale when he climbed slowly into the dock assisted by a policeman."

Standing by his attorney, Reg may have prayed for life behind bars—it was certainly better than what he deserved. And Reg would do anything, or say anything, to avoid the gallows.

Harry Procter stared at John Reginald Christie inside the West London Magistrates' Court on April 1. The day after his arrest, "this monster-like creature" sat relaxed in the defendant's chair, with his arms crossed, listening to the prosecutor. The Crown, led by Attorney General Sir Lionel Heald, was charging him with the murder of his wife; Procter waited in the press box.

The serial killer unnerved the journalist—but he was also thrilled, even exhilarated, because Notting Hill's most wanted murderer had finally accepted his business arrangement. Reg seemed glum until he turned, spotted Procter, and revealed a slight smile. It miffed the journalist—he was forced to treat Reg like a luminary, even though he was a depraved killer. Procter wanted his exclusive story, so he needed to appease Reg. If only he weren't so gauche about it. Reg moaned about the various gifts the *Sunday Pictorial* sent to the jail. He complained about the color of the tie, the size of the dress shirt. The killer's haughty attitude irked Procter, but they were in business now.

"News is news," said Procter. "And I believe that real news should be pursued ruthlessly, accurately, speedily, and completely."

Most of the hacks in the Murder Gang made overtures to "Jack the Strangler," but Harry Procter won the bidding war. Reg agreed to tell his story exclusively to the *Sunday Pictorial* and its fourteen million readers, while the newspaper would pay his defense expenses. "Cheque-book journalism" was the main method to secure the sole rights to a blockbuster story, propagated over the years by editors and owners of the British press. Journalists slipped money to the killer's family, who then paid the tab of the defense team. But Reg posed a problem—he didn't have a family.

"There was no wife of the killer to offer the money to this time," said Procter. "She'd been murdered and buried under the floorboards at No. 10 Rillington Place."

Procter and the rest of the Murder Gang devised a sort of formula for this type of deal-making.

"First you contacted a friend—'no intrusion on private grief,' says the rulebook of the National Union of Journalists— through the friend you contact a relative, preferably a husband, wife, mother, or sister," said Procter. "Then you talk, and talk, and talk, and talk…"

But Reg was estranged from his family—he hadn't seen his siblings for years. His parents were dead. He appeared to have no friends. Fortunately, Procter and Reg's defense attorney were cronies. Forty-nine-year-old Derek Curtis-Bennett was an aggressive lawyer—a brilliant speaker who defended some of Britain's most notorious criminals, including a German theoretical physicist who spied for the Soviets.

Curtis-Bennett granted Procter full access to Reg during the trial, but the journalist was a headache for prison officials. Four months earlier, he had visited a young murderer in prison, pretending to be a relative. Procter had interviewed Christopher Craig and printed the story in the *Sunday Pictorial*. He had shammed prison officials—and now they distrusted him. So when Procter tried to contact Reg in Brixton Prison, they swiftly rejected his request.

"Any further attempts by persons known or suspected to be journalists to establish contact with Christie by letter or visit should be referred for instructions," wrote the governor of Brixton Prison. "No correspondence between Christie and Mr. Proctor (sic) is to be allowed. Mr. Proctor should be so informed, no reasons being given, and his letter should be returned to him."

The *Sunday Pictorial* gave Reg's defense less than two thousand pounds for his story; other papers were offering up to five thousand—that decision spoke to Harry Procter's prominence. The paper would publish his anecdotes over the summer. Reg acquired bravado in prison that he had never shown before. Now he was infamous—journalists jockeyed for his story. Prison officials turned away their gifts of fruit baskets and cigars. Churches sent him literature.

A clinical psychologist administered a Rorschach test. The results claimed Reg was very intelligent but "a sad, unhappy, rather inadequate, anxiety-ridden little man. A good deal of repression, especially of aggression." Newspapers reported he was even given a brain scan. Reporters printed every tidbit of information they could gather, particularly about his life inside prison. Reg appeared to eat well and sleep soundly, and he got along with other inmates. He was allowed to smoke cigarettes. He put on weight. But Reg had few visitors, so he tried to develop his social skills with other prisoners. He boasted that he was a lothario, a seducer of women. He bragged that he "did some of them in." He was incredibly narcissistic—he kept a picture of himself in his cell. Reg enjoyed being compared to serial killer John George Haigh, known as the Acid Bath Murderer, who had disposed of his six victims by submerging them in steel drums of acid.

"It wasn't me who did the chasing. Girls were attracted to me," said Reg. "I'm not like Boris Karloff…more like Charles Boyer (a handsome French film actor of the day)."

Yet, despite his bluster, he was still awkward. A prison officer recalled a time when Reg was taking a bath—he pointed to his penis and explained it was responsible for drawing those crowds to 10 Rillington Place. Reg was finally receiving the attention he craved—he was no longer invisible. Reporters quoted every word he uttered. Gawkers begged for entrance to the court. Women swarmed the prison gate. Newspaper sales soared. The macabre legacy of John Reginald Christie was indelible.

As he rested in his cell, Reg began jotting down notes about his life—scrawled in messy cursive writing—for those pieces in the *Sunday Pictorial*. They were musings—his complaints, and his justifications. He sat in his cell, alone, much of the time. And his narratives for the *Sunday Pictorial* began flowing, one by one. In each story, Reg framed his life very carefully. He was determined to mold the public's last impression of him. He hoped to garner sympathy by explaining how his strict father had abused him, yet he seemed proud of the way he had reclaimed control of his life. But then his thoughts turned dark. Reg described a recurring dream that demanded he kill ten women to fulfill his destiny.

"After victims Four, Five and Six, I now remember how I used to think there are only six more—or only five or four more to make ten, and then I can rest," he wrote.

He blamed cruel teenage girls from his boyhood for mistreating him, damaging his fragile ego.

"Laughter and sneers in a way made me more determined to prove I was a man," he said. "I have proved it."

The *Sunday Pictorial* included the headline "Christie's Own Story" and highlighted phrases like: "My Second Victim…We Kissed and Cuddled." There were four stories and each had a similar tone—arrogance.

"It was thrilling because I had embarked on the career I had chosen for myself, the career of murder," he wrote. "But it was only the beginning. I was perfectly calm. But the dark work which was my destiny had begun."

The stench of Reg's trial drifted into the House of Commons on July 13, 1953—MPs were disgusted that a suspected murderer was allowed to publish his memoirs, particularly to pay for his defense. A Labourite demanded the Attorney General consider introducing legislation that would prevent killers on trial from selling their life stories.

"Is there not a possibility that the enormous sensational publicity given to the Christie memoirs might be conceivably lead other morbid-minded people to imitate the crimes?" asked MP Emrys Hughes.

The Attorney General stood up and refused—he also reminded the lawmakers that censorship was a dangerous suggestion. Reg's stories in the *Sunday Pictorial* would continue to be published—and reporter Harry Procter would proceed with funding the serial killer's legal defense.

❧

Before his trial began, Reg agreed to a meeting with his attorney, Mr. Derek Curtis-Bennett. He knew it was time to build a defense. He would never be free again, but he didn't want to die. The barrister wasn't alone—he asked Reg to meet with Dr. Jack Hobson, a psychiatrist hired by the defense; Hobson was one of the doctors who stood near Beryl and Geraldine's graves as their bodies were exhumed. Reg was reluctant to talk with a "head doctor," but his attorney explained that it was crucial for trial.

Dr. Hobson interviewed Reg about each woman, including Beryl Evans, more than a dozen times. But the psychiatrist and the barrister seemed to focus on her, which seemed odd to Reg. They wanted to know what he remembered about Beryl's murder—*did he do it?* He paused and complained about his fuzzy memory, but finally replied "no." The men looked at each other. Dr. Hobson and Derek Curtis-Bennett began to gently clarify the reason for their question.

"They explained that it was a similarity. It meant that there were two stranglers in one house," remembered Reg, "and that was something which was highly improbable."

Curtis-Bennett was very careful; he didn't ask Reg to lie. *Think hard*, he said. *Could you have killed Beryl and Geraldine, also?* Reg said he couldn't recall. Then came another strange question, about the unsolved murder of a little girl in Windsor during the summer of 1951, seven-year-old Christine Butcher. *Did you visit Windsor recently?*

"No, not for years," replied Reg. He knew what they were implying and now he was resolute: "Mine were all adults."

Reg's previous confessions were irrefutable—he may have spun the stories so he didn't appear to be a monster, but he never denied killing six women, including his wife. And of course, police had found their remains on his property—there was hard evidence. It would be a tough battle for any seasoned defense attorney; Reg was certain to be hanged. So Curtis-Bennett recruited a strange ally—a nineteenth-century killer whose sick mind had caused him to murder.

Daniel M'Naghten was a woodworker who, in 1843, had assassinated a personal secretary to the British prime minister as he walked toward Downing Street. M'Naghten was found to be suffering from paranoid delusions. The Crown prosecutor argued that, though M'Naghten did suffer from "partial insanity," he knew the difference between right and wrong when he shot the victim. The defense put medical experts on the stand that insisted M'Naghten had no control over his actions. The jury felt no need to retire. They returned a verdict of "not guilty on the ground of insanity," and M'Naghten was released to a lunatic asylum. The trial became the benchmark for the country's legal test of criminal insanity, called the "M'Naghten Rules."

Curtis-Bennett believed Reg's jury might save his life, too. A sex-crazed killer who assaulted and murdered women, even a toddler? He would be found guilty and hanged by a jury quickly. But a murderer who slept just feet from his dead wife? A man who took tea in his kitchen, where a wall hid three more bodies? He would have to be insane; the more people he killed, the battier he seemed. And if Reg were insane, he *couldn't* be put to death.

Curtis-Bennett became determined to prove that Reg was, in fact, the only murderer to have resided at 10 Rillington Place. He was convinced that, with a persuasive narrative and a sympathetic jury, Reg might actually avoid the hangman's noose. So, days after that meeting with his attorney, Reg made another confession to police, this time in prison. It differed substantially from his first declaration. And unlike most defendants, his second confession was actually more damning than his first.

Reg's new story began in August 1949, after Beryl and her husband's mistress fought in the top-floor flat. Beryl had told the Christies that she planned to file for separation, and they had offered to adopt little Geraldine. Reg contended that Beryl had declined, saying her mother would take her daughter. *She was so upset*, Reg recalled.

"Mrs. Evans told me that her husband was knocking her about and that she was going to make an end of it," he said, "moaning that she was going to commit suicide."

Shortly after that conversation, according to Reg, he went upstairs to her flat and found her lying on a quilt in front of the kitchen fireplace. The room was filled with gas—he knew she was trying to kill herself by breathing in coal gas from a rubber hose connected to a tap at the fireplace. He was frantic—he flung open the window and she began to awaken, complaining of a headache. He offered her water and left her to recover. The next day, he found himself in her flat again, around lunchtime. This time, she begged him to help her die. She seemed to offer him sex.

"I got on my knees but found I was not physically capable of having intercourse with her owing to the fact that I had fibrositis in my back and enteritis," said Reg. "I turned the gas tap on and as near as I can make out, I held it close to her face. I think that's when I strangled her. I think it was with a stocking I found in the room."

Later that night, Reg said, he had told Tim Evans that his wife had killed herself using coal gas. Reg warned Tim that investigators would immediately suspect the husband, so the Welshman promised to retrieve his work van and take away her body. That was the end of Reg's involvement in the murder, he said. He had no idea what had happened to baby Geraldine—he refused to admit he had killed her. Reg was only willing to play along to a point. Of course, that confession didn't at all jibe with any of Tim Evans' stories, even the confession where he implicated Reg.

In some ways, Reg's confession was a reasonable explanation that answered a lot of the questions for investigators. *How could there be two killers under the same roof?* It seemed impossible, even for a ghetto like Notting Hill. But Dr. Keith Simpson, one of the pathologists at the exhumation of Beryl and Geraldine, was suspicious. His report, the one handed to Reg's defense attorney days earlier, indicated that Beryl likely didn't die from carbon monoxide poisoning—and it didn't appear that she was raped. During the exhumation of her body, pathologists determined that her pubic hair had not been cut—none of the hair in Reg's tobacco tin could be linked to her. In fact, he claimed that they came from his wife and the three women in the kitchen. Dr. Simpson announced that he was highly dubious of Reg's confession involving Beryl's murder.

Still, this confession—and its terrible implications—had to be taken seriously. Police recorded Reg's statement, asked him to sign it, and turned over the massive amount of evidence to the Crown prosecutors. And Reg began to write another article for the *Sunday Pictorial*. In this story, he pondered his relationship with Beryl Evans—a woman he had once vehemently denied killing.

"As I felt at the time of Evans affair normally I could not have done it," he wrote, "but if I was ill mentally I could possibly have killed her, using force that came to me without feeling the pain in my back." It was possible now, according to Reg, that he *did* kill Beryl Evans. He hoped everyone believed him—the public, the press, the jury hearing his case. But his confession to Beryl's murder seemed absurd, an afterthought from a desperate man trying to avoid the gallows. If the jury members believed his story about Beryl, it wouldn't be because of hard evidence linking him to her murder. There was none. They would conclude he had murdered his neighbor's wife because it seemed improbable, maybe even impossible, that two stranglers had lived at 10 Rillington Place at the same time. But most police officers in Notting Hill, who responded daily to cases of deadly rage, knew it was certainly possible—in this case, maybe even likely.

～

He eyed every one of them from the dock, as they stepped into the witness box. He gazed at them—phantoms, vague reminders of his other life. Each person belonged in a category: "neighbor," "coworker," or "police officer." Reg listened closely. They described him in the past tense. He was already dead—a ghost. He nibbled his thin, dry lips. Licked them. His attorney scribbled notes, shuffled papers. Reg jotted down his own notes, and shoved them over to Curtis-Bennett.

"I have run out of fags," wrote Reg. "Can you get me any?"

It was the first day of John Reginald Christie's murder trial, June 23, 1953. Three years earlier, he had testified in that same courthouse; he had told a story that doomed a young husband. Now Reg was sitting in the dock of the Old Bailey. It might have been surreal if he weren't so panicky. The small courthouse was loaded with people—it was a hot summer day. He was uncomfortable. Earlier in the day, Reg had listened as the Attorney General addressed the jurors, reminding them to concentrate on the evidence in court, not stories in the media. No need to worry about his other victims, the five women in his kitchen and garden. Reg was on trial only for killing his wife—Sir Lionel Heald refused to help the defense's insanity claim.

They stepped into the witness box, one after another. Reg listened to those specters of his former life—the years when Ethel was alive, when his neighbors weren't horrible, and when his stomach wasn't twisted, so long ago. The prosecutor's list included the police photographer who snapped photos of the bodies—he would help set the scene. Mr. Burrow, Reg's boss, gave context to his solid work ethic, but also his erratic behavior. His landlord, Charles Brown, described the tension between Reg and his Caribbean neighbors, as well as his tenant's acerbic personality.

Ethel Christie's best friend, Rosina Swan, described her various conversations with Reg about his wife's sudden move to Sheffield. Ethel's brother and sister read Christmas cards they had received after she was already dead. Reg held his hands between his knees. There were short testimonies from service people, chronicling items that Reg had sold, including furniture and jewelry. Neighbors described the strong smell of disinfectant. The Reillys confirmed that Reg had subleased his flat to them before he disappeared. The Attorney General, Lionel Heald, interviewed witnesses who had encountered Reg while he was on the run.

Perhaps the star of the trial that first day was Chief Inspector Albert Griffin, the cop who had interrogated Reg after his arrest. He summarized the grim details of the case for the Crown, including details about the murders of Beryl and Geraldine Evans. Griffin also described Reg's childhood in Halifax, the son of an abusive father and an overbearing mother; Griffin confirmed Reg's struggle with girls as a teenager, and his troubled marriage to Ethel. Reg's war record was decent, said Griffin. But he also detailed Reg's legal troubles, his spotty employment, and his shaky psychiatric history. He summarized medical testimony from the Magistrates' Court, where Reg pleaded "not guilty."

Doctor Lewis Nickolls, director of the Metropolitan Police Laboratory, confirmed that the three last victims, found in the cupboard, had all been exposed to large amounts of coal gas. All three had been sexually assaulted. No sperm was found inside Ethel Christie, but there was also no trace of barbiturates. She had clearly been killed by strangulation—his first confession claimed she had overdosed and he had merely strangled her to help finish her off as a sort of mercy killing; that was a lie. Griffin also recounted Reg's confession of Kathleen Maloney's murder, which Reg had described to police as an act of self-defense.

"I tried to get her out, and she picked up a frying pan and she tried to hit me," he had told Griffin. "The next thing I remember she was lying still in the chair with the rope round her neck." It was an odd point in the narrative to have a lapse in memory. He certainly didn't seem like a reliable witness, even during his own murder trial.

Griffin described how Reg claimed similar memory problems with the other murders. He was vague, cagey, and generally uncooperative with investigators. Both sides then offered details from Tim Evans' murder trial, possibly the most explosive part of an already highly charged testimony. If the jury believed Reg and his attorney, then the wrong man had been put to death for that crime.

The Attorney General insisted that Tim Evans *did* kill his wife—he had confessed to her murder multiple times. He had even admitted he'd killed Geraldine. He had belonged at the hangman's noose in 1950. But during cross-examination, Curtis-Bennett slowly worked to convince the jury that Reg could have been the real killer.

There were the doctors who took the stand to discuss Beryl Evans' exhumation and reexamination. Reg, after all, had claimed that he had killed his young neighbor during a botched suicide attempt: that she had gassed herself using a tap from her fireplace and then he had strangled her—that scenario would fit with his previous murders. But the pathologists' findings were still the same as they had been in Tim Evans' original trial: Beryl was *not* gassed. If she had been, they said, then they would have found evidence of poisoning in her body, even several years later, but certainly during the first autopsy.

Reg also claimed that Beryl's flat was filled with coal gas when he arrived, yet he himself was not overcome—that was a lie. Reg argued that he had strangled Beryl with a stocking, but forensics showed she was likely killed with a rope, as Tim Evans had claimed. There was no visible evidence of sexual intercourse, which was telling because he *had* sexually assaulted all of his other victims, with the exception of his wife. He had even admitted to raping Ruth and Muriel, even though there was no proof—their remains were reduced to bones. Yet pathologists couldn't be certain that Beryl had not been raped, because no semen swab had been taken at the time.

Things came to a head between the Crown and the defense when the Attorney General asked Chief Inspector Albert Griffin, "Have you any grounds for believing, from your inquiries into the case and everything you have heard in this matter, that the wrong man was hanged in the Evans case?"

"None at all," replied the inspector.

Curtis-Bennett leaped up and objected, complaining that it was an improper question. The Crown taunted the attorney, declaring that Reg should be honest—*he never killed Beryl or Geraldine Evans, did he?*

"If my learned friend is asking me to make plain that Christie did not kill Mrs. Evans, I am going to try to make plain the reverse," said Curtis-Bennett.

The defense team tried to make it very clear to the jury—it was their assertion that Reg had, in fact, killed Beryl Evans. It was all part of the insanity defense, Reg's only hope at that point. But it wouldn't be an easy road for his attorney. Mental health experts who examined Reg testified that he was sane during and after the murders—he seemed quite adept at covering them up. He clearly wanted to avoid being caught—an insane man would not have bothered, because he wouldn't have understood the difference between right and wrong. In the middle of the second day, Reg took the stand. He knew Curtis-Bennett's strategy: "The more the merrier," Reg would later tell a prison chaplain.

In preparation for Reg's testimony, the defense attorney issued a strange warning to the jury.

"Although Christie is going to say for the fifth or sixth time that he did not kill that baby," said Curtis-Bennett, "it is open to you to think that it is impossible that there were two stranglers in the house, and it may well be that he killed all the people you heard of."

With that, John Reginald Christie finally took the stand. "Do your best to speak up, Christie," ordered his attorney.

Reg was evasive, in his own meek way. During neutral subjects, like his work history or childhood, he could be very specific. But when asked pointed questions about the murders, his memory was fuzzy.

"I am not quite sure whether I did at the time," he would say, when asked about having sex with Ruth Fuerst in 1943. "I think

I strangled her then," Reg responded to a question about Beryl Evans' death. "It is a very long time since and I do not recollect a lot," he repeated. He didn't seem to remember the order of his victims. But when asked about murdering Geraldine Evans, his response was emphatically "no." Reg blamed his sporadic amnesia on mental health issues—his hysteria. If there was evidence that he killed the women, then he must have, Reg admitted. But he couldn't remember a thing. He showed no shame, no remorse for the victims—gross apathy. There might be more victims, he guessed.

"Is this the first person you've killed in your life?" asked Curtis-Bennett.

"I think so. I don't know," was Reg's reply. He shook his head, like he was trying to remember.

He was so ambiguous—it was riling. He paused for long periods, furrowed his brow to recollect the murders. Reg's voice was low, difficult to hear, so the court installed a microphone. When he heard his voice amplified, his demeanor changed. He sat up tall—his confidence grew. He looked out toward the spectators. Now he was on stage, the star of a popular show. While Reg was giving testimony, journalists took frantic notes.

"An insignificant little mouse of a man," wrote one reporter. He was such a contradictory character; he intrigued the media, like Jekyll and Hyde. Reg stepped down from the chair and walked toward his seat.

Now Dr. Jack Hobson, the psychiatrist Reg's attorney had hired to examine him in prison, took the stand. During cross-examination, the Attorney General said that, during this case, people had used various expressions to describe Reg, including "maniac," "raving lunatic," "mad as a March hare," and "umbrella of total madness," but none of those were scientific terms. Dr. Hobson agreed, but still insisted his patient was nuts and should be institutionalized, not hanged. Reg just might avoid execution. At least he could build a life inside a mental health hospital. On the fourth day of the trial, June 25, both sides presented their closing arguments. The Crown urged the jury to find Reg guilty of murdering Ethel Christie, and send him to the gallows. But the defense reminded jurors that only an insane man would live near corpses for months, even years. *Who was right? Perhaps both?*

Finally, the judge issued his charge to the jury. He lectured for two and a half hours, reminding jurors of the preponderance of evidence against Reg, particularly the testimony that showed how he covered up the crimes. Late that afternoon, just before five o'clock, jury members retired to privately deliberate. They returned with a verdict eighty minutes later—not good news for most defendants. Reg returned to the dock, smiled weakly at the judge.

"Do you find the prisoner at the Bar, John Reginald Halliday Christie, guilty or not guilty?" asked the Clerk of Court.

"We find him guilty."

He listened. The words "but insane" didn't follow. Reg shook his head, gripped the rail before him.

"Have you anything to say why sentence of death should not be passed?" asked the judge. Reg stayed silent, shook his head, then his mouth formed the word, "no."

Reg shifted his weight and closed his eyes. He refused to collapse. The journalists were watching.

"The newspapers cannot say that I fainted or made a scene in the dock," he said, after he was taken away.

CHAPTER THIRTEEN

Legacy

[A] rainy, colossal London smelling of molten metal
and of soot, ceaselessly steaming and smoking in the
fog now spread out before his eyes...while trains
rushed past at full speed or rumpled underground
uttering horrible cries and vomiting waves of
smoke, and while, through every street, monstrous
and gaudy and infamous advertisements flared
through the eternal twilight...
            —*J.-K. Huysmans,* Against the Grain
                      (À rebours), *1884*

It was a quiet summer for smoke abatement advocates—once
the Ministry of Housing announced in May that there would
be a committee to research and report on solutions for air pollution, the issue languished in Parliament. MPs assumed the
government would quickly produce a list of committee members, but as weeks turned to months Norman Dodds became
impatient once again.

   In late July—more than two months after his row with Housing in Parliament—Norman confronted Harold Macmillan's
ministry once again, demanding a progress report on the com-
position of the committee. Winter was coming, and the smog
would again return—there was no time to waste. Once again,
Ernest Marples, the beleaguered parliamentary secretary, stood
in Macmillan's place.

"We have been fortunate in securing the services of Sir Hugh Beaver as chairman," said Marples. "The committee will begin work forthwith, but I cannot predict when it will report."

Beaver was a much-respected industrialist who led the way in the country's rebuilding effort. By his early sixties, Beaver had become one of Britain's most influential engineers and scientists, helping to restore the country after World War II. He led the housing committee to redesign towns leveled by German bombs; he advised the government on constructing new power plants. His leadership would give the committee—known in the press as the "Beaver Committee"—the gravitas it needed to be effective.

While Norman was impressed with the appointment of Hugh Beaver, he was also indignant: *Why had it taken two months for this committee to merely find a leader? What had been done in the way of research and planning? What were the committee's recommendations? What was he to tell his constituents and others who were looking to their government for information to help them prevent the next Great Smog?* This slight progress on a committee wouldn't pacify him.

"Whilst thanking the hon. Gentleman for that information, may I ask if he is aware that there is a good deal of concern that it took five months following the December massacre to decide to set up the committee at all?" asked Norman. "Will he press ahead with this in view of the fact that there might be a worse case in the months ahead, because winter is just round the corner?"

It was sunny outside Westminster; Londoners sat on benches, admired the blue sky. There seemed to be little fear of rain— no real motive to worry about another fog. Or how they might keep warm on a bleak November night. It was dispiriting to reflect on last December's tragedy during a glorious summer day. Marples stood again, ignored Norman's blatant slight, and replied that the speed of the report depended on the committee—he wasn't in charge of its productivity. He later distributed a full list of the members. And with that, the issue of fog was extinguished in the House of Commons, and in the newspapers, for more than three months. MPs trusted that the committee was diligently working on a permanent solution and hoped the government would find a way to help prevent more deaths this winter.

✑

At the end of August 1953, it was rainy and more brisk than usual for a late summer day—lower sixties, with a chilly breeze. Fall seemed to arrive a bit sooner, ushering away a lovely, mild summer for London. But inside the Ministry of Health at Whitehall, any hint of cooler weather was only a warning that winter was nearing. The government was scrambling to find safeguards. Another fog was sure to come in less than three months—it arrived every winter. But even smoke abatement advocates knew that a countrywide conversion to smokeless fuel would take time—it was a long-term goal. The Beaver Committee was still meeting privately. There was no plan for the winter. The government realized that something needed to be done immediately, to protect the vulnerable and to prevent another catastrophe. So the Ministry of Health discussed a proposal that would provide respirators to Londoners with predisposed respiratory or heart conditions. The heavy-duty masks had a sealed system to circulate clean air.

But there were so many questions: *Are they effective against sulphur dioxide and solid particles from smoke? How would health experts decide who needed the respirators the most? How long would patients need to wear them? How would they be distributed?* This wasn't a model solution—the Ministry of Health wasn't convinced that many elderly people, those most susceptible to the fog, would tolerate wearing a respirator for long. Then what good would it do? In an internal memo, a principal medical officer with the Ministry of Health said that the proposal was a good one, even though the respirators could prove useless.

"The Government is certain to be under fire this coming winter for not having produced a scheme for preventing fog deaths," wrote Edmund Martin. "A scheme such as this even though it had little effect would go a long way towards convincing the public that the problem of fog deaths was not just being pigeon-holed."

The respirators may have given some Londoners a peace of mind that might have proved dangerous. It was a callous reaction from a desperate government. Churchill's ministers were determined to show that they had a strategy, even if it was incompetent.

∽

In late September and early October, local governments began to take control of smoke abatement, despite the inertia of the national government. The County Council of the City of London declared "smokeless zones," areas where coal was banned. It also vowed to stop the installation of furnaces in buildings unless they could operate continuously without emitting smoke. Of course, carbon dioxide or sulphur dioxide would continue to spill from the chimneys. More cities and towns, like Manchester and Birmingham, were either creating or increasing their smokeless zones. Harold Macmillan insisted that the Ministry of Housing encourage British cities to create those smokeless zones, but when Salford had applied for a zone in 1951, he had rejected its proposal. It was a confusing message. Did the government really want smokeless zones? Local governments were calling newspapers now, complaining that smoke-producing factories were given priority.

"I believe that the Government should make it financially easier for councils to bring about extensions of smokeless zones," said alderman G. H. Goulden, chairman of the Salford Health Committee. "I realize we cannot perhaps afford this, but we can't afford the loss of four thousand lives. The time for action is now."

The newspapers began printing alarming stories about the potential for another deadly fog with headlines like "Menace of the Dirty Air: London Fog Disaster Could Happen Again," and "London Warned of Smog."

Norman Dodds had such a familiar feeling. Once again, he rested on a green bench in the House of Commons, watching Harold Macmillan. And once again, Norman was ready for a battle. The minister of housing had made a promise more than five months ago that the Conservative government would combat air pollution and prevent another deadly fog. And now here they were—in late October—with no real progress to report. Norman demanded to hear about the government's emergency plan.

"So far as I know the only practicable way of combating 'smog' is to reduce smoke from chimneys," replied Macmillan. "The problem is not one for which it is easy to devise emergency plans. I am of course awaiting the report of the Beaver Committee. Meanwhile a special effort is needed by all those who burn coal to use it efficiently, and as sparingly as possible during fogs."

That was an easy request to make in the cool air of the fall—a frigid winter would be a struggle without coal. Norman jumped up.

"Is not it remarkable that the Government have no plan ready should similar conditions apply again this winter?" he barked. "Would not it be possible to give a warning if weather conditions were likely to be similar to those of last December and to request that domestic open fires and certain industrial processes should be dispensed with during the danger period?"

"I welcome that and any other suggestion that the honourable gentleman might be willing to make to me," replied Macmillan coolly.

Norman was livid. The government's stock reply for months had been *we must wait for the Beaver Report*, followed by more excuses. The rhetoric had grown tiresome. Norman asked Macmillan when a report would be available to the public.

"As one would expect from a Committee presided over by Sir Hugh Beaver, it has lost no time and, I understand, intends to present an interim report shortly," replied Macmillan.

Norman wanted to know what Macmillan meant by "shortly," then reminded him that the committee was given little time to prepare a timely report because it had been organized more than seven months after the smog.

"By 'shortly,' I mean within a few weeks," Macmillan replied. "Honourable and right honourable gentlemen who are *experienced* in the appointment of committees know that it takes some time to get exactly the people one needs."

Norman was annoyed by Macmillan's crowing—the housing minister seemed to enjoy reminding the backbencher that he wasn't a cabinet member. But Norman was pleased that he could continue to pester him in Parliament. And the Tories were also feeling pressure outside the House of Commons.

By late October, the weather turned sharply colder. The wind was brisk. The city's doctors demanded the government work harder to prevent a repeat of last year's fog. A committee representing six thousand physicians was "profoundly alarmed at the lack of any effective response from official quarters to what can truthfully be described as a national disaster." Doctors suggested Londoners fashion their own masks using thick surgical gauze. The media began touting their use. Chemists sold out of the thin material as Londoners snatched up the supplies before winter arrived. Women wrapped their faces with chiffon scarves. The medical officers at the Ministry of Health were frustrated with the doctors, and they were forced to make a statement at the end of October.

"There is certainly no simple universal remedy such as everyone wearing a mask," read the statement from the Health Ministry. "There are also other practical measures which are probably quite as effective as the surgeon's gauze mask and which can be produced in the home, such as a scarf or a towel or other cloth wound round the face."

Iain Macleod, the health minister, reiterated the point in Parliament—gauze wouldn't help.

"I am advised that they would be of little or no value in absorbing the toxic gases," he said.

The next day, the committee of doctors fired back in the newspapers.

"We made it abundantly clear the mask was not a cure-all," read the statement. "It is a partial solution. The Ministry has produced no solution at all." Health experts couldn't even agree on what would stop the smoke and fumes.

If surgical gauze was a poor solution, the government's answer was no better. Health experts came up with a plan to offer simple masks to Londoners. Some US tobacco companies made Britain an offer: free cloth masks with their logos stamped on the outside of each one. The government declined and began running tests on the effectiveness of its own masks, including one called the Martindale.

"It is light and convenient," said Ronald V. Christie, a professor at the Medical College at St Bartholomew's Hospital, "but I am fairly certain that it would only filter off the coarser particles from the fog." The Ministry knew the masks were virtually useless against smoke and deadly gases.

"In my opinion," wrote Professor Christie, "the manufacturers of the 'Martindale' mask should now be asked how many of these they can supply and what is the rate of output."

Now, the government was preparing to sell a mask to Londoners that its own experts deemed to be worthless. The winter's first fog was just days away.

∽

The November air howled outside—what a difference one month made in London. It was in the forties now, cold and biting once again. A clerk put coal on the open grate to warm the room—the fire spit as the smoke wafted up through the chimney and poured out the stack above. The Ministry of Housing was one of the last government buildings in London to use an open fire, an irony that may have been lost on most of the ministers inside as they debated handing out protective masks.

The Ministry of Health emphasized to reporters that the masks were not a long-term solution—they were cheap and generally ineffective, but they might help Londoners with serious health problems living in smoke-laden areas. And they planned to charge patients one shilling for the prescription, the price they might normally pay for medicine. People without a prescription might buy one for two and a half shillings. Yet despite the concern over another anticipated fog, the government refused to stop the sale of nutty slack.

"The consumption of this type of coal is very small in relation to the total consumption and when the weather is windy, as it often is, there is no great harm in burning it along with other coals, and it produces no more smoke," said Geoffrey Lloyd, the minister of fuel and power. "Of course, during foggy conditions, as I said, it is better to avoid banking up with it."

November 17 was bitterly cold—and then the sky darkened by mid-afternoon. The deadly fog was back. Londoners groped their way through the streets, yet again bobbed between a patchwork of grey clouds and vapor. The smoke was rancid. This was supposed to be a triumphant day for the government. Today, the National Health Service began issuing its Martindale masks. Londoners strapped the new masks on their children, even their pets. But the masks weren't helping—the smoke seeped through the fabric. Kids took them off at school and looked inside at the brown gunk. A committee of pollution researchers and representatives from the National Coal Board and the Meteorological Office conducted an emergency meeting about the secret trials. Researchers were trying to figure out how effective they really were.

"It was fully realized that so long as the toxic principles in smog were not known with any degree of certainty, the problem of assessing the efficiency of masks was extremely difficult," read the confidential notes from the meeting.

The results were inconclusive because government scientists had not yet figured out what caused smog. And now they were concerned that vulnerable Londoners might venture out into the next smog wearing the mask, assuming they were protected.

∽

On November 19, Harold Macmillan pondered a memo to the cabinet, which was set to meet the next day. It would be insightful, but confidential—it showed the enormous pressure felt by the Conservative government. He finalized it, and then circulated it to the government's top ministers.

"Today everybody expects the Government to solve every problem," wrote Macmillan. "It is a symptom of the Welfare State. For some reason or another, 'smog' has captured the imagination of the press and the people."

The minister of housing complained that his public relations officer was bombarded with questions about what the government was going to do about the smog.

"Ridiculous as it appears at first sight, I would suggest that we form a committee," wrote Macmillan. "Committees are the oriflamme of democracy. There are some short-term things which we have done, and can do. We can gain popularity by doing them well—the masks, the warning signals, etc."

It did seem ridiculous to many. Another committee? This new committee, one distinct from the Beaver Committee, would coordinate the activities of various departments concerning air pollution. Macmillan also mentioned some longer-term solutions—like better stoves and smokeless fuel—that he recommended the government explore. Macmillan named several ministries, which might later join the new committee, including Health, Fuel and Power, and the Meteorological Office—the same ministries that were involved in the last interdepartmental committee. It seemed redundant.

"We cannot do very much, but we can seem to be very busy and that is half the battle nowadays," wrote Macmillan. "The Beaver Report will be published next week. So we must act at once."

The next day, the Conservative government's cabinet met in 10 Downing Street, with Prime Minister Winston Churchill sitting as chair. Harold Macmillan began the discussion about the fog.

"It's the small things that cause politicians trouble," he said.

He suggested two courses of action: either play down the controversy or boost it up—someone needed to take control, because now several ministries were vulnerable. The secretary of state for Scotland, James Stuart, wondered if they should not wait for the Beaver Report before deciding on a tactic.

"Let us look at the report before we decide," recommended the chancellor of the exchequer, the head of the ministry in charge of budget. "Season of fog is passing."

The minister of fuel agreed, saying the Beaver Committee would likely make some practical suggestions for immediate action—the government should study those first, then they could announce a plan. The minster of health then chimed in.

"Publicity is now on the decrease," said Iain Macleod. "Pity to revive it."

That meeting seemed to sum up the government's stance on the fog—the cabinet hoped the controversy would wane as quickly as possible. As the one-year anniversary of the fog approached, a confidential interdepartmental memo was sent to the parliamentary secretary to the Ministry of Health, Patricia Hornsby-Smith. It written by someone within the Health Ministry who had read a draft of the Beaver Committee's report—and the author was alarmed.

"I am afraid that the government are not going to come out of this too well," said the memo, "and that the interim report of the Beaver Committee, so long delayed and so thin in content, will not receive good press."

The memo detailed how best to write a press release announcing the circulation of the report. But near the middle of the message, the author mentioned something, a suggestion that had not been mentioned in the newspapers. It was a statement the government did not want publicized, fearing it could cause a public panic—a frenzy of demands for even tougher smoke abatement laws.

"Perhaps this would not be a suitable opportunity to correct the mistaken impression spread by Professor Wilkins that the death toll was 12,000 and not 4,000?" it said.

The accusation that the number of victims was twelve thousand, not four thousand, was tucked away in a graph, hidden within the interim Beaver Committee Report. The next year, it vanished from the final version. The real death toll of the Great Smog of 1952 would remain buried for more than fifty years.

Epilogue

> The fog was denser than ever—very black, indeed,
> more like a distillation of mud than anything
> else....So heavy was the gloom, that gas was
> lighted in all the shop-windows; and the little
> charcoal furnaces of the women and boys, roasting
> chestnuts, threw a ruddy, misty glow around
> them. And yet I liked it. This fog seems an
> atmosphere proper to huge, grimy London.
> —*Nathaniel Hawthorne,* Notes of Travel, *1857*

Norman Dodds listened closely in Parliament, straining to
hear over the cackles of the other MPs around him—it was
1953, in the middle of the summer, and warm, even in the early
evening. A Labourite was proposing a bill in the House of Commons and Norman wanted to lend his support. The bill's subject
sparked the most raucous debate in months—Norman voted
aye. The bill that concerned him didn't involve air pollution,
foggy weather, or a bankrupt British government—it was focused on serial killer John Reginald Christie.

Less than a week after Reg was sentenced to death on June
25, Norman Dodds voted yes to a bill that would suspend the
death penalty in Britain for five years. Norman—and much of
Parliament—was disturbed by Reg's confession to the murder
of Beryl Evans. *Had an innocent man been put to death three
years earlier?* There couldn't have been two stranglers, living

in a small building, at the same time, MPs proclaimed—surely Timothy Evans was innocent. Though the preponderance of evidence showed that the two crimes varied in several key aspects—and that Reg had lied about many essential aspects of his confession—the coincidence rattled the populace and politicians alike. The Labour Party pleaded to spare Reg the noose, if only to glean more information about the Evans case. And MPs confessed there was a larger moral issue.

"We have no right, until human judgment is infallible, to pass and execute an irrevocable doom," said MP Sydney Silverman.

Reg was scheduled to step onto the platform of the gallows on July 15, 1953. If the Crown executed him, would the country ever know conclusively who strangled Beryl and Geraldine Evans? Frustrated MPs convinced the government to launch an immediate inquiry. Scott Henderson, a judge in Portsmouth, headed the first investigation, one held in private, without a panel. Henderson interviewed Reg as he awaited execution, along with more than twenty key police investigators, medical experts, and witnesses.

And it was here, staring down the gallows, that Reg offered a fourth confession—a new version of his story about Beryl. Reg told Henderson that he had lied previously when he confessed to killing Beryl Evans—he hadn't found her attempting to gas herself. He had never attempted to sexually assault her. He had no idea who killed Geraldine. Reg described the disturbing meeting he'd had with his attorney and the psychiatrist before his trial—the one where they had convinced him that a confession to all the crimes (even ones he hadn't committed) was his only option to avoid execution; they needed to bolster an insanity defense. Scott Henderson believed him—Reg's admission that he murdered Beryl Evans was unreliable, according to the official report. It was Henderson's belief that the Crown had put the right man to death in the Evans murder case—Tim Evans was a killer. He also agreed that the British government was about to justly execute another man—John Reginald Christie—for a series of different murders. The only common link, Henderson concluded, was the location: 10 Rillington Place. Yes, it was an incredible coincidence that two killers had lived there at the same time, said Henderson—but it was a coincidence all the same.

Scott Henderson's inquiry was broadly criticized for being rushed—it was completed in less than a week. Critics declared it was biased, meant to protect police and prosecutors. "Whitewashed," screamed Timothy Evans' supporters in Parliament, after Henderson's report was published. Tim's execution would never be forgotten.

In 1965, twelve years later, the government launched a second inquiry, thanks to the prodding of an influential journalist. Ludovic Kennedy would in time become famous for reexamining high-profile cases, like the Lindbergh kidnapping. Four years earlier, Kennedy had written a book, *Ten Rillington Place*, which examined the trial and execution of Timothy Evans. The author offered an incredibly convincing account of why he was innocent, though the book also included misleading information, incorrect facts that were later disputed by police and witnesses. Kennedy's book sparked public furor over the case once again—so the second inquiry was held in 1966, this time by high court judge Sir Daniel Brabin.

For more than thirty days, Brabin reexamined all of the evidence. He questioned important witnesses and experts; he produced a comprehensive, well-written narrative that included both Reg and Tim's cases. But his conclusions were confusing. He believed it was "more probable than not" that Tim did strangle his wife, and that Reg's confession was false. But Brabin suspected that Reg did murder little Geraldine. He referenced a conversation with a hospital officer just after his sentencing. During their chat, Reg had boasted that the Crown could have charged him with Geraldine's murder—he had killed her.

"They cannot do anything about it now," he said.

Reg then confessed that Tim had asked him to murder both Beryl and his daughter. The confession was ludicrous—it fit none of the narratives offered by Reg or Tim over the past three years. *Why would he say that?* But then Reg made a curious statement to the hospital officer at the courthouse, just before he was taken back to prison.

"Why don't you tell the newspapers and make some money out of me?" suggested Reg.

It seems likely that Reg simply wanted more media attention—his time in the spotlight was waning quickly. The braggart would be dead soon. Less than a week later Reg denied making that confession, but Judge Brabin believed him when he admitted to Geraldine's death. The judge concluded that there was enough reasonable doubt in the Evans case; Brabin believed if jurors knew about Reg's two bodies, buried in the garden, they would have found Tim Evans not guilty of killing his daughter. Since Tim had been on trial for killing Geraldine, not Beryl, he would be free. But he wasn't innocent of murder, Brabin concluded. He suspected that Tim and Reg had colluded, but he offered no real motive to why Reg would kill the little girl. It seemed a very unlikely scenario.

The UK was already embroiled with talk of abolishing the death penalty—the subject had surfaced every few years for the past century within Parliament. In fact, in 1956 the House of Commons had been in favor of its abolition, but the bill died in the House of Lords. In 1965, the resurgence of the Evans controversy led the newspapers. That same year, the death penalty was suspended in Britain and then later abolished, at least partially because of Tim Evans' case. The following year, Judge Brabin's report persuaded the government to grant Tim a posthumous pardon for Geraldine's murder. His body was exhumed from his Pentonville Prison grave and reburied in a family plot in St Patrick's Roman Catholic cemetery in London.

Hordes of people were still visiting 10 Rillington Place months after Reg's trial. The renters were harassed—they demanded the city rename the street. It was soon called Ruston Close; in 1970, Rillington Place, the entire street, was demolished. In the 1971 movie *10 Rillington Place*, actor Richard Attenborough played Reg—it was an advocacy piece, based on Kennedy's sympathetic book. The film was a hit. In London, Madame Tussaud's Chamber of Horrors displayed a wax figure of Reg preparing to be hanged—forever immortalized for curious visitors.

In 2004, an independent assessor for the British Home Office concluded that Reg likely murdered Beryl and Geraldine—and that Tim Evans had been wrongly executed. The government awarded Timothy Evans' half-sister and sister *ex gratia* payments for their brother's wrongful conviction for murdering his daughter, Geraldine. His family hoped for a complete exoneration of both murders, but the government replied that a new inquiry would be too costly.

But on July 15, 1953, as John Reginald Christie was sitting in his cell, there was little focus on inquiries. The night before, a Labourite politician had requested a meeting with him, trying one last time to save his life—but Reg had refused. Now the executioner stood at his prison door. Albert Pierrepoint retrieved Reg as he received prayers from the chaplain. Pierrepoint was the country's lead executioner—he had killed hundreds of criminals. In fact, he had slipped a noose around Timothy Evans' neck just three years earlier. The morning of the execution, Reg seemed terrified.

"My assistant and I had his skimpy wrists pinioned before he knew fully what was happening," said Pierrepoint. "Faltering pitifully, his movements were not so much a walk, as a drifting forward, his legs stumbling. I thought he was going to faint." That description in the press surely would have devastated Reg.

He stood on the platform, with a hood over his head. Once the trapdoor opened, it took just seconds for his neck to snap. The Beast of Rillington Place was dead. Hundreds of gawkers, including women and children, stood outside Pentonville Prison, waiting to read the posted notice of execution. They laughed, joked, and then surged forward as the paper was affixed to the green prison gate. Six policemen were wedged against the wall. The crowd was celebratory. John Reginald Christie provided no last words, no final wishes. He left a will, gifting almost everything to one of his sisters. At the end of the document, he simply said: "An apology for any trouble I may have brought about."

The press drifted to its next big story.

The murders at 10 Rillington Place will always be enigmatic — a macabre mystery that belongs in an Edgar Allan Poe tale, complete with secluded bodies beneath an eerie fog. There will never be definitive answers. *Could there have been two stranglers living in the same building?* people ask. Yes, particularly in postwar Notting Hill, where domestic violence was prevalent and poverty was endemic. Two *serial killers* living in the same home may have been farfetched. But Tim Evans wasn't a serial killer — he was an abusive husband, very capable of snapping.

There is no conclusion to this case — no real closure. Both men were habitual liars. Both men offered multiple unreliable confessions. Both men were violent. And both men had strong motives, though their impulses were quite different. There's no reliable physical evidence: no vaginal swabs taken from Beryl Evans and no DNA tests conducted on the pubic hairs found inside the tobacco tin—nothing that police could dust for fingerprints. Strangulation was a very common weapon—cheap and effective.

The abundance of circumstantial evidence fueled enormous speculation. The list of coincidences in the murders seems hard to ignore. Beryl and Geraldine were found in the washhouse, and two of Reg's victims were also briefly stored there. Yet Reg never kept the women there for very long; he was scared of being caught. Beryl and Geraldine were there for weeks—Reg was never that sloppy; he prided himself on having a plan. There is no real proof that one man was solely responsible—there were so many conflicting stories and details. There will likely never be a satisfying conclusion.

What may be most disturbing about this case, the saga of 10 Rillington Place, is what remains unknown. To whom did those four sets of pubic hairs really belong? Pathologists concluded that one set likely belonged to Ethel Christie, but that none could have come from any of the three women in the alcove, as Reg had claimed. It's unclear if they could have come from the two women in the garden. Pathologists excluded Beryl Evans as a contributor. Reg was a collector, a serial killer who indulged in keeping mementos of his murders. There's always another space on the shelf for collectors.

And there was another mystery, discovered in Reg's garden by police: four teeth that couldn't be definitively linked to either woman buried in the backyard.

Were there more victims of John Reginald Christie, tucked away somewhere, never to be found?

"It would not surprise me to find that there is someone else," said Reg, in one of his final interviews before his execution. "It would not surprise me."

∽

On December 2, 1953, Minister of Housing Harold Macmillan stood before Parliament, a paper gripped in his hand. It was three days shy of the one-year anniversary of the killer fog, later referred to as the Great Smog of 1952.

"*The Interim Report of the Committee on Air Pollution* is being published today, and the Government have given it careful consideration," announced Macmillan. "As the Committee points out, the problem of air pollution, and of smoke in particular, has been the subject of study and research over a long period."

He paraphrased sections of the interim Beaver Report. The committee of eleven divided the report between two actions: the first was an analysis of the source and effect of air pollution. The second section detailed recommendations for immediate action. Some of those recommendations were already in place, like a meteorological warning system and smog masks for the elderly. But there were other suggestions—both short- and long-term solutions. Members proposed launching a campaign to request Londoners stay inside during smog events. The committee moved for a ban on burning trash and lighting bonfires. It suggested urging the public not to drive their cars into thickly settled urban areas. It pressed the government to encourage the use of smokeless fuel during heavy smog periods.

The committee blamed air pollution on local governments, as well as the country's administrations, past and present. It also targeted the domestic customer, those Londoners who burned coal during the winters. The neighboring factories and generating stations were not the sole source of pollution, said the report—in fact, the average resident held the majority of the responsibility for the smog. Housewives were to blame for blackening their own bedsheets.

"It has been estimated that in the London 'smog' of December, 1952 up to 60 percent of the smoke was due to domestic fires," read the report. "The first objective should be to prevent the emission of coal smoke and oil smoke, and of grit."

The committee admitted this wouldn't be an easy task; the country wasn't producing enough smokeless fuel to replace coal, but it should be possible to distribute cleaner-burning fuel in the worst areas within the next few years.

"To achieve this will, in many cases, involve replacing or modifying existing equipment, and will involve capital expenditure, but it is completely possible," read the Beaver Report.

It demanded more research into smokeless fuels—how to make them both more efficient and more plentiful. The Beaver Report also named the main components of air pollution—smoke from the incomplete combustion of fuel, and oxides of sulphur formed by combustion. A subsidiary source was the fine grit and dust derived from the combustion of fuel. The mixture of pollutants with white fog proved to be deadly. The government refused to publicly acknowledge the sources of air pollution, yet the Beaver Committee provided a list, along with amounts contained in the air during the smog.

The final findings were ghastly. During each day of the fog, almost 4,000 metric tons of pollutants were added to the air— that equated to about 20,000 pounds over five days. There were 1,000 metric tons of smoke particles, 2,000 metric tons of carbon dioxide, 140 metric tons of hydrochloric acid, 14 metric tons of fluorine compounds, and 370 metric tons of sulphur dioxide. The causes were clear: domestic coal-burning fires; coal-fuel locomotives, steam engines, and power stations; and the city's new diesel buses, which replaced the electric tram system. Those pollutants, trapped by a fog layer almost seven hundred feet deep at times, killed thousands of people.

Newspapers around the world quoted the Beaver Committee and its recommendations. Residents read it at their local libraries. International communities were shocked. Yet, the report wasn't unique, or even innovative. All of its recommendations were points constantly heralded by smoke abatement proponents, like Norman Dodds. But the Beaver Report was revolutionary because it coalesced those recommendations into one document that both politicians and lay people could understand—and then demand. The theme of the report was the need for a national Clean Air Act, a piece of legislation that would replace all current provisions to abate smoke. It would also, for the first time, target both domestic and industrial air pollution. The Beaver Report was the impetus for cleaner air in Britain—it would save lives.

But there was something in that report—a small fact, virtually ignored for decades, that was so important, so disturbing and upsetting. The politicians didn't seem to notice it. The media didn't seize on it. The public didn't know.

In 1953, as the Beaver Committee members sifted through loads of data, they were sent a paper. It was written by Dr. E. T. Wilkins, the head of pollution investigations at the government's Fuel Research Station—he was the nation's top pollution scientist. Wilkins included a small graphic, a chart that caught Sir Hugh Beaver's attention.

"In this, there is included a chart which shows a continuing abnormal death rate in Greater London during the 2½ months following the 'smog,' " read the Beaver Report. "Obviously this requires further, and close, investigation."

The chart showed a large spike during the fog in December: the four thousand additional deaths mentioned by the media and the government. That spike declined, beginning December 20th. But the latter part of the graph showed another steady rise from January 1953 through mid-March. The death rate was 50 percent higher than expected. There were eight thousand additional deaths. So there were two large spikes: one during the fog, and the other shortly after. In the graph, Wilkins highlighted them both and underneath printed "Smog Incident, 1952." According to the government's pollution expert, the fog had killed not four thousand Londoners, but twelve thousand.

The following November, the Beaver Committee released its final report, which offered the government a practical plan for smoke abatement, but one that was slightly tempered from its interim report. And that chart was missing.

"The effects of the London fog of December, 1952, which resulted in the deaths of some 4,000 people, have been the subject of a recently published report by an expert committee appointed by the Minister of Health," the final Beaver Report read.

The chart was still in a government report, but in one from the Ministry of Health in 1954 titled *Mortality and Morbidity During the London Fog of December 1952*. In that report, health experts made a change to the graph. Beneath the chart, in the section between January and mid-March, was written "Influenza." The government was now claiming that the additional eight thousand deaths that had occurred in the aftermath of the smog were actually the result of a flu epidemic. This claim was the prevailing conclusion for decades.

But in 2001, epidemiologist Devra Davis and her team from Johns Hopkins and Carnegie Mellon universities researched the number of influenza deaths during the two and a half months after the smog event. The flu was responsible for only a small portion of deaths. Davis' team cited researchers who had studied tissue samples from the victims of the Great Smog before, during, and after the disaster. By looking at the contents of the lungs right before the patients died, scientists found air pollutants inside. Dr. Davis discovered that, if the influenza deaths were excluded, approximately 7,700 more deaths had occurred between January and March. She concluded that twelve thousand people had died from the smog between December and March.

In fact, there was no mention in Parliament of a flu epidemic—no great calamity referenced in the newspapers or in the Ministry of Health's annual report. Of the hundreds of memos, public and confidential, that were reviewed from Iain Macleod's ministry for this book, none suggested that there was a widespread flu epidemic. In fact, the World Health Organization reported that the flu seemed relatively mild for 1952–53.

In 1954, E. T. Wilkins—the creator of that chart—published a paper in the *Journal of the Royal Sanitary Institute.* In it, he targeted W. P. D. Logan, the country's chief medical statistician, for claiming that those eight thousand additional deaths were caused by the flu.

"Logan and others have suggested that this secondary peak, which lasted for most of January and February, was influenced by factors other than the smog, including an outbreak of influenza," wrote Wilkins.

He said that the secondary peak of deaths corresponded almost perfectly with the secondary peak of pollution during the same time period.

"It was thus a second pollution shock to Londoners whose powers of resistance may have been reduced by the earlier smog incident."

But it was too late. The government had already shared the narrative with the public—the number stood at four thousand. Both the media and the government largely chose to ignore the fog deaths; they were nonetheless forced to admit that four thousand people had died. Still, it might have been difficult to believe that Londoners continued to die, months afterward. And they were also more likely to die from heart or respiratory diseases, even years later.

Thanks to the efforts of the Beaver Committee in 1954, backbenchers, including Conservatives, pushed through Parliament a Private Members Bill on domestic coal burning. It would be called the Clean Air Act of 1956, the world's first air pollution act enacted by a government that uniformly restrained pollution nationwide—it tightened restrictions on industrial smoke and banned coal in many domestic and industrial areas across the country. It shifted sources of heat toward cleaner fuels, like electricity and gas. In November 1955, Parliament debated the bill for six hours. Critics claimed it was a watered-down version of what could have been a tougher bill—that was true.

"A miserable hypocritical shadow of a Bill," said one Labour MP. "A little mouse of a Bill," claimed another.

MPs made many concessions to ensure it would pass, like allowing industries to receive a temporary exemption from the changes, under some circumstances. But the bill passed and the amount of air pollutants in Britain was immediately reduced.

The 1956 Clean Air Act became a blueprint for the rest of the world to follow—the first comprehensive legislation to attack air pollution. And it seemed to have an immediate impact. The Meteorological Office tracked the number of fog events in London every year. In 1956, the year the bill was enacted, there were almost forty fogs, including one that killed more than one thousand people in London. The following year, there were about half the number of fogs. The same was true for industrial and domestic smoke. Eventually, coal was replaced in Britain with gas, oil, and electricity.

The Clean Air Act couldn't accept all of the credit—the severity of air pollution had been declining in the UK for years. But now, the dirty fogs slowly began to disappear. The new regulations helped, but in December of 1962 another smog settled over London for four days, killing 750 people. The governments of the past simply didn't act quickly enough. And killer fogs were still happening around the world. In 1963, a two-week-long fog in New York City killed almost four hundred people.

Thanks to the Clean Air Act of 1956, the Great Smog was the last major air pollution event in Britain's history. Norman Dodds was pleased—his tenacity had saved lives, although the story of London's Great Smog quickly disappeared from headlines and became virtually forgotten. Four years after the deadly fog, Minister of Housing Harold Macmillan was appointed prime minister after Sir Anthony Eden resigned. When a journalist asked him what was the most difficult thing about his job, Macmillan famously replied, "Events, dear boy, events." The deadly fog of 1952 was just another ephemeral event for Harold Macmillan, a scandal that failed to spoil his successful career in British politics. But another public humiliation did—in 1963, Macmillan resigned as prime minister after the Profumo affair, a British sex scandal involving his secretary of state for war and a nineteen-year-old model. The next year, Macmillan returned to his family's publishing house, as chairman.

Minister of Health Iain Macleod enjoyed a twenty-year career in the government, and briefly became the leader of the House of Commons and the chancellor of the exchequer. Norman Dodds remained an MP until his death in 1965—he became an advocate in Parliament for those suffering from mental health issues; he also broadcasted the plight of the Gypsies in England. The Labour Party campaign center and headquarters building in Northumberland Heath is named the Norman Dodds House in his honor. Met Police cadet Stanley Crichton was eventually transferred from North London. His wife, Maura, suffered from asthma for the rest of her life—Stanley believed she died prematurely thanks to the 1952 fog. Rosemary Sargent failed to pass her O-level exams, so she wasn't able to move forward to college. She became a secretary and, eventually, a parent. She and her siblings never again spoke about the fog. Dr. Donald Acheson became a physician and epidemiologist who specialized in public health. He was the chief medical officer for England in the 1980s, a crusader who helped Britain lead the way in innovative research and public education during the AIDS epidemic.

Air pollution is still a crisis around the world. Exhaust fumes from vehicles have usurped chimneys filled with coal smoke. A US study from 2015 found that smog kills more than four thousand people in China *every day*, about 17 percent of deaths in the country. In 2016, atmospheric chemistry experts at Texas A&M University began a joint study with several universities in China, hoping to solve one mystery about the Great Smog of 1952. The researchers measured air pollution in two large cities in China, Xi'an and Beijing, and then used lab tests to isolate the chemicals that made London's fog so lethal.

The scientists discovered that two coal byproducts, sulphur dioxide and nitrogen dioxide, had formed sulfate particles in the clouds. When the fog dissipated, it left behind acid particles in the air that were deadly to susceptible Londoners. More than sixty years later, the Great Smog prompted important research in vulnerable countries like China. But like Winston Churchill's cabinet in Great Britain, the Chinese government has opted to largely ignore the problem.

Women in some rural regions of China as well as India and Africa develop lung cancer and respiratory ailments at rates typically found in smokers because of their chronic exposure to indoor cooking fires. And air quality is still a worry in London. In December 1991, more than 150 people died from a smog event.

Recent studies found that the long-term effects of the 1952 smog are terrible; the fog was linked to asthma and developmental problems in children and babies in the womb at the time. Low levels of pollution are damaging the health of millions of people worldwide.

In 1953 London, the story of John Reginald Christie and the eight bodies found at 10 Rillington Place enthralled a public fascinated with grisly crimes. And it offered valuable and disturbing lessons about the legal system. But of the two killers, society may be better served to heed the lessons of the Great Smog—and remember its estimated twelve thousand victims, along with the millions of people who have suffered since.

Acknowledgments

One of the most exciting things about this book, as the author, is that I was able to bring these characters to life, thanks to contributions of many people I've met over the past few years. The most important, certainly, are Stanley Crichton, Rosemary Sargent (now Merritt), and Len Trevallion. I asked them to recount, in great detail, some fairly traumatic moments in their lives. I'm so grateful to each of them—Rosemary and I spoke for hours over the phone and I was thrilled to finally meet her in person during a research trip to London. Stanley, a former cop, was wonderfully candid about his experiences in the Great Smog—he helped bring his wife, Maura, to life. Len Trevallion, who passed away in December 2016 at the age of 102, was generous with his time on the phone with me, recalling his interactions with both Tim Evans and John Reginald Christie. Likewise, Christine Dodds provided me with context concerning her father-in-law, Norman Dodds. She also sent me valuable family papers that supplemented his story.

There are numerous repositories in London, and I'm indebted to several of them, particularly the Wellcome Trust and the National Archives. The Wellcome Trust offered several wonderful films about the Great Smog, as well as pictures and papers. I spent hours researching both the fog and John Reginald

Christie's case at the National Archives in Kew in southwest London. I also scoured the Barking and Dagenham Archives and Local Studies Centre, the Library and Learning Centre, the University of East London, and the Hartley Library at the University of Southampton. At the Museum of London, curators Georgina Young and Jackie Keily pointed me toward their unique exhibit on crime, where they displayed evidence in the John Christie case. I'm thankful to Paul Bickley, the former curator of the Met's Crime Museum, who was a font about crime in 1950s London.

Professor Robert Maynard, the former head of the Air Pollution and Noise Unit of the Health Protection Agency in the UK, provided me with some valuable resources about the history of air pollution. One of my most useful resources was the Hansard archive, the official transcripts of the House of Commons, but there were times when I needed guidance. For that, Myf Nixon of mySociety was a huge help.

Jonathan Oates, author of *John Christie of Rillington Place: Biography of a Serial Killer,* was invaluable as a resource, a sounding board, and a fact-checker for the Christie sections. Journalist Phyllis Oberman provided context for the sections about London media—she was a wide-eyed print reporter on Fleet Street during the 1950s. Maxwell Vernon, once a teenaged Met police cadet, gave me a detailed description of life in Scotland Yard's Information Room during the 1952 smog.

My incredible fact-checker, Joyce Pendola, was an able safety net. Former defense attorney and law professor David Sheppard was a fantastic listener and adviser. Meteorologists Kris Wilson and Troy Kimmel, both professors at the University of Texas at Austin, helped guide my meteorological knowledge, which was very limited. Philippa Levine, the codirector of the University of Texas Program in British Studies, was a great resource.

For guidance on medical assessments for the Christie case, I consulted pathologist Emily DeSantis at Clinical Pathology Associates in Austin and Melissa Brassell, MD, assistant medical examiner, Office of the Chief Medical Examiner, Baltimore.

One of my most favorite books was *London Fog: A Biography*, written by the talented Christine Corton at the University of Cambridge. I'm grateful that she agreed to read over my book—and even more grateful that she enjoyed it. There are two researchers who deserve recognition. Peter Brimblecombe's book, *The Big Smoke*, provided a fantastic snapshot of the history of air pollution in London. Devra Davis' book, *When Smoke Ran Like Water*, provided much-needed context regarding the history of the 1948 smog in Donora, Pennsylvania. Davis also exposed the British government's fabricated flu epidemic through diligent research, published in 2001. Brimblecombe and Davis have been very supportive of this book.

I would be remiss to not thank some folks at the University of Texas, particularly the dean of the Moody College of Communication, Jay Bernhardt, School of Journalism Director R.B. Brenner and Associate Director Kathleen McElroy, along with Glenn Frankel, former director and Wanda "Fluffy" Cash, former associate director. I've received generous funding for several years from the Maureen Healy Decherd '73 Teaching Endowment for Journalism, for which I am grateful. I'm also so happy to see my cousin, Diana Dawson, most days at UT. She inspired me to become a journalist years ago and her support has been invaluable. And I'm so pleased to trade students with the most talented journalism faculty in the country, particularly with fellow authors Kevin Robbins and Bill Minutaglio. Writing might have been a much shorter career for me, had it not been for them. And some other scribes who have influenced me are Bryan

Burrough, Pam Colloff, Stephen Harrigan, Skip Hollandsworth, and Joe Drape. I'm honored to call them friends.

A shout-out to Genuine Joe Coffeehouse in Austin, Texas, my third office when there were too many distractions at the other two—Victor Levi and Dave Swainston are wonderful hosts. Thanks to Becka Oliver, the executive director of the Writers' League of Texas, who was a fantastic cheerleader from the beginning—and her organization is outstanding. Likewise for KUT—Emily Donohue has been so supportive.

I'm honored to be with Hachette Book Group. I've been surrounded with a talented, passionate group of people that quite honestly love and support this book, particularly Mauro DiPreta, publisher; Michelle Aielli, associate publisher; Betsy Hulsebosch, marketing director; and Lauren Hummel, assistant editor. I will forever be indebted to executive editor Michelle Howry—from the moment we spoke on the phone, I knew she was the right person for this book. She is truly a gifted editor, a wonderful visionary, and a genuine friend.

To my literary agent, Jessica Papin with Dystel, Goderich & Bourret (who deserves her own paragraph): I'm blessed to have her as my stalwart advocate and a devoted friend. She's been my support system in the bewildering world of books and I'm so pleased about that! P.S. to Jessica: Yes, I know there are too many adjectives.

To the group of Texas girls I've known for thirty years— thanks for the love, laughs, and margaritas.

And finally to Jen, Ella, and Quinn, as well as my parents, Lynn and Jack Lefevre, my in-laws Sandra and Charlie Winkler, and my brother-in-law Chuck Winkler—I'm honored to be a part of this amazing family.

Notes

PROLOGUE

The teenager in the bombing sites comes from more than one dozen interviews with Rosemary Sargent (Merritt), now a seventy-seven-year-old grandmother.

The Morrison bomb shelter comes from Sargent's interviews, along with archival photos.

The V-1 bomb: Reginald Victor Jones' *Most Secret War: British Scientific Intelligence, 1939–1945*, along with archival photos.

Background of King George VI: Denis Judd's book *King George VI* (p. 190).

Seventy thousand civilians killed, according to the 2013 update by the Commonwealth War Graves Commission.

Britain in the Korean War comes from The National Archives exhibit entitled *Korea, 1951*.

Interviews with several Metropolitan police officers from 1952 provided anecdotal evidence of crime in London. More specific data will be addressed in a later chapter.

Prewar coal production details were provided by the Department of Energy and Climate Change, "Historical Coal Data: Coal Production, 1853–2014."

Information on coal-fired power plants in London in 1952 came from a government report called the "Environmental Impact of Power Generation," by the Royal Society of Chemistry (Great Britain) from 1959 (p. 22).

Coal accounted for 60 percent: "50 Years On," *Greater London Authority*, December 2002.

"The Politics of Big Coal…" was supplemented with remarks by Professor Roy Parker, from the Centre of Social Policy, and his contribution to the 2002 panel discussion titled "The Big Smoke: Fifty Years after the 1952 London Smog," sponsored by the Centre for History in Public Health. The idea that the Conservative government was bracing for a potential regime change was certainly known, but Parker was able to tie that fear to the potential public backlash over air pollution. (p. 16).

"The government was selling its best coal…": House of Commons, *Parliamentary Debates*, 17 February 1949, vol. 461 cc1315–7; House of Commons, *Parliamentary Debates*, 10 June 1952, vol. 502 cc22–3W; House of Commons, *Parliamentary Debates*, 7 July 1952, vol. 503 cc879–80.

"Nutty slack typically included lignite…": *Encyclopedia Britannica* search for "lignite."

"Black coal, anthracite, had carbon content…": *Encyclopedia Britannica* search for "anthracite."

In the section that begins: "In 1952, London entered winter with its largest stock of coal in any postwar year," the amount of 19½ million comes from a Parliamentary debate led by MP Gerald Nabarro, which can be found here: House of Commons, *Parliamentary Debates*, 1 December 1952. Vol. 508 cc1244–54.

CHAPTER 1

Description of the Gulf Stream was greatly helped along by the guidance of two outstanding meteorologists, Troy Kimmel and Dr. Kristopher Wilson. Its history comes from various sources, but the most thorough was *The Ocean World Encyclopedia* by Donald G. Groves and Lee M. Hunt.

There is a rather interesting debate about whether the Gulf Stream actually warms Western Europe—a minority of scientists contend that the current is just one of many factors. For the purposes of this book, we'll stay with conventional wisdom.

Details about postwar life were gleaned from various sources: magazines and newspapers, as well as *Life in 1950s London*, by Mike Hutton. Most helpful were the memories of interviewees, who could confirm or deny my many assumptions.

The UK's first test of an atomic bomb: "British Atomic Weapon Exploded," from the *Times* (London), October 3, 1952. (Unless otherwise stated, the *Times* refers to the *Times of London*.)

Harry Truman's speech: January 9, 1952, entitled "Annual Message to the Congress on the State of the Union"; British Pathe film: *Truman Speech to Congress*, 1952.

Lynmouth flooding: "31 Believed Dead," *Times* (London), August 18, 1952.

The Farnborough Air Show: "27 killed at Farnborough Air Display," *Times*, September 8, 1952.

Details from the Harrow and Wealdstone railway crash were culled from numerous sources, including articles from the London *Times* and the *Manchester Guardian*. The accusation that fog was the reason for the crash comes from the Ministry of Transport's *Report on the double collision which occurred on 8th October 1952 at Harrow and Wealdstone Station*, published by Her Majesty's Stationery Office. Each disaster was also well documented on British Pathe, a helpful repository for film footage of most major British news stories.

The sections involving Parliament were supported by numerous sources: Norman Dodds' book *Gypsies, Didikoid, and Other Travellers*, Johnson Publications, 1966 (pp. 11–15); Christine Dodds, Norman's daughter-in-law and only surviving relative, provided more personal details. Dodds' voting record and list of debates can be found on the Hansard website.

"Harold Macmillan's main idea was to keep me quiet for a few months": Dodds, *Gypsies, Didikoid, and Other Travellers*.

Customs of Parliament: www.parliament.uk; I also asked many, many questions of Ms. Myf Nixon, the marketing and communications manager of mySociety, an organization that strives to provide UK citizens with online tools to discover more about democracy. I watched a fantastic four-part documentary series on the BBC entitled *Inside the Commons*. I also visited Parliament.

The details about fireplaces in the Palace of Westminster: House of Commons, *Parliamentary Debates*, 3 February 1953. Vol. 510 cc1628–9.

Details about the weather: the London *Times'* Index page, where the daily weather forecast was given.

Details about the Press Gallery were provided by the official Parliament website, "the Parliamentary Press Gallery." The lovely Phyllis Obermann, an active journalist on Fleet Street in 1952, provided some of the commentary about life as a Parliamentary reporter. Charles Dickens' quote: "I have worn my knees by writing on them on the old back row of the old gallery of the House of Commons," comes from his 1865 speech to the Newspaper Press Fund.

The goose comment: House of Commons, *Parliamentary Debates*, 3 December 1952. Vol. 508 cc1565–667. The *Times* did a nice job of providing color commentary, which can be found in a December 4, 1952, article, "Angry Scenes in Commons."

Dodds, "They expect me to deny it...": Greatorex, Wilfred, "Back-bencher Who Asks the Awkward Questions," *John Bull* magazine, July 5, 1952. (p. 15).

Fifteen hundred oral questions: Greatorex, "Back-bencher Who Asks the Awkward Questions" (p. 15).

"I cannot make up my mind as to whether he agreed to this as a helpful contribution in dealing with this social problem...": Dodds, *Gypsies, Didikoid, and Other Travellers,* (pp. 51–52).

The anticyclone section was supplemented by data from Britain's Meteorological Office, which churned out daily reports of London's weather; they included a narrative summary and levels of barometric pressure, temperature, and wind readings. They can be found in MH 55/2659. *Smog of December 1952: Meteorological Reports.*

John Reginald Christie is first introduced here. The descriptions of the bush root and the newspaper scrap come from my visit to the Museum of London's fascinating exhibit "The Crime Museum," where the items were on display; and Francis E. Camps, *Medical and Scientific Investigations in the Christie Case,* Medical Publications Limited, Anchor Press, 1953 (p. 47).

The physical description and life story of Ruth Fuerst came from the police statements of two friends, Ernestine Zagier and Alice Trater, and her former employer Alfred Goddard: National Archives, CAB 143/TS 58.

Christie's details about the murder of Ruth Fuerst come from his June 5, 1953, confession to police, along with his story in the *Sunday Pictorial,* published July 5, 1953; Tennyson F. Jesse, *Trials of Timothy John Evans and John Reginald Christie* (pp. 187–89).

"The beauty of a corpse" comes from Christie's story in the *Sunday Pictorial,* July 12, 1953.

The brother-in-law's visit comes from Jesse, *Trials of Evans and Christie* (p. 188).

The National Coal Board: Peter Thorsheim, *Inventing Pollution, Coal, Smoke, and Culture in Britain since 1800,* Ohio University Press, 2006 (p. 161).

The anticyclone section can be found in *Smog of December 1952: Meteorological Reports,* MH 55/2659.

CHAPTER 2

Horatio Nelson descriptions come from a photo of his column, enveloped by the fog in December 1952, posted by Getty, along with a summary by the *Times,* December 6, 1952, "Fog Delays Air Services." Facts about Nelson come from the *Encyclopedia Britannica*; Hitler's desire to move the column comes from Colin White's *The Nelson Companion,* Royal Naval Museum Publications, in association with Sutton, 2005. (p. 129).

The temperature decrease and barometric pressure rise come from the government's meteorological reports, produced daily by the Air Ministry during December 1952.

General fog problems in London come from several articles printed on December 6, 1952, including "Fog Delays Air Services" by the *Times* and "Traffic Delayed by Fog" by the *Manchester Guardian.*

MPs in the House of Commons debated from 11 a.m. to 4:30 p.m., a shortened session, according to Hansard's record from December 5, 1952.

The assaulted woman cleaner comes from a news brief from the *Times,* December 6, 1952.

Macleod's decision to curtail medical staff comes from "Limitation of Hospital Staffs," by the *Times* on December 5, 1952.

Compulsory crash helmets and the new royal stamps come from a *Times* news brief, December 6, 1952.

"The first real fog of the year has enveloped London today, an old-fashioned peasouper..." came from a *Manchester Guardian* article, December 6, 1952.

Description of West End Christmas lights comes from the *Times*, December 6, 1952, "Fog Delays Air Services."

The pollution levels were recorded by the government and distributed in the Ministry of Health's *Report on Public Health and Medical Subjects, No. 95, Mortality and Morbidity During the London Fog of December 1952*, Table 3 on page 3 (Lambeth, County Hall reading). Table 12 of the same document shows the number of patients admitted for respiratory and cardiac diseases.

Eight thousand diesel buses: David Laskin, "The Great London Smog," *Weatherwise* magazine, November/December 2006 (p.44).

Rosemary Sargent's recollections come from her various interviews—the same for former police officer Stanley Crichton.

Nutty slack and coal supply: Roger Fouquet, "The Demand for Environmental Quality in Driving Transitions to Low-Polluting Energy Sources," London School of Economics, 2012 (p. 27).

"Until the thirteenth century, wood was the main fuel source in London...": Peter Brimblecombe, *The Big Smoke: A History of Air Pollution in London Since Medieval Times* (p. 17).

"Londoners then collected 'sea coal' that washed ashore off the northeast coast of England, near Newcastle...": Brimblecombe, *The Big Smoke* (p. 7).

"It was used to churn out a variety of products...": Eric Ashby and Mary Anderson, *The Politics of Clean Air*, Oxford University Press, 1981 (p. 1).

"Lime kilns blasted...": Brimblecombe, *The Big Smoke* (p. 16).

"In 1257, the British royals were warming...": Brimblecombe, *The Big Smoke* (pp. 8–9).

"Seventeenth-century astrologer John Gadbury kept a daily weather diary...": Brimblecombe, *The Big Smoke* (pp. 59–60).

Vitamin D deficiency: Peter Brimblecombe, "It All Changed with Chimneys," *New Scientist*, July 9, 1987 (p. 56); "Rickets on the Increase?," University of Leeds, *Research News*, http://www.leeds.ac.uk/youarewhatyouate/news/news-rickets.html.

"In 1661, influential writer John Evelyn distributed a treatise, one of the earliest works on air pollution, entitled: *FUMIFUGIUM*...": Brimblecombe, *The Big Smoke* (pp. 47–50).

"In the 1600s, the Church of England's Archbishop of Canterbury, William Laud, fined several coal-burning brewers, so he could repair smoke damage to Saint Paul's Cathedral...": Brimblecombe *The Big Smoke* (pp. 41–42).

"By the nineteenth century, more than a million Londoners....": David Urbinato, "London's Historic 'Pea-Soupers,'" *EPA Journal*, 1994.

"During World War I, smoke became a defense strategy...": Thorsheim, Peter. *Inventing Pollution, Coal, Smoke, and Culture in Britain since 1800*, Ohio University Press, 2006 (p. 159).

"The National Smoke Abatement Society...": Thorsheim, *Inventing Pollution*, (p. 160).

"Factory owners began to force their steam boilers...": Thorsheim, *Inventing Pollution* (p. 159).

"In 1873, smog smothered the city for days...": Urbinato, "London's Historic 'Pea-Soupers.'"

"Londoners in the East End were usually the most affected because...": Christine L. Corton, *London Fog: The Biography*. Belnap Press of Harvard University Press, 2015 (p. 20).

Smoke as a defense and factories increasing productivity: Thorsheim, *Inventing Pollution* (pp. 159–60).

Descriptions of Christie's backyard come from various contemporary pictures, provided by Getty Images, as well as reports from police officers on the scene.

The thighbone detail comes from Christie's June 5, 1953, confession to police. National Archives, CAB 143 and TS 58.

Description of Eady comes from various pictures submitted into evidence.

Murder of Muriel Amelia Eady comes from Christie's June 5, 1953, confession to police, along with his story in the *Sunday Pictorial*, July 12, 1953; Jesse, *Trials of Evans and Christie*. (pp. 189–90).

Note about Ethel Christie's employment: She was trained as a shorthand typist, so that was likely her job at Osram's light bulb factory. Additional info: Ludovic Kennedy, *Ten Rillington Place*, Simon and Schuster, New York, 1961.

Christie's various quotes about Eady's death come from the *Sunday Pictorial*, July 12, 1953.

Eady's clothing and physical description come from a missing persons report made by her cousin, Wilfred Dunn, on November 4, 1944—stored in police evidence at the National Archives, CAB 143 and TS 58.

Christie's injured arm comes from his medical history, submitted into evidence. The list, made by Dr. S. Fazekas, mentions "able to do work not involving strain on right arm." Stored in the National Archives, CAB 143 and TS 58. Five days before Eady's murder, he also complained of bronchitis.

CHAPTER 3

Information Room: interviews with former police cadet Max Vernon, who was sixteen years old when he worked in Scotland Yard during the smog. British Pathe also has two great films on Scotland Yard, *New 999 Information Room at Scotland Yard* (1957) and *999-Scotland Yard* (1948). Descriptions of the Yard on the embankment: numerous archival pictures available on the internet.

History of Scotland Yard: *Encyclopedia Britannica*; "A Brief History of Scotland Yard," *Smithsonian*, September 27, 2007; "Scotland Yard," the Metropolitan Police online archives.

"The Whitehall Mystery": *Times*, "The Murder at Westminster," October 23, 1888.

The pollution levels were recorded by the government and distributed in the Ministry of Health's *Report on Public Health and Medical Subjects, No. 95, Mortality and Morbidity During the London Fog of December 1952*, Table 3 on page 3 (Lambeth, County Hall reading). Later in the chapter, the data comes from Westminster readings.

The temperature decrease and barometric pressure rise come from the government's meteorological reports, produced daily by the Air Ministry during December 1952.

General details about fog chaos: "Traffic Delayed by Fog," *Manchester Guardian*, December 7, 1952.

Automobile Association comments: "Fog and Ice: Cars Left by Roadside," *Observer*, December 7, 1952.

Police using bikes and white jackets: "London Blacked Out Again," *Manchester Guardian*, December 9, 1952.

General crime: "London Fog Tie-up Lasts for 3D Day," *New York Times*, December 8, 1952.

"Girl stabbed": "Much Crime in London's Bad Fog," *Barrier Miner*, December 9, 1952; "London Blacked Out Again," *Manchester Guardian*, December 9, 1952.

Details about the workers killed by train: "London Fog Crash of Train Kills 2," *New York Times*, December 7, 1952.

Responding ambulances: "Transport Dislocated by Three Days of Fog," *Times*, December 8, 1952.

The judge's injuries: "Chaos Again in Fog," *Times*, December 9, 1952.

Number of police in 1952: *The Report of the Commissioner of Police of the Metropolis for the Year 1952*, published by HMSO, 1953.

Details about the size of the police force before and after the war and the number of cases cleared: "Detection and Prevention of Crime," *Times*, December 4, 1952.

Rosemary Sargent's recollections come from her various interviews.

"In the West End, on the corner of Mortimer and Cleveland streets, sat Middlesex Hospital...": "Frederick Cayley Robinson's Acts of Mercy Murals at the Middlesex Hospital, London" by J. H. Baron, *BMJ* (journal), 24–31 December 1994. Middlesex descriptions come from two YouTube videos, one produced by British Pathe, *Middlesex Hospital 1964.*

Acheson's recollections come from his 2007 autobiography, *One Doctor's Odyssey, The Social Lesion*, and an in-depth 2002 panel: "The Big Smoke: Fifty Years after the 1952 London Smog."

"He was one of the city's nearly two thousand general practitioners...": William Wise, *Killer Smog, The World's Worst Air Pollution Disaster*, Rand McNally, 1968 (p. 130).

Acheson's biography: "Sir Donald Acheson: Obituary," the *Telegraph*, January 13, 2010.

National Health Service history: Martin Gorsky's *Social History of Medicine*, 2008.

Christie's resignation letter comes from police evidence, stored in the National Archives, CAB 143 and TS 58.

The Ladbroke Grove station note is speculation; it's the most likely Tube station Christie used, but he couldn't remember names of Underground lines very well. His neighbors mentioned that he tended to use that station. Details of his resignation come from trial transcripts, both Christie's and Burrow's testimonies, stored in Jesse, *Trials of Evans and Christie* (pp. 137–38, 205).

The history and description of 10 Rillington Place: Christie's trial transcripts and archival photos, provided by Getty Images. Jonathan Oates' *John Christie of Rillington Place: Biography of a Serial Killer* was also an excellent guide, along with *Life in 1950s London* by Mike Hutton.

"Reg's home was the last at the end of the cul-de-sac...": Ludovic Kennedy, *Ten Rillington Place*, (p. 21).

"There is not enough room to swing a dead cat in the kitchen": Christie's defense attorney Derek Curtis Bennett during his trial. Jesse, *Trials of Evans and Christie* (p. 184).

"Police hurried to domestic violence calls, sometimes involving former servicemen who smuggled their service weapons...": Steve Chibnall, *Law and Order News: An Analysis of Crime Reporting in the British Press*, Tavistock Publications, 1977 (p. 52).

"And the number of working class, young criminals in prison increased...": Chibnall, *Law and Order News* (p. 55).

The reconstruction of Christie's Saturday comes from reports about how the fog affected the entire city—dirt, grime, black flecks, and soot-blanketed homes—with no exceptions. Ten Rillington Place was so poorly constructed that the fog would have had no trouble entering the building. In a letter to her sister dated December 15, Ethel Christie discusses how ill the fog made them. It's stored in the National Archives, CAB 143 and TS 58.

History of Notting Hill and the West Indies immigrants comes from the Museum of London's series *Where Do Londoners Come From? London's Communities 1675–Present*; a series by the British Library, *Timelines: Sources from History: Windrush*; and a National Archive series, *Bound for Britain: Experiences of Immigration to the UK*. In addition, a British Pathe film entitled *Jamaicans Come to Britain to Look for Work* (1948); the BP film *Notting Hill Tension* (1959) shows "Keep Britain White" signs.

Christie's social behavior: *News of the World*, dated June 28, 1953.

Christie's physical description was reconstructed from various sources, including archival pictures and witness testimony — all consistent. They can be found in the National Archives, CAB 143 and TS 58.

Note about mustard gas comes from Jesse, *Trials of Evans and Christie* (p. xli). In contrast, Kennedy believed that Christie's reactions to the gas were from hysteria: Kennedy, *Ten Rillington Place* (p. 32).

Ethel Christie's physical description was reconstructed from various sources, including archival pictures; the testimony of her brother, Henry Waddington; and Christie's own testimony, describing their relationship.

Charles Brown's ownership of the building: Brown's testimony in Jesse, *Trials of Evans and Christie* (p. 138).

"Nervous types": Dr. Matthew Odess' testimony in Jesse, *Trials of Evans and Christie,* (pp. 165–69); police statements and a list of medicines prescribed to the Christies in National Archives, CAB 143 and TS 58. Odess knew the Christies' complaints about the neighbors and their physical ailments.

"When Mr. Brown took over the house…": Christie's testimony in Jesse, *Trials of Evans and Christie,* (p. 194).

Christie's complaints to the city were recorded in a letter dated April 7, 1952, and stored in CAB 143 and TS 58.

"If we could only get somewhere else to live it would be better for us," comes from Ethel Christie's letter to her brother, dated October 10, 1952, and stored in and stored in CAB 143 and TS 58.

Christie's various quotes about his teenage years come from the *Sunday Pictorial*, published July 12, 1953.

Details about Christie's exam with a psychiatrist come from Dr. Dinshaw Petit's police statement on April 2, 1953, stored in the National Archives, CAB 143 and TS 58.

Note about Christie's photo shoot with prostitutes: Maureen Riggs' police statement, March 31, 1953, stored in the National Archives, CAB 143/TS 58.

CHAPTER 4

Rosemary Sargent's recollections come from personal interviews.

Details about the weather: the *Times'* Index page, where the daily weather forecast was given.

Disruption in transportation and sporting events: "Transport Dislocated by Three Days of Fog," the *Times* (London), December 8, 1952.

Images and facts about rat catchers and "fluffers" were found during a Getty Images search of the London Underground in the 1950s.

The pollution levels were recorded by the government and distributed in the Ministry of Health's *Report on Public Health and Medical Subjects, No. 95, Mortality and Morbidity During the London Fog of December 1952*, Table 3 on page 3 (Lambeth, County Hall reading).

"The most recent case…": "Transport Dislocated by Three Days of Fog," *Times*, December 8, 1952.

"And yet, on the hills of London…" comes from William Wise's *Killer Smog: The World's Worst Air Pollution Disaster*. (p. 137).

Monet in London and his quote come from Anna and T. Novakov's "Eyewitness: The Chromatic Effects of Late Nineteenth-Century London Fog," *Literary London Journal*, 2006.

"That Sunday, the *New York Times* published a flattering…": Herbert F. West, "A Dingy, Haunting Beauty," *New York Times*, December 7, 1952.

"The fog is as thick as any Northerner…": "London Sunday Night," *Manchester Guardian*, December 8, 1952.

John Christie at postal office comes from a document titled "Antecedents of John Reginald Halliday Christie," National Archives, CAB 143 and TS 58.

Weather on November 8, 1948, comes from the *Times* daily forecast in "The Index."

Christie's doctor visit, physical condition, and prescriptions: Dr. Matthew Odess' testimony in Christie's trial transcripts, in Jesse, *Trials of Evans and Christie*.

Note: This section was written from Christie's point of view, using his trial testimony and his police statements during the Timothy Evans murder trial. Police were unaware that Christie had buried two women in his garden; he was considered a good witness.

John and Ethel Christie's story about the bump in the night comes from their police statements and trial testimonies, in Jesse, *Trials of Evans and Christie*, (pp. 30–45). *Note*: The Christies mentioned no "bump" in their initial police statements on December 1, 1949. They only recalled the noise during their second statements on December 5, 1949, after Timothy Evans confessed to killing his wife and child. I find their second statement to be dubious. Based on the police evidence given about this particular night, there's no way to conclude whether the Christies were telling the truth. It's left to the reader to decide if John Christie is a reliable narrator.

Tim and Beryl Evans' background: Jesse's *Trials of Evans and Christie* (pp. i–vi).

"All the time the Evans' have lived…": Ethel Christie's police statement, December 1, 1949, in National Archives, CAB 143 and TS 58.

"Mrs. Evans has told my wife…": John Reginald Christie's police statement, December 1, 1949, in National Archives, CAB 143 and TS 58.

"We think he is a bit mental…": John Reginald Christie's police statement, December 1, 1949, in National Archives, CAB 143 and TS 58.

"I thought that it sounded a bit like heavy furniture…": John Reginald Christie's testimony, from Jesse's *Trials of Evans and Christie* (p. 31).

"Within hours, one burglar had ransacked…": *Times*, "Street Attacks in Fog," December 8, 1952.

Stanley Crichton's section comes from personal interviews.

Physical requirements for Met police in 1952: *Times*, "Detection and Prevention of Crime," December 4, 1952.

"Oh, yes, they died peacefully in their sleep…" reported by William Stott, medical officer of health for Southwark, to Bradley of the Ministry of Health, dated February 20, 1953. National Archives, MH 55/58.

London's Fleet Street section comes from interviews with journalist Phyllis Oberman; British Pathe video *Printing the Daily Express* (c. 1948); journalist Harry

Procter's book *The Street of Disillusion* (1958); and "The Newspaper Trade in the 1950s," by David Hall in *Epsom and Ewell History Explorer.*

"Just two days earlier, the Number Nine red double-decker bus…": "Fleet Street in Smog," by Edward Miller, Getty Images.

"Reporters began to specialize…": Steve Chibnall, *Law-and-Order News: An Analysis of Crime Reporting in the British Press,* Tavistock Publications, 1977 (p. 50).

"Third Day of a London Particular," *Manchester Guardian,* December 8, 1962.

"London Fog Tie-Up Lasts for 3D Day," *New York Times,* December 7, 1952.

"The business of the city cannot cease…": "London Sunday Night," *Manchester Guardian,* December 8, 1952.

Different cultures spell "bogeyman" in various ways; in the US, it's typically boogeyman or boogieman. "Bogeyman" is the British version.

CHAPTER 5

La Traviata: "Opera Discontinued," *Times,* December 9, 1952, along with an undated article found in the Sadler's Wells Theatre Archives website.

"Cinemas closed": "London Monday Night," *Manchester Guardian,* December 9, 1952.

Position of anticyclone and forecast: the government's meteorological reports, the Air Ministry, December 8, 1952.

Section on London in the fog was supplemented by "London at a Standstill," *Daily Express,* December 8, 1952; "Chaos Again in Fog," *Times,* December 9, 1952; "Third Day of a London Particular," *Manchester Guardian,* December 8, 1952; "London Fog Returns after Brief Respite," *New York Times,* December 9, 1952.

Power cuts: "First Power Cuts and Winter," *Times,* December 9, 1952.

"Another lovely day in the country…": Harold Macmillan, *The Macmillan Diaries: The Cabinet Years, 1950–1957,* Vol. 1, Pan Macmillan, 2014 (p. 198).

Dodds' debates: House of Commons, *Parliamentary Debates,* December 8, 1952. Series 5, vol. 509.

Murray's question: House of Commons, *Parliamentary Debates,* December 8, 1952. Vol. 509 c12W.

Rationing and nutty slack energy efficiency: "The Demand for Environmental Quality in Driving Transitions to Low-Polluting Energy Sources," by Roger Fouquet of the London School of Economics; Basque Centre for Climate Change (2012).

Advertisements for nutty slack appeared in the *Times* on November 25, 1952, and December 11, 1952.

"More than one million tons…" House of Commons, *Parliamentary Debates,* February 2, 1953. Vol. 510 cc1460–2.

"Housewives were cleaning a layer of greasy grime that coated every surface in the house…": "Our London Correspondence," *Manchester Guardian,* December 9, 1952.

Position of anticyclone and forecast come from the government's meteorological reports, produced daily by the Air Ministry, December 9, 1952.

Stanley Crichton's section provided by his interviews.

Description of 10 Rillington Place: PC Thomas Watson in Jesse, *Trials of Evans and Christie* (p. 133).

The following statements come from National Archives, CAB 143 and TS 58:

John Christie's December 8, 1949, police statement comes from Ethel Christie's police statement, December 1, 1949; manhole cover story comes from DC John Corfield, October 20, 1965.

DC Gwynfryn Howell Evans' description of Tim Evans: Jesse, *Trials of Evans and Christie* (p. 46).

The Met telegram is stored in the National Archives, MEPO3-3147.

Tim Evans' first statement, November 30, 1949: Jesse, *Trials of Evans and Christie* (p. 47).

Tim Evans' literacy: Journalist Tennyson F. Jesse pointed out that an illiterate lorry driver would have a difficult time because he couldn't read the signs on the road—though he might have been in the habit of asking for directions. She also added that he couldn't have "signed his name as well and easily as he always did, or filled in his pools." Jesse, *Trials of Evans and Christie* (p. viii).

"Terrible liar...": Brabin, *The Case of Timothy John Evans* (p. 8).

"He finally explained that he had handed over the child...": Jesse, *Trials of Evans and Christie* (p. 49).

"The drain which you say you put your...": Jesse, *Trials of Evans and Christie* (pp. 48–49).

"The only part that is not true in the statement...": Jesse, *Trials of Evans and Christie* (pp. 49–52).

The section that begins, "the detective interviewed the Lynches...": Brabin, *The Case of Timothy John Evans* (pp. 6–13).

"I don't intend to keep him anymore..." Brabin, *The Case of Timothy John Evans* (pp. 6–13).

"When did you last see your wife..." Jesse, *Trials of Evans and Christie* (p. 52).

"I do not think you are saying the truth..." Jesse, *Trials of Evans and Christie* (p. 53).

Description of Evans stepping off train at Paddington Station in Getty Images. Much has been said about this photo. Evans' defenders say he was scared while in custody, the reaction of an innocent man. Police (and Brabin) say Evans was startled by the numerous flashbulbs of waiting photographers: Brabin, *The Case of Timothy John Evans* (pp. 48–49).

"Now Detective Inspector James Neill Black, a twenty-two-year veteran of the Met, took over the interrogation...": Testimony of DI James Neil Black found in Jesse, *Trials of Evans and Christie* (p. 59), along with his statement from October 15, 1965, in evidence in the National Archives, CAB 143 and TS 58.

Ethel Christie's statement in kitchen: Details come from the statement of DS Philip John Fensome on August 18, 1952, in National Archives, CAB 143 and TS 58. Ethel's recollections come from her testimony in Jesse, *Trials of Evans and Christie* (pp. 41–45).

"I have seen nothing to suggest that Mrs. Evans had had a miscarriage...": in Ethel Christie's statement to DS Fensome on December 1, 1949, in National Archives, CAB 143 and TS 58.

"After Beryl disappeared, Tim bemoaned her absence...": in John Christie's statement to DS Corfield and DI Black on December 1, 1949, in National Archives, CAB 143 and TS 58.

"I'm going off the track...": Clarke Vincent's statement to police on December 7, 1949, in National Archives, CAB 143 and TS 58.

The section which begins with, "on December 1, 1949, Notting Hill police investigators closed...": Brabin, *The Case of Timothy John Evans*, (pp. 6–13).

"How often have I said to you that when you have eliminated the impossible, whatever remains, however improbable, must be the truth?": Arthur Conan Doyle, *The Sign of Four,* Spencer Blackett, 1890.

CHAPTER 6

Smithville cattle show: "Fog Causes Slaughter of Cattle at Smithville Show," *Manchester Guardian*, December 9, 1952; Devra Davis, *When Smoke Ran Like Water: Tales of Environmental Deception and the Battle against Pollution*, Basic Books, 2002 (p. 43); "More Deaths at Cattle Show," *Times*, December 9, 1952.

Section on London in the fog was supplemented by "Record Fog Ends in London," in *Newcastle Morning Herald and Miners' Advocate*, December 10, 1952; "London 'Obliterated' by Worst Fog in Memory," *Advocate*, December 9, 1952; "London Clear of Fog," *Times*, December 10, 1952; "London Clear of Fog," *Manchester Guardian*, December 10, 1952; and "London Reviving After Fog," *New York Times*, December 9, 1952.

Parliament, full list of debates: House of Commons, *Parliamentary Debates*, December 9, 1952. Series 5, vol. 509. Coal dust debate: House of Commons, *Parliamentary Debates*, December 9, 1952, vol. 509 cc421-30. Side note: The debate on compulsory X-rays concerned only 250,000 of the 700,000 miners who worked in British mines. That group of workers was considered to be the most affected by coal dust.

The section that begins "The Automobile Association reported…": from "London 'Obliterated' by Worst Fog in Memory," *Advocate*, December 9, 1952.

Smoke Abatement Society: "London 'Obliterated' by Worst Fog in Memory," *Advocate*, December 9, 1952.

"Hit by Duck" and the dog track stories come from "Freak Accidents in London Fog," *Sydney Morning Herald*, December 8, 1952.

Drowning story from "Fears of Loss of Life in London Fog," *Canberra Times*, December 9, 1952.

Pollution data: *The Ministry of Health's Report on Public Health and Medical Subjects, No. 95, Mortality and Morbidity During the London Fog of December 1952*, Table 3 on page 3 (Lambeth, County Hall reading).

Insurance claims: Davis, Devra, and Michelle Bell. "Reassessment of the Lethal London Fog of 1952: Novel Indicators of Acute and Chronic Consequences of Acute Exposure to Air Pollution," *Environmental Health Perspectives*, June 2001.

Rosemary's section was supplemented by her interviews. Rosemary's note from her teacher to her mother comes from her personal files.

Notes about florists and undertakers come from David Laskin's "The Great London Smog." *Weatherwise* magazine, November/December 2006, and the Channel 4 documentary *Killer Fog*, 2012.

Information about parlors: "19th Century Mourning" exhibit, National Museum of Funeral History.

Emergency Bed Service: *The Ministry of Health's Report on Public Health and Medical Subjects, No. 95, Mortality and Morbidity During the London Fog of December 1952*, page 30, Table 12.

Acheson's recollections come from his 2007 autobiography, *One Doctor's Odyssey, The Social Lesion* (pp. 104–6) and an in-depth 2002 panel: "The Big Smoke: Fifty Years after the 1952 London Smog."

Milkman and pregnant woman: "Phantom Fog City London's New Role," *Brisbane Telegraph*, December 8, 1952.

Autopsies in pubs: http://hidden-highgate.org/flask-public-house/; http://www.casebook.org/dissertations/rip-victorian-autopsy-2.html.

Coal men details: British Pathe film *Coal and the War*, 1941; and *Kings Gift of Coal*, 1945.

Ethel and the coal man: police statement of Henry Frederick Willcox, coal man, March 6, 1953, at the National Archives CAB 143 and TS 58.

Ethel writes to Lily: John Christie's testimony, Jesse, *Trials of Evans and Christie* (pp. 196–7; 205–6).

Jennings opens the washhouse: Brabin, *The Case of Timothy John Evans* (p. 38); Jesse, *Trials of Evans and Christie* (pp. xv, 53–59).

"We have been using this place daily…": Brabin, *The Case of Timothy John Evans* (pp. 38–39).

Reg paces in the garden: Jesse, *Trials of Evans and Christie* (p. xv).

Tim Evans' final confession, December 2, 1949, description and statement come from: Jesse, *Trials of Evans and Christie* (pp. 53–60).

"She was incurring one debt after another…": Jesse, *Trials of Evans and Christie* (pp. 53–54).

The detail about Black putting his arm around Evans comes from Brabin, *The Case of Timothy John Evans* (p. 51).

"It is a great relief to get it off my chest…" Jesse, *Trials of Evans and Christie* (pp. 54–57).

Len Trevallion's recollection of his conversation with Evans comes from my multiple interviews with him, a statement before Justice Brabin dated 10/12/1965, and a summary of his interactions with Evans in Brabin, *The Case of Timothy John Evans* (p. 53).

Evans' confession to Dr. Matheson: Brabin, *The Case of Timothy John Evans* (pp. 60, 66–67).

Details about Old Bailey: www.oldbaileyonline.org

The cases of Geraldine and Beryl were intertwined, so the prosecutor requested that the judge allow evidence from Beryl's murder case. The judge agreed, an unusual ruling that devastated Tim's defense team.

The Crown's case: Brabin, *The Case of Timothy John Evans* (pp. 89–90); Jesse, *Trials of Evans and Christie* (p. lvi).

Newspaper clipping: "Alleged Murder of Wife," *Times*, December 5, 1949.

"Fish and Chippy": Harry Procter, *The Street of Disillusion*, Revel Barker, 1958 (p. 170).

"You will bear in mind that he begins with a story…": Jesse, *Trials of Evans and Christie* (p. 13).

Dr. Donald Teare's testimony: Jesse, *Trials of Evans and Christie* (pp. 14–15).

"The murder weapon used to kill…": Jesse, *Trials of Evans and Christie* (p. 15); Brabin, *The Case of Timothy John Evans* (p. 40).

"Beryl wore a dress, blouse and jacket…": Brabin, *The Case of Timothy John Evans* (p. 40).

"There was also considerable swelling on her right eye and mouth…": Brabin, *The Case of Timothy John Evans* (pp. 40–43); Dr. R. Donald Teare, "Post Mortem Examination," December 2, 1949, in CAB 148.

"Then one of the most unfortunate mistakes in the case was revealed…": Brabin, *The Case of Timothy John Evans* (pp. 44–46).

No evidence of sexual assault: There was debate over Dr. Teare's exam. The court reporter recorded that she might have been assaulted "post-mortem," or after she died. Kennedy contended that this proved Christie was the killer. But Dr. Keith Simpson explained that Dr. Teare actually said the assault might have happened ante-mortem (before death) and the elderly court reporter had heard it incorrectly. Kennedy, *Ten Rillington Place* (p. 131); Keith Simpson, *Forty Years of Murder*, Charles Scribner's Sons, 1979 (p. 205).

Dr. John Matheson: Brabin, *The Case of Timothy John Evans* (pp. 60–61).

Evans' mother visits: Brabin, *The Case of Timothy John Evans* (pp. 61–64).

John Christie's testimony comes from Jesse, *Trials of Evans and Christie* (pp. 16–41).

"If you can find anyone better to do the job then get him…" through "he admitted to them all…" comes from Jesse, *Trials of Evans and Christie* (pp. 16–41).

"Could you keep your voice up?" comes from the Timothy Evans trial transcripts found in Jesse, *Trials of Evans and Christie*, (p. 18).

"I went to the doctor, so it would be impossible." Dr. Odess' records proved Reg kept his appointment that Tuesday afternoon.

"What a wicked man…" Procter, *The Street of Disillusion* (p. 171).

Discrepancies over repair work: Brabin, *The Case of Timothy John Evans* (pp. 80–88).

Ethel Christie's testimony from "she described Tim's fury.…": Jesse, *Trials of Evans and Christie* (pp. 41–45).

Violet Lynch (Tim's aunt): Jesse, *Trials of Evans and Christie* (pp. 45–46).

Timothy Evans' testimony from "Did you strangle your baby daughter Geraldine?" through "Tim said he told them all to protect Reg": Jesse, *Trials of Evans and Christie* (pp. 60–81).

Closing speech for prosecution: Jesse, *Trials of Evans and Christie* (pp. 81–82).

Closing speech for defense: Jesse, *Trials of Evans and Christie* (pp. 82–91).

"Even if Christie had been responsible for the woman's death…": Jesse, *Trials of Evans and Christie* (p. 82).

"It is not impossible if Christie is an abortionist…": Jesse, *Trials of Evans and Christie* (p. 83).

Jury instructions: Jesse, *Trials of Evans and Christie* (pp. 92–117).

"Should have it said of him because seventeen years ago he was in trouble…": Jesse, *Trials of Evans and Christie* (pp. 111–12).

Christie crying: Procter, *The Street of Disillusion* (p. 171).

"Murderer, murderer…": Jesse, *Trials of Evans and Christie* (p. xxviii).

"I didn't do it. Christie done it…": Kennedy, *Ten Rillington Place* (p. 196).

"Worst since war": "London 'Obliterated' by Worst Fog in Memory," *Advocate*, December 9, 1952.

"Thugs added terror to the fogs…": "Phantom Fog City London's New Role," *Brisbane Telegraph*, December 8, 1952.

CHAPTER 7

Weather notes come from the December 10th Index in the *Times*.

Ethel writes to Lily described in John Christie's testimony in Jesse, *Trials of Evans and Christie* (pp. 196–97, 205–6); Ethel's original letter is stored in the National Archives, CAB 143 and TS 58.

Christie's personal background: "Antecedents of John Reginald Halliday Christie," National Archives, CAB 143 and TS 58; "My Dream and My First Victim," *Sunday Pictorial*, July 5, 1953; John Christie's testimony, Jesse, *Trials of Evans and Christie* (pp. 185–87).

"I always lived in dread of my father…": "My Dream and My First Victim," *Sunday Pictorial*, July 5, 1953.

Married life with Ethel: "Girls Laughed at Me," *Sunday Pictorial*, July 12, 1953.

Maud Cole episode: Met police record dated May 10, 1929, in the National Archives CAB 143/TS 58; Jonathan Oates, *John Christie of Rillington Place: Biography of a Serial Killer,* Wharncliffe, 2013 (p. 20); Jesse, *Trials of Evans and Christie* (p. xlii).

Cole is often referred to as a prostitute, which appears to be untrue. I suspect this came from the Met police report detailing Christie's assault on her. In it, she is referred to as a "prosecutrix," which is a female plaintiff. I suppose the rumor might have originated from that report. She held a full-time job and there's no evidence she was a prostitute.

"At the visit she said it was a question of divorce...": Oates, *John Christie of Rillington Place* (p. 25).

"Humans never seemed to understand me quite, but animals always did,": "My Dream and My First Victim." *Sunday Pictorial*, July 5, 1953.

"My wife and I were really happy together...": "My Dream and My First Victim," *Sunday Pictorial*, July 5, 1953.

"A very polite man who never talks to anyone very much," Oates, *John Christie of Rillington Place* (p. 98).

"I am a quiet, humble man, who hates rows or trouble": "My Dream and My First Victim." *Sunday Pictorial*, July 5, 1953.

The following memos came from the Ministry of Health, *Correspondence and Reports with Coroners*. National Archives, MH 55/2661:

"My pathologists report that the great majority...": Dr. William Heddy, December 11, 1952; "A physician in Kensington explained that...": Dr. Brian Rhodes, December 17, 1952; "The Medical Officer of Health for Walhamstow...": Dr. A. T. W. Powell, December 18, 1952; "The total deaths of all ages for Stepney...": Dr. F. R. O'Shiel, December 23, 1952; "They were instructed to look into the question...": Dr. Tudor Lewis, December 23, 1952; "Fog deaths...": C. Grant Nicol, December 29, 1952; "*Fog Deaths.* I have no doubt about it whatsoever..." Dr. L. F. Beccle, December 13, 1952; "the medical officer for Hammersmith separated...": Dr. F. M. Day, January 9, 1953; list of Battersea victims comes from a chart submitted by Dr. Tutor Lewis to the Ministry of Health, January 7, 1953.

1950s public health statistics: Davis, *When Smoke Ran Like Water* (p. 47).

Analysis from Dr. Donald Acheson comes from "The Big Smoke: Fifty Years after the 1952 London Smog," 2002 panel.

"Doctors would later find out that bronchitis was the most common cause of death during the fog...": David V. Bates, *A Citizen's Guide to Air Pollution,* McGill-Queen's University Press, 1972, Canadian Society of Zoologists (pp. 53–54).

"Our newspapers recently reported that a severe smog existed over part of England...": George D. Clayton, Ministry of Health, *Correspondence and Reports with Coroners*, December 18, 1952. National Archives, MH 55/2661.

Meuse Valley: J. Firket, "Fog Along the Meuse Valley," *Lancet,* March 31, 1936; "The Meuse Valley Fog of 1930: An Air Pollution Disaster," *Lancet,* 2001; Devra Davis and Michelle Bell, "Reassessment of the Lethal London Fog of 1952: Novel Indicators of Acute and Chronic Consequences of Acute Exposure to Air Pollution." *Environmental Health Perspectives* (journal), June 2001.

Donora, Pennsylvania, event: Davis, *When Smoke Ran Like Water* (pp. 15–18).

Lethal fluoride: Davis, *When Smoke Ran Like Water* (p. 23).

Clean air movement: "Unveiling a Museum, a Pennsylvania Town Remembers the Smog That Killed 20," *New York Times,* November 1, 2008.

Smog as a new term: "The Danger of 'Smog,'" *Times,* November 6, 1948.

U.S. Steel lawsuits: "Unveiling a Museum, a Pennsylvania Town Remembers the Smog That Killed 20," *New York Times,* November 1, 2008.

US inquiry: Davis, *When Smoke Ran Like Water* (p. 24).

"Health Visitor's Questionnaire: Fatalities Possibly Associated with Fog—

December 5th/8th, 1952" can be found in Ministry of Health, *Correspondence and Reports with Coroners*. National Archives, MH 55/2661.

"The maximum fog density is not known for six of...": from the Director of Fuel Research, December 15, 1952, in the Ministry of Health, *Correspondence and Reports with Coroners*. National Archives, MH 55/2661.

The section that begins, "The Welsh politician gripped the tabloid in his hand..." can be found here: House of Commons, *Parliamentary Debates*, December 12, 1952, vol. 509 cc837-904.

Lord Beaverbrook: "Daily Express: A Chequered History," *BBC News*, January 25, 2001.

"It was unusually dense and long-lasting...": "Lung Ills in London Rise in Wake of Fogs," *New York Times*, December 12, 1952.

MP Tim Driberg from House of Commons, *Parliamentary Debates*, December 16, 1952, vol. 509 c188W.

MPs Fort and Williams and Iain Macleod from House of Commons, *Parliamentary Debates*, December 18, 1952. Vol. 509 c237W.

"The *Manchester Guardian* relegated that story to a brief of less...": "Death Rate Rose During Fog," *Manchester Guardian*, December 19, 1952.

MPs Driberg and Molson: House of Commons, *Parliamentary Debates*, December 17, 1952. Vol. 509 c221W.

National Smoke Abatement Society history: Thorsheim, *Inventing Pollution* (pp. 153–57).

NSAS releases data to the media: "Inquiry into London Fog Suggested," *Times*, December 20, 1952.

Details about Macmillan and Marples: Anthony Sampson, *Macmillan: A Study in Ambiguity*, Penguin Press, 1967 (pp. 94–95).

"On the whole it seems impossible to refuse...": diary of Harold Macmillan, Sunday, October 28, 1951, found in *The Macmillan Diaries: 1950–57*, Macmillan, 2003.

MP Dodds questions Marples from House of Commons, *Parliamentary Debates*, December 18, 1952, vol. 509 c265W.

Smokeless fuel: Eric Ashby and Mary Anderson, *Politics of Clean Air* (p. 105).

Ethel Christie writes Lily Bartle: Letter dated December 15, 1952, in the National Archives, CAB 143 and TS 58.

Ethel Christie's murder: John Christie's testimony, in Jesse, *Trials of Evans and Christie* (pp. 195–96); Christie's March 31, 1953, confession to police, in the National Archives, CAB 143 and TS 58.

Details about Ethel's death come from the pathology report from Dr. Francis Camps, "Body No. 4," dated March 25, 1953, held in the National Archives in CAB 143; Camps, *Medical and Scientific Investigations in the Christie Case* (p. 190).

A note about Christie's collection of his wife's pubic hairs: this material comes from his June 8, 1953, confession to police, the National Archives, CAB 143 and TS 58; and testimony of Dr. Lewis Nickolls, director of the Met Police lab, in Jesse, *Trials of Evans and Christie* (pp. 173–74).

Harry Waddington's Christmas card: not dated, found in police evidence in the National Archives, CAB 143 and TS 58; John Christie's testimony, in Jesse, *Trials of Evans and Christie* (pp. 196–97).

"After she had gone...": from Oates, *John Christie of Rillington Place* (p. 93).

CHAPTER 8

Christmas tree in Trafalgar Square: "Christmas Festivities in Trafalgar Square," *Times*, December 6, 1952; "The Bell-Ringers of Fairford London's Tree from Oslo," *Times*, December 22, 1952.

Shopping: "Buying the Last Few Presents," *Times*, December 24, 1952.

The Queen's Christmas Address was broadcast on BBC radio on December 25, 1952; "Broadcasting Programmes for Christmas," *Times*, December 24, 1952.

Rosemary Sargent's recollections of Christmas 1952 come from interviews.

Christie's sleeping arrangements: John Christie's March 31, 1953, confession to police, which can be found in the National Archives, CAB 143 and TS 58.

Ethel Christie's laundry slip, dated December 12, 1952, in evidence at the National Archives, CAB 143 and TS 58. Coal man: police statement from Henry Frederick Willcox on March 26, 1953, also at the National Archives, CAB 143 and TS 58.

Milkman: statements from Anthony Sanders and Arthur Cook on April 6, 1953, located in the National Archives, CAB 143 and TS 58.

The sections that begins, "Reg began making plans, a scheme...": John Christie's March 31, 1953 confession to police, which can be found in the National Archives, CAB 143 and TS 58.

The section about Rosina Swan in Christie case: Swan's testimony in Jesse, *Trials of Evans and Christie* (pp. 138–39); Swan's police statement in the National Archives, CAB 143 and TS 58; Rosina Swan's police statement in Evans case in the National Archives, CAB 143 and TS 58; William Swan's police statement in Evans case in the National Archives, CAB 143 and TS 58.

The section that begins, "He tried out several different lies to explain Ethel's absence...": police statements from Jennie Grimes on March 29, 1953, Gladys Oliver on March 28, 1953, and Margaret Sergison on March 25, 1953.

Story about teenager and Christie: Margaret Sergison's police statement on March 25, 1953, in the National Archives, CAB 143 and TS 58.

Ethel's aunt: Emily Legg police statement, April 2, 1953, in the National Archives, CAB 143 and TS 58.

"I noticed that he was disinfecting the place...": Lena Louise Brown, March 26, 1953 in the National Archives, CAB 143 and TS 58.

Christie sat in dark: Florence Newman police statement, March 29, 1953 in the National Archives, CAB 143 and TS 58.

Weather and church services: "Christmas Day Sunshine," *Times*, December 27, 1952; "Changeable Weather," *Times*, December 27, 1952.

Second fog: "London Struck Again by Lung-Stinging Fog," *New York Times*, December 27, 1952; "Fog, Ice and Snow," *Times*, December 29, 1952.

"I was paying a heavy price to my neighbours' indulgence...": Caroline Haslett, *Times*, Letters to the Editor, December 12, 1952. Biography: "Dame Caroline Haslett: Outstanding Woman Engineer," *Times*, January 5, 1957.

"It is a blessed thing perhaps to feel so secure in virtue...": E. Moberly Bell, *Times*, Letters to the Editor, December 17, 1952.

"But may I quote from the last report of the Director of Fuel Research?" Eric Bellingham, *Times*, Letters to the Editor, December 16, 1952.

"In 1952, it was estimated that two-thirds of gas sold by the North Thames Gas Board came from plants...": Thorsheim, *Inventing Pollution* (p. 178).

"Reducing smudge": Ernest Fisk, *Times*, Letters to the Editor, December 16, 1952.

"Conservative Arnold Gridley wrote the editor...": Arnold B. Gridley, *Times*, Letters to the Editor, December 22, 1952.

"Converting an old-fashioned fireplace to burn gas would cost between ten and twenty pounds...": Thorsheim, *Inventing Pollution* (p. 176).

Dr. Stross versus Macmillan can be found here: House of Commons, *Parliamentary Debates*, December 19, 1952, vol. 509 cc289-90W.

Norman Dodds' background and life at home come from the intro of his book, *Gypsies, Didikoid, and Other Travellers*; interviews with his daughter-in-law, Christine Dodds; an article with Eva Dodds, his wife: "Woman Will Help Smooth Change to Decimals," *Brandon Sun,* April 20, 1976; and "Mr. Norman Dodds, Obituary," *Times,* August 23, 1965.

"Publicity is the lifeblood of a back-bench M.P.": Wilfred Greatorex, "Back-bencher Who Asks the Awkward Questions," *John Bull,* July 5, 1952 (p. 15).

Dodds and the Donora Report: "Donora Report to Aid Britain in Smog Fight," *New York Times,* December 28, 1952.

Donora investigation: Davis, *When Smoke Ran Like Water* (pp. 22–27).

CHAPTER 9

Len Trevallion's recollections come from various interviews and his autobiography, *Policeman, Pilot and a Guardian Angel,* Four O'Clock Press, 2008.

A note about the cabinet papers: They are part of a collection held by the National Archives, called "The Cabinet Papers: 1915–1988." When I refer to cabinet meetings, minutes, or dialogue, the information comes from this source.

Description of Cabinet Room: https://www.gov.uk/government/history/ 10-downing-street#cabinet-room; various stock photos; https://www.historicengland.org.uk/listing/the-list/list-entry/1210759; number10.gov.uk's section entitled "The Cabinet Room"; and Charles Eyre Pascoe, *No. 10 Downing street, Whitehall,* London: Duckworth & Company, 1908.

The section that begins: "for this Cabinet meeting, Winston Churchill was absent..." Churchill Cabinet, "The Cabinet Papers: 1915–1988," National Archives, January 14, 1953.

Debt: ukpublicspending.co.uk/spend- ing_chart_1930_1953UKb_09c1li001mcn_G0t_UK_National_Debt_As_Pct_GDP

Iain Macleod's admission in Parliament: House of Commons, *Parliamentary Debates*, December 18, 1952, vol. 509 c237W.

"Vital Statistics: Deaths in the Fog," *British Medical Journal,* January 3, 1953.

Six thousand deaths: Thorsheim, *Inventing Pollution* (p. 168).

"The fog, 'was a catastrophe of the first magnitude,'": Logan, W. P. D. "Public Health," *Lancet,* February 1953.

London County Council: "Worse Than 1866 Cholera, Deaths After Fog," *Manchester Guardian,* January 31, 1952.

"We have also been under fire...": S. G. G. Wilkinson, Ministry of Health, *Smog of December 1952,* January 1, 1953. National Archives, MH 55/58.

Iain Macleod: Richard Shepard, *Iain Macleod: A Biography,* London: Hutchinson, 1994 (p. 38); "Sir Richard Doll, the Scientist Who Linked Smoking to Cancer, Dies." *Independent,* July 24, 2005.

Dodds requests updated numbers: House of Commons, *Parliamentary Debates,* January 21, 1953, vol. 510 cc41-2W.

"The Minister of Health is anxious to find out the actual number...": Author unknown, Ministry of Health, *Smog of December 1952,* January 6, 1953. National Archives, MH 55/58.

Numbers from statistician: "4,000 London Fog Deaths," *New York Times,* February

12, 1953; W. P. D. Logan, "Mortality in the London Fog Incident, 1952," *Lancet*, February 14, 1953 (p. 336).

"Mr. Wilkinson is innocently asking a number of unanswerable questions...": George Godber, Ministry of Health, *Smog of December 1952* January 6, 1953. National Archives, MH 55/58.

"I am not very clear for what purpose you want the answers...": Michael Reed, Ministry of Health, *Smog of December 1952,* January 8, 1953. National Archives, MH 55/58.

"We merely want it for our own use in considering...": S. G. G. Wilkinson, Ministry of Health, *Smog of December 1952,* January 22, 1953. National Archives, MH 55/58.

The National Smoke Abatement meeting: "Note of Meeting Held at Ministry of Health, Savile Row on 14th January, 1953 between representatives of the Ministry of Health and the Secretary of the National Smoke Abatement Society." Ministry of Health, *Smog of December 1952*. National Archives, MH 55/58.

Emergency Bed Service: "Hospital Admissions During Fog," *Times*, January 24, 1953; "The Cost of Fog," *Manchester Guardian*, January 31, 1953.

Emergency Bed Service numbers: Thorsheim, *Inventing Pollution* (p. 164).

"A smoky atmosphere is a dangerous killer of the old and sickly...": "The Cost of Fog," *Manchester Guardian*, January 31, 1953.

"London Fog Deaths, Investigations in Progress," *Times* (London), January 2, 1953.

"Clamor Rises in London for Smog Relief," *Washington Post*, January 25, 1953.

Nuclear plant: "Atom Electricity Pushed in Britain," *New York Times,* January 27, 1953.

"There is no reason why nuclear reactors...": House of Commons, *Parliamentary Debates*, January 26, 1953, vol. 510 cc673-6; House of Commons, *Parliamentary Debates*, April 30, 1953, vol. 514 cc121-2W; "First Nuclear Power Plant to Close," *Guardian*, March 21, 2003.

"Mass extinction" and other phrases: Lieutenant-Colonel Marcus Lipton debates Macleod: House of Commons, *Parliamentary Debates*, January 22, 1953, vol. 510 cc382-3.

"Heart and lung diseases....": House of Commons, *Parliamentary Debates*, January 22, 1953, vol. 510 cc382-3.

"Really, you know...": House of Commons, *Parliamentary Debates*, May 8, 1953, vol. 515 cc841-52.

"I fear that they may now approach you...": by D. Emery, Ministry of Health, *Smog of December 1952,* February 9, 1953. National Archives, MH 55/58.

"We in the United Kingdom have a desperate need for more coal...": House of Commons, *Parliamentary Debates*, 26 January 1953, vol. 510 cc803-12.

National Assistance Board: R. E. C. Jewell, *The Report of the National Assistance Board, 1952.*

Macmillan's background: gov.uk (official portal for all things UK government), "Past Prime Ministers: Harold Macmillan"; BBC's History page: "Harold Macmillan biography"; Spartacus Educational: Second World War, Political Figures, Harold Macmillan.

"I hate uneducated people having people...": Alistair Horne, *Harold Macmillan,* Viking, 1989 (p. 286).

"He has grown in stature during the war more than anyone...": Lynne Olson, *Troublesome Young Men: The Rebels Who Brought Churchill to Power and Helped Save England,* Macmillan, 2008 (p. 355).

"He would put his hands on the lapels of his coat and turn to the backbenches behind him for approval and support...": Emrys Hughes, *Macmillan: Portrait of a Politician,* George Allen and Unwin, 1962 (p. 66).

For the section about Margaret Thatcher and her relationship with Norman Dodds, I used several different sources. Their debates via *Grantham Journal* were frequent from September 1949 through February 1950.

Thatcher's tango with Dodds comes from Charles Moore's excellent book, *Margaret Thatcher: The Authorized Biography, Volume One: Not For Turning*; along with an article in the Dartford *Chronicle* entitled "Political Truce for One Evening," October 7, 1949.

"I was lucky to have an opponent like Norman Dodds," comes from Thatcher's autobiography, *The Path to Power*, HarperCollins, 1995.

"It turned out to be an exhibition dance: everyone left the floor to watch us...": *Evening Post,* January 17, 1950.

Lipton, Dodds, and Macmillan debate: House of Commons, *Parliamentary Debates*, 27 January 1953, Vol. 510 cc828-31.

Description of Christie's coal cupboard comes from various pictures in police evidence, stored in the National Archives, TS 58; testimony of Percy Law, chief inspector at New Scotland Yard with the photographic department: Jesse, *Trials of Evans and Christie* (pp. 136–37); Brabin, *The Case of Timothy John Evans* (p. 114).

A note about the timeline of Christies' next two victims: There's confusion over who was killed first, Kathleen Maloney or Rita Nelson. The murders appeared to happen so close together that it's difficult to figure which was the predecessor. Christie was an unreliable source, so I've depended on the accuracy of witnesses to create a timeline.

Kathleen Maloney and Christie: Brabin, *The Case of Timothy John Evans* (pp. 115–16); John Christie's testimony in Jesse, *Trials of Evans and Christie* (pp. 198–99); Christie's confession from June 8, 1953. National Archives, CAB 143/TS 58.

The section that begins with Catherine Struthers: Catherine Struthers' police statement, March 26, 1953. National Archives, CAB 143/TS 58.

"She had no place to live and went home at night with...": Catherine Struthers' police statement, March 26, 1953. National Archives, CAB 143/TS 58.

"She was always drunk...": Christina Maloney (Grainger) police statement, March 27, 1953. National Archives, CAB 143/TS 58.

Maloney's police record: Brabin, *The Case of Timothy John Evans* (pp. 115–16).

"That night, around nine o'clock, the door to the Westminster Arms...": This section benefited from the police statement of Augustine Murray (potman), recorded March 27, 1953, and stored in the National Archives, CAB 143/TS 58.

"He wore horn-rimmed glasses...": Maureen Riggs' police statement, March 31, 1953. National Archives, CAB 143/TS 58.

Fish-and-chips shop: Brabin, *The Case of Timothy John Evans* (pp. 115–16); Christie's confession from June 8, 1953, stored in the National Archives, CAB 143/TS 58.

"She then asked the man to give her two shillings..." Catherine Struthers' police statement, March 26, 1953. National Archives, CAB 143/TS 58.

Rita Nelson and Christie: Brabin, *The Case of Timothy John Evans* (pp. 115–16); John Christie's testimony in Jesse, *Trials of Evans and Christie* (pp. 199–200); Christie's confession from June 8, 1953, stored in the National Archives, CAB 143/TS 58.

Physical descriptions of Rita Nelson come from various pictures in police evidence stored in the National Archives, CAB 143/TS 58. Her family background comes from the police statement of her sister, May Langridge, on March 30, 1953, stored in the National Archives, CAB 143/TS 58.

"Rita looked nice in her blue cardigan and pretty dress...": from the pathology report of "Body No. 3, Rita Nelson," made by Dr. Francis Camps on March 24, 1953.

"She said it would help her and her friend...": Christie's confession from June 8, 1953, stored in the National Archives, CAB 143/TS 58.

CHAPTER 10

1953 East Coast flood: The UK's Met Office, the country's national weather service, offers a wonderful synopsis: http://www.metoffice.gov.uk/news/in-depth/1953-east-coast-flood; "The Meteorological Magazine: Weather of January 1953"; *Meteorological Office*, vol. 82, no. 969, March 1953 (p. 95).

"The film footage, running nightly on the television...": British Pathe news footage titled "East Coast Floods," 1953.

"Flood Havoc in Holland," February 15, 1953; "Cost of Flood Disaster," *Times*, February 20, 1953.

"Every necessary expenditure by local authorities on the restoration of coast...": Harold Macmillan, March 14, 1953. National Archives, CAB/129/60.

"It was very hard to make out just what was the extent of the Great Flood," Macmillan, *The Macmillan Diaries*, vol. 1 (p. 210).

Dodds debates Marples: House of Commons, *Parliamentary Debates*, 3 February 1953, vol. 510 cc1659-71.

"I got a telephone call...": Macmillan, *The Macmillan Diaries*, vol. 1 (p. 211).

Description of Christie shoving another body into coal cupboard comes from his June 8, 1953, police confession and from the pathology report of "Body No. 1, Hectorina MacLennan," made by Dr. Francis Camps on March 24, 1953, both stored in the National Archives, CAB 143/TS 58, along with graphic police photos of MacLennan's body in the cupboard before it was removed.

Scratches on her back: Jesse, *Trials of Evans and Christie* (p. xxxv).

MacLennan's background: Brabin, *The Case of Timothy John Evans* (p. 116); statements from family members, stored in the National Archives, CAB 143/TS 58, including Benjamina MacClennan on March 29, 1953, Donald MacClennan on March 26, 1953, and Robert MacClennan on March 25, 1953.

MacLennan's meeting with Christie: Christie's testimony in Jesse, *Trials of Evans and Christie* (pp. 200–2); Christie's confession from June 8, 1953, stored in the National Archives, CAB 143/TS 58.

"I told you not to tell anyone...": police statement from Alexander Baker, Hectorina's boyfriend, on March 25/26, 1953. National Archives, CAB 143/TS 58.

"He waited for her at a café for nearly three hours, he complained...": police statement from Baker on March 25/26, 1953. National Archives, CAB 143/TS 58.

"I venture to think that from the point of view of practicability of remedial action...": author unknown, addressed to Sir John Charles of the Ministry of Health, dated February 13, 1953.

Million tons of nutty slack: House of Commons, *Parliamentary Debates*, February 2, 1953, vol. 510 cc1460-2.

"Is the Minister aware that to charge more than 5 shillings a hundredweight for this rubbish is bare-faced robbery?": Willie Hamilton, House of Commons, *Parliamentary Debates*, February 2, 1953, vol. 510 cc1460-2.

"Does the right hon. Gentleman still maintain that the use of nutty slack, which seems to produce smoke without fire...": House of Commons, *Parliamentary Debates*, 16 February 1953, vol. 511 cc857-9.

"One Tory demanded to know why three million tons...": House of Commons, *Parliamentary Debates*, 16 February 1953, vol. 511 cc857-9.

"The results of the Donora report have been studied and are being borne in mind...": House of Commons, *Parliamentary Debates*, February 24, 1953, vol. 511 cc1912-3.

"Churchill says it is a gamble...": Macmillan, *The Macmillan Diaries,* vol. 1 (p. 114).

Ministry of Health committee: Thorsheim, *Inventing Pollution* (p. 166).

"Investigations are continuing...": House of Commons, *Parliamentary Debates*, May 7, 1953, vol. 515 c552.

"The Minister was greatly concerned at the suggestions that the marketing of 'nutty slack' was associated with a fog producing an abnormally high death rate...": "Minutes of a meeting held on February 24, 1953, for Preliminary Consideration of the Possibility of Further Action to Reduce Atmospheric Pollution," *Ministry of Fuel and Power*, National Archives, MH 55/58.

Nutty slack on sale in December: Advertisements for nutty slack appeared in the *Times* on November 25, 1952, and December 11, 1952.

"Although there sometimes contained a high content of finely divided carbon...": "Minutes of a meeting held on February 24, 1953, for Preliminary Consideration of the Possibility of Further Action to Reduce Atmospheric Pollution," *Ministry of Fuel and Power*, National Archives, MH 55/58.

"There is now an urgent need for a comprehensive review of the problem, covering effects, causes and cure..." J. Syman to F. Armer, March 28, 1953. National Archives, MH 55/58.

Iain Macleod refuses to join Macmillan's committee: F. Armer to J. Syman, April 28, 1953. National Archives, MH 55/58.

"Unless much more is done to correct those things which have not been done...": House of Commons, *Parliamentary Debates*, March 19, 1953, vol. 513 cc189–90.

Queen Mary: British Pathe film entitled *Scenes in London at Death of Queen Mary* (1953).

"She discharged the duties of her high station with a dignity which was truly queenly...": "Queen Mary, A Lifetime of Gracious Service," *Times*, March 25, 1953.

"I rise to move the adjournment of the House...": House of Commons, *Parliamentary Debates*, March 24, 1953, vol. 513 cc801-2.

Christie owed rent: Charles Brown testimony in Jesse, *Trials of Evans and Christie* (p. 138).

Christie owed for coal and milk: police statements from Henry Frederick Willcox (collector for coal company) on March 26, 1953, and Anthony Sanders (milkman) on April 6, 1953. National Archives, CAB 143/TS 58.

Forged Ethel's signature: Frederick Henry Snow (bank manager) testimony in Jesse, *Trials of Evans and Christie* (p. 142).

Life insurance: police statement of Sidney Frank Denyer (insurance agent) on March 26, 1953. National Archives, CAB 143/TS 58.

Unemployment payments: a timeline, created by Chief Inspector Albert Griffin, showed that Christie received £2.14.0 per week from the Unemployment Exchange until March 18, 1953, two days before he disappeared. That timeline can be found in police evidence, stored in the National Archives, CAB 143/TS 58.

Christie tries to lure women: police statement of Charles Lee, café manager, on March 25, 1953, and Margaret Forrest (café customer) on March 25, 1953. National Archives, CAB 143/TS 58.

Euthanized dog: police statement from Ernest Jacobs (veterinarian) on March 28, 1953. National Archives, CAB 143/TS 58.

"Those repairs I did myself...": police statement of Mary Margaret Reilly on March 24, 1953. National Archives, CAB 143/TS 58.

Details about the Reillys' encounter with Christie comes from Mary Reilly's police statement; her testimony in Jesse, *Trials of Evans and Christie* (pp. 144–45); and from John Reilly's testimony (Ibid., p. 145).

Rosemary Sargent's recollections come from her various interviews.

Brown's recollection of discovering the bodies: Beresford Brown's police statement, March 24, 1953. National Archives, CAB 143/TS 58.

"Reg's alcove provided almost perfect conditions for preservation: cool, dry with a bit of air flow." Simpson, *Forty Years of Murder* (p. 194).

Photos of crime scene taken by police photographer PC Thomas Watson, stored in the National Archives, DPP2/2246 and MEPO 2/9535. "Police Pose," photo by Charles Lay for Getty Images. Descriptions of kitchen alcove and the removal of the bodies come from these.

"I lifted the floorboards and noticed that the earth under...": Albert Griffin's police statement, page three, April 12, 1953, stored in the National Archives, CAB 143/TS 58. Griffin also detailed the time delays in removing each body; the police worked all night, removing and categorizing evidence.

Sampling of earth and ashes: Chief Inspector Albert Griffin's police statement, page seven, April 12, 1953, stored in the National Archives, CAB 143/TS 58.

Digging for bones: DI Lawrence Kelly's police statement, pages two and three, April 12, 1953, stored in the National Archives, CAB 143/TS 58.

News photographers snapped various photos from atop rooms, including a Getty Image entitled "Crime, London, England, 1953, Police Search the Rear Garden."

Skull broken into nearly a hundred pieces: from police summary written by Albert Griffin at Notting Hill station on May 16, 1953 (page 2). "A skull was reconstituted from 92 pieces of broken bone and showed evidence of burning." National Archives, CAB 143/TS 58.

Note about dental crown: Jesse, *Trials of Evans and Christie* (p. xxxix).

Animal bones: Camp, *Medical and Scientific Investigations in the Christie Case* (p. 61).

Police Sergeant Len Trevallion's recollections come from our interviews and his autobiography, *Policeman, Pilot and a Guardian Angel*.

"Three Women Found Dead in Flat...": *Times*, March 25, 1953.

"Nationwide Search for Tenant of Murder Flat," *Daily Telegraph*, March 26, 1953; "Murder Unlimited," *Daily Express*, March 26, 1953; "Police Hunting for 'Man with Inane Laugh,'" *Sydney Morning Herald*, March 27, 1953.

"Jack the Strangler" and "The Notting Hill Killer...": in story headlined "Fifth Murder Feared," *Sydney Morning Herald*, March 28, 1953.

"Search for Moon-Mad Killer..." and "A new examination of the mutilated bodies suggests he is...": from *The Mail (Adelaide, SA: 1912–1954)*, Saturday, March 28, 1953.

"Once again the cry was heard...": Procter, *The Street of Disillusion* (p. 169).

The following are found in the National Archives, CAB 143/TS 58:

"I have to inform you that Hotels and Boarding Houses in this town have been visited in an attempt to trace John Reginald Christie, so far without success...": Captain W. J. Hutchinson, March 27, 1953.

Families of missing women, one example: A memo from Buxton police on March 30, 1953, of a husband searching for his wife; article "Rillington Place, the Hunt Moves to the Files," *Evening Standard*, undated.

"The first was that of a young girl sitting at a table...": "Arrest of London 'Landru,'" *Le Soir*, April 4, 1953.

Color system: letter from Charles Zwiep of Amsterdam to New Scotland Yard, March 31, 1953.

"Any person who finds this communicate with New Scotland Yard…": note to Oxfordshire police received in April 1953; author unknown.

"You will never get me. I am leaving England, good-bye, Staring Eyes…": note received by Met police on March 28, 1953; author unknown.

"I cannot remember his face very well…": undated note, unsigned, sent to Met police.

"How is the public to deal with the sordid, squalid and revolting…": House of Commons, *Parliamentary Debates*, May 8, 1953, vol. 515 cc748-806.

Beresford Brown's death threats: "'Murder House' Yields New Hidden Secrets," *Sydney Morning Herald*, March 29, 1953.

"The discovery of what seemed to be the bones of a sixth woman victim added horror…": "London Murder Home May Yield 6th Victim," *New York Times*, March 29, 1953.

Christie's life on the run: Christie's testimony in Jesse, *Trials of Evans and Christie* (pp. 202–5).

Christie gave his real name: police statement of Harold Cooper (Rowton House), April 7, 1953.

Description of Rowton House: http://www.workhouses.org.uk/Rowton/.

"He looked tired and sallow and appeared as if he had not washed…": "London's Wanted Man Arrested," *Sydney Morning Herald*, March 31, 1953.

"What are you doing, looking for work?" Police statement of Police Constable Thomas Ledger on March 31, 1953.

Physical description of PC Ledger: "London Arrest," *Sydney Morning Herald*, April 1, 1953.

Clip from Evans' trial in Christie's pocket located in evidence stored in the National Archives, CAB 143/TS 58.

CHAPTER 11

"Sex, scandal, surprise, sensation, exposure, murder…": Procter, *The Street of Disillusion* (p. 141).

"The Murder Gang": "The News of the World and Fleet Street's Dark Era," *BBC News Magazine*, July 8, 2011.

Harry Procter: Neil Root, *Frenzy!: How the Tabloid Press Turned Three Evil Serial Killers into Celebrities,* Random House, 2011 (p. 66).

The Crime Reporters Association: Steve Chibnall, *Law and Order News* (p. 50).

A throng descended: "A black van, surrounded by public (Getty); Crowd outside court: "Christie hearing" (Getty); Press outside court: "Photographers wait" (Getty); "Christie in car" (Getty).

String of Pearls: James Rymer and Thomas Prest, *The String of Pearls: A Romance,* penny dreadful, 1850.

"Your pipe is drawing sweetly…": George Orwell, "Decline of the English Murder," *Tribune-GB, London,* February 15, 1946.

"The Skeleton Mystery," *Daily Express*, April 30, 1953.

"Mad Strangler," *Sydney Morning Herald*, March 28, 1953.

"He smiled, a sickeningly, silly smile, and he gave me an unforgettably…": Procter, *The Street of Disillusion* (p. 170).

"He appeared to be very upset because Evans had told the jury he believed Christie to be the real killer…": Procter, *The Street of Disillusion* (p. 171).

"He smiled at me as a proud son might smile at his parents on speech day...": Procter, *The Street of Disillusion* (p. 171).

"You may have seen that Mr. Norman Dodds, MP...": S. G. G. Wilkinson, addressed to D. Emery, May 6, 1953. National Archives, MH 55/58.

"Futile to think that air pollution can be abolished overnight..." from internal
memo entitled "Air Pollution: Brief for Adjournment Debate on 8th May, 1953,
" May 8, 1953. National Archives, MH 55/58.

"Sulphur Dioxide was also estimated and whereas the normal November concentration of this gas is between 0.05 and 0.15 parts per million..." comes from a
memo, dated December 15, 1952, from the Director of Fuel Research to the Ministry of Health. National Archives, MH 55/58.

The Hound of the Baskervilles: Arthur Conan Doyle, *The Hound of the
Baskervilles*, George Newnes, 1902 (p. 81).

Len Trevallion's story about Christie in a jail cell comes from various interviews I've
conducted, along with his autobiography, *Policeman, Pilot and a Guardian
Angel* (p. 140).

"We certainly have had a very busy day and we have certainly seen some very
shabby tricks...": House of Commons, *Parliamentary Debates*, May 8, 1953,
vol. 515 cc841-52.

Beryl's exhumation: Photos: "The Exhumation of Beryl Evans" (Alamy), "Gravesite
of Beryl Evans During Exhumation" (Alamy); Simpson, *Forty Years of Murder*
(pp. 192–93); Camps, *Medical and Scientific Investigations in the Christie Case*
(p. 136).

"Will the right honourable gentleman give some indication of how long that...":
House of Commons, *Parliamentary Debates*, May 19, 1953, vol. 515 cc1859-60.

Queen Elizabeth's coronation: the YouTube video *The Coronation of Queen Elizabeth II*; "50 facts about the Queen's Coronation," royal.uk (official website of
the royal family), March 25, 2003.

"Journalists, dressed in their best and fully hatted...": from Phyllis Oberman's article entitled "I Remember...Coronation Day."

CHAPTER 12

"The Murder House of Notting Hill": "London Man on Trial in Death of 4
Women," *New York Times*, April 23, 1953.

Christie's confession to Chief Inspector Albert Griffin is reconstructed from Griffin's
testimony: Jesse, *Trials of Evans and Christie* (pp. 148–51); Christie's confession
from March 31, 1953 is stored in the National Archives, CAB 143/TS 58.

"I sat up and saw that she appeared to be convulsive...": Christie's confession from
March 31, 1953. National Archives, CAB 143/TS 58. (p. 1).

Final three victims: Christie's confession from March 31, 1953. National Archives,
CAB 143/TS 58. (pp. 2–5).

"A queue began to form at 9 a.m. for seats in the public gallery...": "Remand for
Christie," *Sydney Morning Herald*, April 2, 1953.

"This monster-like creature...": Procter, *The Street of Disillusion* (p. 173).

"Reg seemed glum until he turned...": Procter, *The Street of Disillusion* (p. 171).

"News is news...": Procter, *The Street of Disillusion* (p. 140).

"Reg agreed to tell his story exclusively to the *Sunday Pictorial*": Procter, *The Street
of Disillusion* (p. 173).

Cheque-book journalism:" Procter, *The Street of Disillusion* (p. 172); Chibnall,
Law-and-Order News (pp. 57–58).

"There was no wife of the killer to offer the money to this time…": Procter, *The Street of Disillusion* (p. 172).

"First you contacted a friend—'no intrusion on private grief'…": Procter, *The Street of Disillusion* (p. 172).

Procter's relationship with Curtis-Bennett: Procter, *The Street of Disillusion* (p. 171).

Curtis-Bennett bio: "Curtis-Bennett Dies," *New York Times*, July 23, 1956.

Christopher Craig: Chibnall, *Law-and-Order News* (pp. 58–59).

"Any further attempts by persons known…": memo entitled "Governor, Brixton Prison," April 15, 1953. National Archives, CAB 143/TS 58.

"The *Sunday Pictorial* gave the defense less than two thousand pounds for his story:" Procter, *The Street of Disillusion* (p. 173).

"A sad, unhappy, rather inadequate, anxiety-ridden little man…": from test given by Dr. Stephen H. Coates on August 8, 1953, stored in the National Archives, CAB 143/TS 58.

Brain scan: "Doctors Give Christie Secret Brain Test," *Empire News*, June 1953.

The section about Christie's life in prison: Dr. Desmond Curran's testimony, Jesse, *Trials of Evans and Christie* (p. 232).

"It wasn't me who did the chasing…": Oates, *John Christie of Rillington Place* (p. 142).

"He pointed to his penis…": Oates, *John Christie of Rillington Place* (p. 142).

"After victims Four, Five and Six, I now remember how I used to think there are only six more—or only five or four more to make ten, and then I can rest…": John Reginald Halliday Christie, "My Dream and My First Victim," *Sunday Pictorial*, July 5, 1953.

"Laughter and sneers in a way made me more determined to prove I was a man…": Christie, "Girls Laughed at Me," *Sunday Pictorial*, July 12, 1953.

"Christie's Own Story": Christie, "Girls Laughed at Me."

"It was thrilling because I had embarked on the career I had chosen for myself, the career of murder," Christie, "My Dream and My First Victim."

"Is it not possible that the enormous sensational publicity given to the…": House of Commons, *Parliamentary Debates*, July 13, 1953, vol. 517 cc1699-701.

"Before his trial began, Reg accepted a meeting with his attorney, Mr. Curtis-Bennett.…": Scott Henderson, *Scott Henderson Inquiry,* Home Office, 1953 (p. 68).

"They explained that it was a similarity…": *Scott Henderson Inquiry* (p. 71).

Christine Butcher: *Scott Henderson Inquiry* (p. 71).

"Mine were all adults," Oates, *John Christie of Rillington Place* (p. 165).

"So Curtis-Bennett felt he had no choice he turned to the McNaughton Rules…": Brabin, *The Case of Timothy John Evans* (p. 120).

Daniel McNaughton: T. V. Asokan, "Daniel McNaughton (1813–1865)," *Indian Journal of Psychiatry*, 2007.

"Mrs. Evans told me that her husband was knocking her about and that she was going to make an end of it…": June 8, 1953, confession. National Archives CAB 143/TS 58 (p.2).

"I got on my knees but found I was not physically capable of having intercourse…": June 8, 1953, confession. National Archives CAB 143/TS 58 (p.2).

"Keith Simpson, one of the pathologists at the exhumation, was suspicious. His report, the one handed to Reg's defense attorneys days earlier…": Simpson, *Forty Years of Murder* (pp. 201–2).

A note about the pubic hairs: All three pathologists present during Beryl Evans' exhumation and examination concluded that the hairs in the tobacco tin were unlikely to belong to her; they contended that her hair showed no signs of being trimmed and the hairs in the tin were frayed—cut at both ends. On the stand, Dr. Jack Hobson, the psychiatrist hired by Christie's team, said that it was still possible that the hairs belonged to Beryl because, perhaps, they came from a different part of her body. The three pathologists strongly disagreed and there remains no definitive answer.

"As I felt at the time of Evans affair normally I could not have done it, but if I…": John Reginald Halliday Christie, "I Turned Off the Gas…," *Sunday Pictorial*, July 9, 1953.

Nibbling his lips: Jesse, *Trials of Evans and Christie* (p. lvi).

"I have run out of fags…" Jesse, *Trials of Evans and Christie* (p. lvii).

Christie's demeanor on the stand: "Christie in Witness Box, in Tears Over Wife's Murder," *Sydney Morning Herald*, June 24, 1953; Jesse, *Trials of Evans and Christie* (p. lx).

Sir Lionel Heald's speech: Jesse, *Trials of Evans and Christie* (pp. 121–32).

"The parade of witnesses included the police photographer who snapped photos of the bodies—he would help set the scene…": Thomas Watson's testimony in Jesse, *Trials of Evans and Christie* (p. 133).

Mr. Burrow's testimony in Jesse, *Trials of Evans and Christie* (p. 137).

Charles Brown's testimony in Jesse, *Trials of Evans and Christie* (p. 138).

Rosina Swan's testimony in Jesse, *Trials of Evans and Christie* (pp. 138–39).

Henry Simpson Waddington and Lily Bartle's testimony in Jesse, *Trials of Evans and Christie* (pp. 139–41).

"Reg sat with his legs crossed…": "Christie's Doctor Gives Evidence," *Sydney Morning Herald*, April 20, 1953.

Various service people and their testimonies in Jesse, *Trials of Evans and Christie* (pp. 141–48).

Chief Inspector Albert Griffin's testimony in Jesse, *Trials of Evans and Christie* (pp. 148–65).

"Medical experts examined the tufts of pubic hair, which Len Trevallion found inside that shiny two-ounce tin…": Simpson, *Forty Years of Murder* (p. 196).

Dr. Lewis Nickolls' testimony in Jesse, *Trials of Evans and Christie* (pp. 173–75).

"I tried to get her out, and she picked up a frying pan and she tried to hit me…": in Jesse, *Trials of Evans and Christie* (p. 150).

Tufts of hair: Dr. Lewis Nickolls' testimony in Jesse, *Trials of Evans and Christie* (pp. 173–75).

Beryl's autopsy: Simpson, *Forty Years of Murder* (pp. 194–98).

"Have you any grounds for believing, from your inquiries into the case…": in Jesse, *Trials of Evans and Christie* (p. 164).

"If my learned friend is asking me to make plain that Christie did not kill Mrs. Evans…": in Jesse, *Trials of Evans and Christie* (p. 164).

Dr. Matthew Odess' testimony: in Jesse, *Trials of Evans and Christie* (pp. 165–69).

Mental health experts: in Jesse, *Trials of Evans and Christie*: Dr. John Matheson's testimony (pp. 222–31); Dr. Desmond Curran's testimony (pp. 231–39).

"Although Christie is going to say for the fifth or sixth time that he did not kill that baby…": Derek Curtis-Bennett's opening speech for the defense, in Jesse, *Trials of Evans and Christie* (p. 184).

"The more the merrier…": *Scott Henderson Inquiry* (p. 18).

"Do your best to speak up, Christie…": testimony of John Reginald Halliday Christie in Jesse, *Trials of Evans and Christie* (p. 185).

"I am not quite sure whether I did at the time…": testimony of John Reginald Halliday Christie in Jesse, *Trials of Evans and Christie* (p. 188).

"It is a very long time since and I do not recollect a lot...": testimony of John Reginald Halliday Christie in Jesse, *Trials of Evans and Christie* (p. 193).

"An insignificant little mouse of a man...": Oates, *John Christie of Rillington Place* (p. 151).

"Maniac," "raving lunatic," "mad as a March hare," and "umbrella of total madness...": testimony of Dr. Jack Hobson in Jesse, *Trials of Evans and Christie* (p. 217).

"On the fourth day of the trial, June 25...": in Jesse, *Trials of Evans and Christie.* (pp. 240–96).

"He lectured for two and a half hours...": "Christie Sentenced to Death," *Daily Telegraph,* June 26, 1953.

"Do you find the prisoner at the Bar...": in Jesse, *Trials of Evans and Christie.* (p. 296).

"Gripped the bar...": "Christie Sentenced to Death," *Daily Telegraph,* June 26, 1953.

"The newspapers cannot say that I fainted...": memo from J. A. Roberts, June 26, 1953, stored in the National Archives, CAB 143/TS 58.

CHAPTER 13

Dodds debates Marples over committee members: House of Commons, *Parliamentary Debates,* July 21, 1953, vol. 518 cc201-3.

Sir Hugh Beaver: Geoffrey Heyworth, "Sir Hugh Beaver," *Journal of the Royal Statistical Society,* vol. 130, no. 4. 1967 (p. 594); "Obit. Sir Hugh Eyre Cambell Beauer, KBE, LLD, 1890–1967," *Institute of Civil Engineers Publishing.*

Weather forecasts for August and November,1953 come from the *Times* "Index."

Health debates useless respirators: memo from Edmund Martin, August 31, 1953, addressed to Professor Bedson. National Archives, MH 55/58.

"The Common Council of the City of London decided to declare 'smokeless zones...' ": "Smokeless Zone in London," *Times,* October 7, 1953.

"I believe that the Government should make it financially easier for councils..." "Something Nasty in the Coalshed," *Manchester Guardian,* October 2, 1953.

"Menace of the Dirty Air: London Fog Disaster Could Happen Again," *Manchester Guardian,* October 16, 1953.

"London Warned of Smog," *New York Times,* October 27, 1953.

Dodds and Macmillan in Parliament: House of Commons, *Parliamentary Debates,* October 20, 1953, vol. 518 cc1791-3.

"Profoundly alarmed at the lack of any effective response from official quarters to what can truthfully be described as a national disaster...": from "Fog as 'National Disaster,' " *Times,* October 28, 1953.

U.S. Tobacco offer: Davis, *When Smoke Ran Like Water* (p. 46).

Chemists sell out of gauze: "Use of Anti-Fog Masks," *Times,* October 29, 1953.

"There is certainly no simple universal remedy such as everyone wearing a mask...": "Use of Anti-Fog Masks," *Times,* October 29, 1953.

"I am advised that they would be of little or no value in absorbing the toxic gases...": House of Commons, *Parliamentary Debates,* October 29, 1953. Vol 518 cc407-8W.

"It is light and convenient...": memo from R. V. Christie to Sir John A. Charles, October 20, 1953. National Archives, MH 55/58.

"The manufacturers of the 'Martindale' mask should now be asked how many of these they can supply...": memo from R. V. Christie to Sir John A. Charles, October 30, 1953. National Archives, MH 55/58.

Burning coal in Ministry of Housing: House of Commons, *Parliamentary Debates*, January 26, 1954, vol. 522 c1578.

One shilling for the prescription: memo from the chancellor of the exchequer to Iain Macleod dated November 9, 1953. National Archives, MH 55/58.

"The consumption of this type of coal is very small in relation to the total consumption and when the weather is windy...": House of Commons, *Parliamentary Debates*, November 23, 1953, vol. 521 cc17-9.

November 17 fog: "25 Counties of Fog Belt," *Times*, November 18, 1953.

Children and dogs with masks: British Pathe film entitled *The Smog Menace*, 1953.

"It was fully realized that so long as the toxic principles in smog were not known with any degree of certainty...": confidential memo entitled "Minutes of Meeting to Consider Protection Against Smog," November 17, 1953. National Archives, MH 55/58.

"Grave doubts" comes from a confidential memo entitled "Minutes of Meeting to Consider Protection Against Smog," November 17, 1953. National Archives, MH 55/58.

"Today everybody expects the Government to solve every problem...": memo by Harold Macmillan to cabinet, entitled "Smog", November 18, 1953. National Archives, CAB/129/64.

"It's the small things that cause politicians trouble...": Cabinet Minutes, November 19, 1953. National Archives, CAB/195/11.

"I am afraid that the government are not going to come out of this too well...": author unknown, titled "Secretary," November 25, 1953. National Archives, MH 55/58.

EPILOGUE

Death penalty debate: House of Commons, *Parliamentary Debates*, July 1, 1953, vol. 517 cc407-19.

"We have no right, until human judgment is infallible, to pass and execute an irrevocable doom...": House of Commons, *Parliamentary Debates*, July 1, 1953, vol. 517 cc407-19.

"Hanging of Christie May Be Put Off," *Daily Mirror*, July 1, 1953.

Scott Henderson background: "Obituary, Mr. John Scott Henderson," *Times*, November 7, 1964.

Number of Henderson witnesses: Jesse, *Trials of Evans and Christie* (p. lxxv).

"Reg told Henderson that he confessed to killing Beryl Evans...": *Scott Henderson Inquiry* (p. 68–72).

"The Henderson Inquiry was widely criticized for being rushed...": "Obituary, Mr. John Scott Henderson," *Times*, November 7, 1964.

Henderson never questioned the workmen who were doing repairs on 10 Rillington Place when Beryl and Geraldine Evans were murdered. Evans' defense attorney believed that their testimony would have proved that Tim didn't kill Beryl and Geraldine because the men had been working inside the washhouse at the time he claimed to have killed them. But the Crown contended that the workmen's timesheets were not reliable and neither were their memories. Also, Dr. Matthew Odess, Christie's physician, told Henderson that Christie came to his office suffering from fibrositis on November 12, 1949, days after Beryl was killed. Dr. Odess even said that the injury could have been caused by carrying a heavy weight down flights of stairs. During the trial, Dr. Odess indicated that Christie's back pain had been ongoing since the beginning of November. Jesse, *Trials of Evans and Christie* (pp. lxix, lxxiii, lxxviii).

Ludovic Kennedy: Kennedy, *Ten Rillington Place.*

"They cannot do anything about it now...": memo from J. A. Roberts, June 26, 1953. National Archives, CAB 143/TS 58.

"More probable than not...": Brabin, *The Case of Timothy John Evans,* (p. 153).

"Brabin's report convinced the government to grant Timothy Evans...": "The Murders at Rillington Place Recalled," *Times,* November 23, 1965; "Posthumous Free Pardon for Timothy Evans," *Times,* October 19, 1966.

"The UK was already embroiled with talk of abolishing the death penalty...": "Milestones in the Campaign to Abolish Hanging," *Times,* November 9, 1965.

"His body was removed from his Pentonville Prison grave...": "Timothy Evans to be Reburied," *Times,* November 6, 1965.

"That same year, the death penalty was suspended in Britain and then later abolished...": *Murder Act of 1965,* London: Her Majesty's Stationery Office, 1965.

Ruston Close: Tom Vague, *Getting It Straight in Notting Hill Gate: A West London Psychogeography Report.* Bread and Circuses. 2012.

"In the 1971 movie *10 Rillington Place,* actor Richard Attenborough played Reg...": "Christie's Ghost Returns," *Times,* May 18, 1970; demo of 10 Rillington Place: British Pathe film *Demolition Workers—Kensington* (1971).

Mr. Justice Collins and Mr. Justice Stanley Burnton, Mary Westlake (claimant) v. Criminal Cases Review Commission (defendant), *Royal Courts of Justice,* November 17, 2004.

"The night before, a Labour MP requested a meeting...": "John Christie Hanged for Murder of Wife," *Sydney Morning Herald,* July 16, 1953.

"My assistant and I had his skimpy wrists pinioned before he knew fully what was happening..." Oates, *John Christie of Rillington Place* (pp. 168–69).

"Hundreds of gawkers, including women and children...": "Christie Hanged at Pentonville," paper unknown, July 16, 1953.

Christie's will, entitled "Copy: Will of J. R. H. Christie." July 14, 1953. National Archives, CAB 143/TS 58.

"It would not surprise me to find that there is someone else": *Scott Henderson Inquiry* (p. 72).

"One of the pathologists concluded that one set likely belonged to Ethel Christie...": Simpson, *Forty Years of Murder* (p. 206).

Four teeth: Camps, *Medical and Scientific Investigations in the Christie Case* (pp. 70–72).

"*The Interim Report of the Committee on Air Pollution* is being published today, and the Government have given it careful consideration...": House of Commons, *Parliamentary Debates,* 2 December 1953, vol. 521 cc1160-2.

"It has been estimated that in the London 'smog' of December, 1952 up to 60 percent of the smoke was due to domestic fires...": Hugh Eyre Campbell Beaver, *Committee on Air Pollution, Interim Report, Presented to Parliament by the Minister of Housing and Local Government, the Secretary of State for Scotland and the Minister of Fuel of Power, etc.,* government publication, 1953 (p. 6).

"To achieve this will, in many cases, involve replacing or modifying existing equipment, and will involve capital expenditure, but it is completely possible...": Beaver, *Committee on Air Pollution, Interim Report* (p. 7).

"The main sources of air pollution...": Beaver, *Committee on Air Pollution, Interim Report* (p. 7).

"Amounts contained in the air during the smog…": Beaver, *Committee on Air Pollution, Interim Report* (charts on pp. 18–19).

Final findings: Met office's official notes on smog at http://www.metoffice.gov.uk/learning/learn-about-the-weather/weather-phenomena/case-studies/great-smog.

Newspapers report on Beaver Committee: "Cozy Fireside Is Cast as Villain in British War on Air Pollution," *New York Times,* November 25, 1954; " 'Clean Air Act' Urged by Beaver Committee," *Times,* November 26, 1954.

"In this, there is included a chart which shows a continuing abnormal death….": Beaver, *Committee on Air Pollution, Interim Report* (p. 19).

Death rate 50 percent higher: Davis, *When Smoke Ran Like Water* (p. 49).

"The effects of the London fog of December, 1952, which resulted in the deaths of some 4,000 people…": Hugh Eyre Campbell Beaver, *Committee on Air Pollution Report, Presented to Parliament by the Minister of Housing and Local Government, the Secretary of State for Scotland and the Minister of Fuel of Power, etc.,* government publication, 1954 (p. 8).

"It demanded more research into smokeless fuels…": Ashby and Anderson, *Politics of Clean Air* (p. 110).

"Yet, the report wasn't extraordinarily unique, or even that innovative…": Ashby and Anderson, *Politics of Clean Air* (p. 107).

National Clean Air Act: Ashby and Anderson, *Politics of Clean Air* (p. 107).

"In this, there is included a chart which shows a continuing abnormal death rate in Greater London during the 2½ months following the 'smog…' ": Beaver, *Committee on Air Pollution Report, Interim Report* (p. 19).

"The chart was still in a government report, but one from the Ministry of Health in 1954…" Health, Ministry of. *Report on Public Health and Medical Subjects, No. 95, Mortality and Morbidity During the London Fog of December 1952.* 1954. (p. 12).

Epidemiologist Devra Davis' findings: Devra Davis and Michelle Bell, "Reassessment of the Lethal London Fog of 1952: Novel Indicators of Acute and Chronic Consequences of Acute Exposure to Air Pollution," *Environmental Health Perspectives,* June 2001.

"The World Health Organization reported that the flu seemed relatively mild in 1953…": Davis, *When Smoke Ran Like Water* (p. 53).

"Logan and others have suggested that this secondary peak, which lasted for most of January and February…": "Air Pollution and the London Fog of December, 1952," *Journal of the Royal Sanitary Institute,* January 1954 (p. 11).

Clean Air Act of 1956: Thorsheim, *Inventing Pollution* (pp. 173, 180–82). While technically the US Air Pollution Control Act of 1955 was the first on a national scale, it really wasn't. That US Act allowed the federal government to provide information, but gave all the power to the states. And it wasn't very effective. The Clean Air Act of 1956 was a federal mandate and I want to make that distinction.

1956 fog: "Mortality from Fog in London, January, 1956," *British Medical Journal,* March 31, 1956.

"A miserable hypocritical shadow of a Bill…": Ashby and Anderson, *Politics of Clean Air* (p. 114).

Blueprint for the rest of the world to follow: John McCormick, *British Politics and the Environment,* Earthscan, 1991 (p. 143).

Number of fog events: Ashby and Anderson, *Politics of Clean Air* (pp. 116, 118).

1962 fog: House of Commons, *Parliamentary Debates,* February 2, 1968, vol. 757 cc1801-8.

Harold Macmillan: gov.uk series called "Past Prime Ministers: Harold Macmillan."

Iain Macleod: "Iain Macleod Dies," *Times,* July 21, 1970.

Norman Dodds: "Obituary: Mr. Norman Dodds," *Times*, August 23, 1965; "M.P. Dies, Cutting Labor's Lead to 2," *New York Times*, August 22, 1965.

Donald Acheson: "Sir Donald Acheson," *Guardian*, January 15, 2010.

China smog: "Air Pollution in China Is Killing 4,000 People Every Day, a New Study Finds," *Guardian*, August 13, 2015.

"Women in some rural regions of China…": "Household Air Pollution and Health Fact Sheet," World Health Organization, February 2016.

Study of the Great Smog's cause: "Studying Chinese Pollution Unraveled the Mystery of London's Lethal Great Smog," *Chicago Tribune*, November 17, 2016; "Researchers Dive into the Science of London's Deadly Fog," Smithsonian.com, November 21, 2016.

Long-term effects: "Great smog of 1952 may have blighted lives of thousands of children," *Telegraph*, March 23, 2016; "London's Great Smog of 1952 Linked to Asthma Surge," *Pantagraph*, July 8, 2016.

Low pollution levels: Davis, *When Smoke Ran Like Water* (p. 56).

1991 fog: "Health Advisers Meet in Secret over Deadly Smog of 1991," *Independent*, June 25, 1994.

Index

A Q&A with

Kate Winkler Dawson, author of
Death in the Air

Q: How did you discover these two relatively unknown stories? What first caught your attention and why did you decide to braid them into one narrative?

A: During my senior year of college, I studied in London while working at United Press International, and I fell in love with the city. I feel so comfortable there. When I was searching for compelling stories for my debut book, I discovered the story of the Great Smog and was immediately intrigued. The smog was a story that no one had written about—it is one of the most forgotten environmental disasters in history—which made it all the more alluring. I knew I had to write about.

As I was delving into the research, I began digging through newspaper archives for 1953. (The smog happened in December of 1952, but the debates in Parliament began in January 1953.) As I searched through the headlines looking for smog news, I began to see headlines like "Murder House" or "Third Body Found." They were, of course, in reference to John Reginald Christie, one of the most infamous serial killers in history. I began exploring John Reginald Christie's story and realized that Christie and the smog were two killers with many parallels.

The smog ultimately killed 12,000 people and Christie claimed at least eight victims of his own—many by asphyxiation. Individually, each story is fascinating, atmospheric, and creepy—together, they are a writer's dream.

Beyond this, I also became interested what happened *after* the smog and Christie's arrest, as the parallels between these two stories continued. Politicians in Parliament debated air pollution and the death penalty during the summer of 1953, sometimes on the same day. Most lawmakers seemed more alarmed by Christie's various confessions than by the emerging death toll from the smog. The public, too, reacted so differently to these two killers (sensationalizing Christie while minimizing the smog's death toll).

Q: America has a growing fascination with true crime. What fuels this fascination? What about true crime captivates our attention so much? Why are *you* drawn to writing about it?

A: I think true crime fascinates readers for various reasons. Some people are drawn to lurid, true stories of murder the way a sci-fi fanatic relishes the next *Star Trek* movie. My mother's bookshelves are still filled with crime novels and true crime tomes from when I was a kid, like *The Alienist, Blood and Money,* and *In Cold Blood*, so I imagine it all started with her. Ultimately, true crime really shines a light on society and culture—what we value (money, fidelity, family, honesty) and the incredible problems with our legal system. True crime stories are cautionary tales told against rich backgrounds, providing readers with important historical context about important issues like crime, race relations, and government corruption.

Q: What sort of research did you do for the book?

A: I spent few weeks in London at different repositories, most notably the National Archives in Kew. I have a specific approach to research—I don't enjoy sitting in a library, slowly thumbing through mounds of information until I find something of interest. This probably reflects the journalist in me, but I order all of the research in a specific order, ranking their importance in case I run out of time, and then I systematically take photos of Every. Single. Thing. It's not even remotely relaxing. I don't think I read a single archived document in London; I just continued to orders dozens of cartons containing thousands of papers from both the fog and the killer—I took photos of everything and then organized them on the ten-hour plane ride home.

While I was in London, I visited almost all of the locations in my book: Notting Hill, where John Reginald Christie lived; Trafalgar Square; Parliament; and North London. I timed the dates of my trip to correspond with the smog in London in 1952. It was so important to me to connect with that time period and the atmosphere of the places. I wanted to feel the winter wind as I walked along the Thames; I loved standing below Admiral Nelson's statue in Trafalgar Square.

Q: You relied on several first-person interviews in your research, including Rosemary Sargent who was thirteen during the Great Smog and Stanley Crichton, who was a police constable during the Great Smog. Both stories are prominent in the book and bring a critical human element to your story. Why did you choose their stories? How did you connect with Rosemary and Stanley?

A: Rosemary Merritt was 13-years-old when her father struggled to walk home through the fog. Later, she tried to save his life as he lay dying. Her story appeared briefly in a British documentary about the smog, just one of many, but she was really compelling. I spent a few weeks tracking her down and we connected over the phone. She was reticent to recount the whole ordeal at first, but we talked about how important her story is and she eventually agreed. When I visited London, we met at The Admiralty pub in Trafalgar Square and bonded over fish pie and cider.

Perhaps the smartest thing I did in preparation for the book was to connect with various retirement associations of several professional groups in London: police officers, nurses, doctors, and journalists. They sent out email blasts to their members that indicated that I was writing a book about the Great Smog and needed characters that were working during that time, and I received hundreds of responses. Former Police Constable Stanley Crichton's story was so interesting because he played several different roles during the smog: he located dead bodies, he patrolled the streets, and he encountered criminals. His wife, Maura, was suffering from asthma and he was forced to leave her. I loved that he was really embedded in the fog.

Norman Dodds was a Labour politician who battled Churchill's ministers over air pollution in Parliament. He had only one living relative, his daughter-in-law, Christine. I hoped to connect with Christine, but she has no email or social media. I called her church in Scotland and talked to her minister, who told me she had retired to a remote village in the Scottish Highlands. He called her on my behalf and she and I finally talked on the phone. She was invaluable with background details.

Q: Not only is *Death in the Air* a truly creepy and captivating story, but it's also a fascinating historical window into postwar London. What did you learn about the city during your research and writing?

A: I didn't realize just how dire things were in the city after World War II. Dirty, grimy—the war left many women without husbands, as single mothers. The government was just trying to dig out of war debt. There were remnants of bombed out buildings across London while the government tried to rebuild. Londoners were literally shell-shocked from the war. Clean-burning fuel was expensive and not very realistic at the time, so it was a city covered in soot from cheap coal. These factors led not only to the smog itself, but the government's almost desperate attempts to downplay the contributing factors of the smog and blame the deaths on an influenza epidemic. In each of the interviews I conducted with survivors, they seemed to share the same sentiment: "It was London, we had smog." As I say in the book, coping with days of smog was the price Londoners paid for living in the most populated, industrialized city in the world. Once the fog blew away, Londoners just tried to move on. The Great Smog was yet another disaster they were forced to survive.

Q: What are some of the themes in the book that resonate today?

A: I think the themes are universal and timely: miscarriage of justice, government corruption, the death penalty, pollution, the effects of war on society, and our fascination with serial killers in contrast to our general apathy about environmental issues.

As of 2018, there have been more than 2,000 exonerations in America. A new report shows the epidemic of false confessions under police pressure. The mystery around the Timothy Evans case is a good example of poor police work, regardless of the reader's belief of his innocence. His case might challenge a reader's views on the death penalty.

Another resonant idea is that many voters don't trust their governments, British or American—government corruption and apathy aren't surprising. But those phrases are generic; they don't resonate loudly until you read those confidential memos from politicians. "Today everybody expects the Government to solve every problem," complained the book's main antagonist, Minister of Housing Harold Macmillan. "We cannot do very much, but we can seem to be very busy." Many more notes, never before seen, depict a government that seemed to care little about the health of Londoners.

The effects of the war certainly had an impact on the public's reaction to the smog. Londoners had become experts at coping with a crisis—there were no protests, or even complaints. They wanted to move forward.

Serial killers are certainly more alluring to newspaper readers than pollution—a smog can't sneak into your house and stab you in the middle of night. A deadly fog won't hide in your closet, ready to pounce. The fog wasn't a freak, just a consequence of living in London, something expected. A serial killer is always a surprise. And I do think many people like to be a little scared—I know I do.

Q: What affect did the Great Smog have on clean-air legislation in the UK and around the world?

A: The fog resulted in the 1956 Clean Air Act, which became a blueprint for the rest of the world to follow—the first comprehensive legislation to attack air pollution. And it seemed to have an immediate impact. The Meteorological Office tracked the number of fog events in London every year. In 1956, the year the bill was enacted, there were almost forty fogs, including one that killed more than one thousand people in London. The following year, there were about half the number of smogs. The same was true for industrial and domestic smoke. Eventually, coal was replaced in Britain with gas, oil, and electricity.

The Clean Air Act couldn't accept all of the credit—the severity of air pollution had been declining in the UK for years. But now, the dirty fogs slowly began to disappear. The new regulations helped, but in December of 1962 another smog settled over London for four days, killing seven hundred and fifty people. Past governments simply didn't act quickly enough. And killer fogs were still happening around the world. In 1963, a two-week-long fog in New York City killed almost four hundred people.

Thanks to the Clean Air Act of 1956, the Great Smog was the last major air pollution event in Britain's history and it inspired America's Clean Air Act of 1970—which was landmark for the US in cleaning up the air.

Q: The United States is not immune to clean-air issues. Donora, Pennsylvania had its own smog crisis that killed twenty people in 1948. In 2017, President Trump signed an executive order to reduce environmental protections, including clean air and water; he also began dismantling the Environmental Protection Agency. What do you make of this?

A: I think that no matter who is in power in government, politicians will seek to find a balance between preserving the environment and appeasing big business—some political parties are more concerned about clean energy than others.

President Trump has called climate change "a hoax." Of course, that's ridiculous—government studies prove climate change exists. He rolled back fuel-economy standards for vehicles and lifted a moratorium on coal leasing on US federal lands.

He's gutting the Environmental Protection Agency and proposing deep cuts to its enforcement branch. In 2017, he announced that the US would pull out of the Paris Climate Accord. Regardless of who is president, the decisions that politicians make about air pollution are crucial. What happened in London could happen to a town in America, under the right conditions. This is a critical time for our country as we choke in dirty air.

Q: Wrongful conviction seems to be a passion of yours: you're on the board of the Texas Board for Actual Innocence, an organization your father founded at the University of Texas School of Law and you co-taught a clinical class entitled the Actual Innocence Clinic in which journalism students and law students investigated claims of innocence from convicted prisoners. It seems like it's no accident that wrongful conviction is a theme in the book. What effect did John Reginald Christie's case have on conviction and the judicial process in the UK?

A: In 1965, a resurgence of the Evans controversy led the newspapers when a high court judge revisited the case. There was a tremendous amount of attention on the capital punishment in the UK. That same year, the death penalty was suspended in Britain and then later abolished, at least partially because of Tim Evans's case (and John Reginald Christie's confessions). Evans's execution is considered one of the most extreme cases of wrongful conviction.

My opinion of the Evans/Christie case is unique and likely controversial in the UK. Conventional wisdom has it that Tim Evans was innocent of killing his wife and daughter and that Christie was the real killer. The hanging of Evans became synonymous with wrongful conviction. But after sorting through all of the evidence and consulting attorneys, criminal psychologists, and pathologists, it seems more likely that Evans did, in fact, kill his wife and daughter and Christie gave a false confession. My work with the Actual Innocence Clinic seems to contradict that conclusion, but we're taught to go where the evidence takes us.

Q: You own an anthology of American criminals (*Bloodletters and Badmen: A Narrative Encyclopedia of American Criminals from the Pilgrims to the Present*), which absolutely marks your initiation into the stable of authentic true-crime writers. Tell us more about this book! What have you learned? Any trends you've noticed?

A: I adore that book. It lists many of the major criminals in America, beginning with the first killer who was a Mayflower pilgrim! The book provides a short summary of the history of the criminals, along with pictures or illustrations.

It's chronological, so it was very reflective of America's history. For example, there were quite a few train robbers until the late 1800s. And there were an awful lot of mobsters until about the 1930s. Women began poisoning their husbands in the Victorian Era—arsenic was sold to the public by chemists! Obviously plane hijackers arrived more than one hundred years later. There are different themes in crime that begin and end over the history of crime, so it was interesting to see which crimes flourished during certain time periods.

Q: What was the most surprising or gratifying part about publishing *Death in the Air*?

A: I think it must be the wonderful response the book received, particularly with people whom I met during my book tour. The story really seemed to resound with readers and it's gratifying to educate folks about two important issues: the environment and the death penalty. Both storylines have their place in history, so I'm blessed to have been able to bring them both to readers around the world. They both have value and both resonate with us today, which is unfortunate because there are so many issues with environmental protection and the criminal justice system. But I think there are also themes in the book about perseverance and strength, which were wonderful to explore.

About the Author

Kate Winkler Dawson is a senior lecturer of journalism in the Moody College of Communication at The University of Texas at Austin and a fellow with the Society of Junior Fellows in British Studies at the University of Texas at Austin. She is a seasoned documentary producer and news writer, whose work has appeared in the *New York Times, Dallas Morning News,* United Press International, WCBS News, ABC News Radio, Fox News Channel, *PBS NewsHour,* and *Nightline.* She's on the board of the Texas Center for Actual Innocence and lives in Austin, Texas, with her family.